SPEED MATTERS

A MUST-READ GUIDE FOR FUTURISTIC EXECUTIVES AND MANAGERS

SPEED MATTERS

WHY BEST IN CLASS BUSINESS LEADERS PRIORITIZE WORKFORCE TIME TO PROFICIENCY METRICS

POWERFUL LESSONS UNPACKED FROM WORLD'S BEST ORGANIZATIONS

DR. RAMAN K. ATTRI

Copyrights © 2021 Raman K Attri and Speed To Proficiency Research: S2Pro©

All rights reserved. No part of this publication may be reproduced, distributed, or transmitted in any form or by any means, including photocopying, recording, or other electronic or mechanical methods, without the prior written permission of the author and publisher, except in the case of brief quotations embodied in critical reviews and certain other noncommercial uses permitted by copyright law.

ISBN: 978-981-18-0536-3 (e-book)
ISBN: 978-981-18-0535-6 (paperback)
ISBN: 978-981-18-0534-9 (hardcover)

Published in Singapore
Printed in the United States of America

https://www.speedtoproficiency.com
info@speedtoproficiency.com

National Library Board, Singapore Cataloguing in Publication Data

Name(s): Attri, Raman K., 1973-
Title: Speed matters : why best in class business leaders prioritize workforce time to proficiency metrics / Dr. Raman K. Attri.
Description: Singapore : Speed To Proficiency Research, [2021] | Includes bibliographical references and index.
Identifier(s): OCN 1241069112 | ISBN 978-981-18-0534-9 (hardback) | ISBN 978-981-18-0535-6 (paperback) | ISBN 978-981-18-0536-3 (ebook)
Subject(s): LCSH: Core competencies. | Performance--Management.
Classification: DDC 658.4--dc23

To Efren Lopez

&

my outstanding training teams at KLA Corp

"You need to know the level of performance required to do the job and how long it takes to get there ... when you can get employees up-to speed in far less time, productivity rises at far less expense."

Steve Rosenbaum and Jim Williams (2004)

FOREWORD

A request from Dr. Attri for me to write a forward for Speed Matters initiated a reflection on a body of research now thirty years in the making. His contemporary research, found within the pages of this new book, provides a significant addition to the subject of speed to proficiency and the important argument for business leaders to bring the topic of workforce proficiency to the boardroom.

The two words in the title of this book are profound.

SPEED, for example, is such an important word given the intention of a proficient workforce. All businesses must operate under one ever-present constraint, the intractable passing of twenty-four hours each and every day. How this time is utilized within a business becomes the highest order of strategies for decision-makers. Operating and competing in a hyper-competitive environment, therefore, depends on the collective proficiency of all employees within an organization. The time required to reach measured proficiency therefore becomes the competitive fulcrum. Raman Attri offers proof of this competitive position through his exhaustive research and intricate quantitative measurements. My research from 20 years ago uncovered the same advantage. However, the proficiency rates of the late 1990's could be seen in gaining a time advantage measured in hours; the advantage now is in seconds as businesses compete in a ceaseless cycle for customer acquisition, delivery and retention.

I believe it is important for leaders and decision-makers to fully comprehend the aspect of measuring speed to proficiency. The measure is a rate assessing the extent of organizational [change-in-employee proficiency] over a specific period of time. Essentially, speed to proficiency measures the number of people in a targeted job role reaching proficiency -- with the capability to perform at a desired level -- and how quickly this transformation takes place. My work on this topic now extends to a fourth decade and I still have not found a more effective instrument to measure the overall competitiveness of an enterprise.

MATTERS. This word brings Raman's entire body of research into focus. Consider this question: For whom does speed to proficiency matter? The commonsensical answer is the leader, or leaders, of an organization directing capital and human resources while making key decisions regarding how to compete and grow. Leaders can utilize the rate of capability change as a key indicator of the rate of improvement and the overall capacity to compete. But there is another key constituent regarding why speed to proficiency matters, the employee. The full engagement of any individual in an organization is vital to both the employee and the organization. According to recent research from the Gallup Organization, just over 30% of employees are engaged in the workplace. This trend has not improved for nearly two decades. The speed by which an individual can learn and contribute to the organization or team is an immutable driver of engagement. Dr. Attri has shown ample evidence of how reaching proficiency quickly is of direct benefit to the employee and its lasting impact on loyalty, retention and performance.

Dr. Raman K. Attri has earned and assumed the chief responsibility of global thought leader on the subject of time to proficiency. This book is his latest chapter, and I can only assume that he will continue to provide us with discoveries and refinements on the topic. I anxiously await his next publication.

Charles L. Fred

Chairman and Chief Executive Officer, TrueSpace

Jossey-Bass Author, *Breakaway*, 2002

May 2021

PREFACE

I was born a normal kid to poor parents in a remote place where there was hardly any access to education or medical facility. Amidst those conditions, I got infected with poliovirus when I was barely six months old, which took away my ability to walk for good. As I was growing up as a disabled kid among the healthy kids around me, I probably realized very little about what I was lacking back then.

However, primary school was the place where I started realizing the sheer lack of "speed." I had to go to school limping on one leg. I could hardly match with the pace of the other kids. Subsequently, the lack of speed troubled me at various points in life so much that it was the only thing in my mind during most of my early childhood years, so much so that speed became my greatest obsession for several decades to come. At times, I used to tell myself that if I could not have speed in walking, I will find speed in something else.

My immediate experiments were on my speed of learning because I strongly believed that it was the best means to master "speed." I gave in all that I had and tried different ways to learn things, which other kids may not have even thought of. It took me several years of failing and succeeding, but there came a moment when I figured out the science and art of learning faster. At the age when kids would typically read comics, I began reading Dale Carnegie. I read books from all genres, poetry to palmistry, physics to psychology. Once I mastered the ways to learn fast, there was hardly any boundary of subject, discipline, or genre for me. Some of the things I learned were five to eight years ahead of my age. I remember reading university physics in my high school times itself.

That's pretty much how I set on a course to focus on speed. Eventually, the lack of speed became my niche that led me to become a learning scientist a couple of decades later. As I continued my academic journey in that path, I earned over a hundred international academic credentials, which include 2 doctorates, 3 masters, and several international certifications.

When I stepped into the professional world, my focus shifted from learning to job performance. My primary concern as a disabled person was to make sure that I sped up my job performance. I had to figure out ways to stay ahead and stay visible. I had the constant anxiety to learn and master job-related skills faster than my peers.

So, I set on a fresh course to figure out ways to speed up professional performance, not merely learning. As I moved into leadership roles, I observed that my team members were taking an incredibly long time to reach the desired speed in their essential job skills. I realized that it was the same across all business units. As I reached out to several forums and consulted with some of the leading professional bodies in the learning and performance field, I realized that it was a systemic issue across industries.

While human performance is the foundation of businesses, I also understood how badly the majority of the organizations were equipped to develop employee performance at the desired speed. I noticed how poorly the professional skills were being delivered through inefficient corporate training. I found the training programs to be outdated, old-styled, and stuffed with volumes of content. As opposed to acting as accelerators to performance, these inefficient training programs were, in fact, acting as decelerators to speed.

Why are speed-savvy organizations doing such a poor job in speeding up the performance of their workforce? I said to myself, and there ought to be a better way. Is there an art that they don't know? Is there a science no one taught them?

That one question led me to pursue an intensive doctoral study on "speeding up the time to employees' proficiency." As it stands today, I am the only one in the world who has conducted an in-depth doctoral study on this significant business challenge. Today, I am one among the handful of global experts on speed in professional learning and performance.

I have the privilege of reaching out to the world's best organizations and renowned leaders to learn, understand, and extend the art and science of speed to proficiency. I deeply explored how best-in-class organizations could stay ahead in the game by leveraging time and speed.

I realize that time is the only thing that is available to all organizations or businesses in equal quantity. How strategically an organization uses that available time determines its market positioning. Charles Fred, the author of Breakaway and arguably the father of the term "speed to proficiency," said two decades ago that 'Speed to proficiency is the most devastating competitive weapon in a world where the competitive forces of scale, automation, and capital are subordinate to the power of a proficient workforce.' This statement is far more valid now than it was two decades ago. The speed with which innovations and technologies are changing our lives is incredible. By the time we adapt to one technology, the next generation of the same technology is already knocking at the door. The cut-throat competition among global organizations is too fierce to ignore. While serving as a learning leader at a 50-billion-dollar semiconductor giant, I saw that a delay by merely a day in launching a product cost the company millions of dollars. It is not an overstatement to say that the universal need across all businesses is "speed matters."

In today's fast-paced world, with a high degree of skill obsolesce, massive technological innovations, and rapid changes, it is important that global leaders develop their employees' performance to be at par with the speed of businesses. This book aims to make that "speed" as the priority of futuristic leaders, executives, and managers to stay ahead in the competition.

Ironically, the need for speed is understood only when the absence of speed is irrevocably established. That's the hard part. There is hardly any science available today to define and establish time-related metrics that could allow organizations to figure out how long it is taking their employees to reach the desired performance level. Correspondingly, front-line managers find it hard to build a solid business case to start projects to shorten time to proficiency or speed up employee trajectories. The biggest reason these projects do not hold ground is that more often time to proficiency is hardly measured systematically in organizations.

That's the precise reason I wrote this book as a one-stop portal for forward-thinking leaders and managers to learn about the importance of shortening workforce time to proficiency. This book is the first and the only one until now that has revealed some alarming figures on time to proficiency metrics, which you, as a distinguished leader, cannot afford to ignore.

This book is a distilled wisdom derived from an extensive research on 66 start-to-end project success stories spanning 28 industries, contributed by 85 best-in-class business leaders from 7 countries for whom "speed mattered" a lot as a competitive weapon.

This book gives you in-depth insights as to why and how the best-in-class global business leaders prioritize and institute time to proficiency metrics in their business dashboards. As a reader, you will learn to data-based evidence to present compelling business cases to implement those metrics in your organization.

In particular, this book will enable you with the answers to some crucial questions –

- ❖ How can you go about being a "speed-savvy" visionary leader?
- ❖ Why should you focus on developing employee proficiency?
- ❖ Why should the speed of employee development matter to you as a leader?

- How are global organizations using the new time to proficiency metrics?
- How alarming is the time to proficiency of workforce in your industry?
- What drives the best-in-class leaders to prioritize time to proficiency metrics in their dashboards?
- What tangible business gains can organizations derive from a shorter time to proficiency?

If speed matters to you and you want to learn science-based secrets to bring speed to your organization, follow me on any social media platforms and my blog. Find the links to the same at the end of the book. I would encourage readers to read my other books to read about proposed models or frameworks: *Modelling accelerated proficiency in organisations* (2018), *Designing Training to Shorten Time To Proficiency* (2019), *Speed to Proficiency in Organizations* (2019), *Models of Skill Acquisition and Expertise Development* (2019) and *Accelerated Proficiency for Accelerated Times* (2020).

Dr Raman K Attri

April 2021

CHAPTER 1
INTRODUCTION

THE BUSINESS OF TIME AND SPEED

1.1	WHAT IS THE PROBLEM?	3
1.2	WHY THIS BOOK?	4
1.3	HOW THE BOOK IS ORGANIZED	6

CHAPTER 2
THE STUDY

THE RESEARCH STUDY ON TIME TO PROFICIENCY

2.1	THE RESEARCH STUDY	11
2.2	RESEARCH OUTCOMES	34

CHAPTER 3
THE PROFICIENCY

THE ROLE OF PROFICIENT PERFORMANCE AT THE WORKPLACE

3.1	NATURE OF WORKPLACE PERFORMANCE	37
3.2	PROFICIENCY AND PERFORMANCE	41
3.3	NOVICE-TO-EXPERT PROGRESSION	46
3.4	PROFICIENCY SCALING	58
3.5	PROFICIENT PERFORMANCE IN ORGANIZATIONS	64
3.6	EXPERT PERFORMANCE	83
3.7	WHAT IT MEANS TO YOU	88

CHAPTER 4
THE METRICS

IMPORTANCE OF TIME TO PROFICIENCY METRICS IN ORGANIZATIONS

4.1	TIME TO PROFICIENCY (TTP)	93
4.2	SPEED TO PROFICIENCY	97
4.3	ACCELERATED PROFICIENCY	99
4.4	DEFINING TTP METRICS	103
4.5	DRAWING THE BOUNDARIES	107
4.6	WHAT IT MEANS TO YOU	119

CHAPTER 5
THE TRIGGERS

THE MAGNITUDE AND SCALE OF TIME TO PROFICIENCY

5.1	MEASURING TTP	125
5.2	THE MAGNITUDE OF TTP	126
5.3	COMPARATIVE ANALYSIS OF TTP	142
5.4	THE SCALE OF TTP	144
5.5	WHAT IT MEANS TO YOU	153

CHAPTER 6
THE DRIVERS

THE BUSINESS DRIVERS TO REDUCE TIME TO PROFICIENCY

6.1	TIME-RELATED PRESSURES	162
6.2	SPEED-RELATED COMPETITIVENESS	164
6.3	SKILL-RELATED DEFICIENCIES	168
6.4	COST OR FINANCIAL IMPLICATIONS	173
6.5	INTERPLAY OF DRIVERS	177
6.6	WHAT IT MEANS TO YOU	186

CHAPTER 7
THE BENEFITS

THE BUSINESS BENEFITS OF REDUCING TIME TO PROFICIENCY

7.1	MAGNITUDE OF REDUCTION IN TTP	191
7.2	BENEFITS OF A SHORTER TTP	210
7.3	WHAT IT MEANS TO YOU	221

CHAPTER 8
THE SYSTEM

THE CLOSED-LOOP OF TIME TO PROFICIENCY

8.1	THE CLOSED-LOOP OF TTP	225
8.2	WHAT IT MEANS TO YOU	228

PUBLICATIONS	231
REFERENCES	233
INDEX	257
THE AUTHOR	279

CHAPTER 1
INTRODUCTION

THE BUSINESS OF TIME AND SPEED

In recent times, the business world has shown a clear need for what I call as *Accelerated Proficiency*. At various points in this text, I will use variants of this term as *accelerating proficiency, accelerating time to proficiency,* or *accelerating speed to proficiency*, to mean the same thing.

My objective behind writing this book is to educate business leaders about this emerging and highly pressing business challenge that cannot seem to wait. I have written this book for business leaders, performance experts, organizational leaders, direct managers, and human resource strategists.

1.1   WHAT IS THE PROBLEM?

Of late, the business world is not only changing at a very fast pace but is also becoming overly complex. As a result, the skills and knowledge acquired become irrelevant or obsolete quickly. The employees need a new set of skills for new technologies and products. The time they take to learn the new skills could delay the launch of new products. In certain industries like semiconductors, a delay by merely a day in launching a new product may cost millions of dollars to a company simply because its competitors may be far ahead of it. The cutthroat competition between global organizations has been an everlasting reality. In this context, organizations cannot wait for long for their employees to become proficient in the critical skills required to support their businesses and customers. This is where the emerging concepts of *accelerated proficiency, time to proficiency* (TTP), and *speed to proficiency* are making rounds at several business forums. Nevertheless, business leaders find it

CH1 / INTRODUCTION

difficult to understand this problem completely, in particular how these metrics influence or drive businesses.

In the last 25 years, I have worked on a range of projects and initiatives that required speeding up the acquisition of proficiency in complex job roles. Time and speed inherently intrigued me in my personal and professional life. In this era of digital revolution, where the time-to-market is being highly squeezed, TTP is a very important metric that all organizational leaders and performance professionals must care about for the support and sustenance of their current and future businesses. A leader's job is to support the employees in achieving proficiency at the fastest rate possible.

I have seen that organizations are now shifting their focus on 'how to shorten the TTP of their employees and bring them up to speed to the required performance.'

1.2   WHY THIS BOOK?

I have written this book to reveal some eye-opening findings from a large-scale study that I conducted on TTP (the *TTP study* hereinafter). I conducted the study with 85 world-renowned leaders who have demonstrated leadership and experience in reducing TTP in their respective settings. I conducted the study across 66 project cases from 15 functional job roles and covered over 21 business sectors and 30 industries. It helped me understand the nature and meaning of accelerating the TTP in organizations under various settings. The study also revealed some shocking truths. The major one among those was that the TTP in some roles could be as long as

3 years. The studies conducted previously have not mentioned or discussed such alarming.

Time is money; therefore, a reduction in time should be the first goal of any training program or employee development initiative. This is the foundational premise of the book. In particular, I have designed this book to explore the following questions that are concerned with the business value of developing employee performance and proficiency:

1. What is the meaning and nature of the process of accelerating proficiency in workplaces?
2. How does the TTP metrics manifest in organizations?
3. What are the drivers or factors that push organizations to think about shortening employees' TTP?
4. What are the business benefits accrued from shortening the TTP?
5. Why should organizations and their leaders care about shortening TTP?

In this book, I discuss the concept and measurement of the acceleration of proficiency; four business drivers that trigger the need for reduced TTP; and four business benefits of shortening it.

Notably, to date, only four books are available on this subject area, apart from mine: *Breakaway: Deliver Value to Your Customers—Fast!* (Fred 2002); *Learning Paths: Increase Profits by Reducing the Time it takes Employees to get Up-to-Speed* (Rosenbaum & Steve 2004); *Speed to Proficiency: Creating a Sustainable Competitive Advantage* (Bruck 2015); and *Up-to-Speed: Secrets of Reducing Time to Proficiency* (Rosenbaum 2018).

CH1/INTRODUCTION

The authors of these books have identified "shortening TTP" as a crucial business challenge.

I highly encourage the readers to check out my other books to get a comprehensive grasp of the concepts, models, and methods of speeding up employee proficiency. I have added significantly to this know-how in my doctoral thesis and several of my books: *Modelling accelerated proficiency in organisations: Practices and strategies to shorten time-to-proficiency of the workforce – Doctoral Thesis (2018); Designing Training to Shorten Time To Proficiency: Online, Classroom and On-the-Job Learning Strategies from Research (2019); Speed to Proficiency in Organizations: A Research Report on Model, Practices and Strategies to Shorten Time to Proficiency (2019); Accelerated Proficiency for Accelerated Times: A Review of Concept and Methods to Accelerate Proficiency (2020),* and *The Business of Time and Speed: How Leading Organizations Reduce Time to Proficiency (forthcoming).*

1.3 HOW THE BOOK IS ORGANIZED

I have organized the book into eight chapters.

Chapter 1 introduces the preamble and background of the book.

Chapter 2 introduces the *TTP study* that I conducted across a large sample of world-renowned leaders to investigate the strategies and practices to accelerate proficiency in organizations. I discuss the findings of this study in the subsequent chapters, elaborating on the various aspects of accelerated proficiency.

Chapter 3 provides the foundational understanding of the concept of proficiency. The chapter presents the role of proficiency in employee performance and sets the grounds for defining and outlining proficient performance, as suggested by various researchers. The chapter also discusses in detail the four characteristics of proficient performance at the workplace and establishes the construct of job-role proficiency.

Chapter 4 broadens the understanding of the concept of accelerated proficiency. It explains the metrics such as time to proficiency, time to competence, time to full productivity, speed to proficiency, and relates them back to the concept of accelerating proficiency. The chapter also describes the five characteristics of accelerated proficiency, which emerged from the *TTP study*.

Chapter 5 describes how the magnitude and scale of TTP act as triggers for organizations to rethink about shortening it. It establishes the importance and mechanism of measuring TTP. The chapter analyzes the TTP numbers across various contextual parameters such as job type, complexity, critical skills, economic sectors, business sectors, and industry groups. The chapter also raises an appeal as to why organizational leaders cannot ignore the magnitude and scale of TTP.

Chapter 6 presents the findings of the *TTP study* on the factors that drive organizations to institute projects to shorten TTP. The chapter reveals four drivers, namely time-related pressures, speed-related competitiveness, skill-related deficiencies, and cost or financial implications.

Chapter 7 outlines the findings of the *TTP study* and provides a deeper understanding of the benefits accrued by organizations from

CH1/INTRODUCTION

a shorter TTP. The chapter discusses the four business benefits, namely business gains, cost savings, improvements in operational metrics, and productivity improvement. The chapter also provides a sense of the range and extent to which leaders can expect a reduction in TTP.

Chapter 8 concludes the book with a big picture which ties the triggers, drivers, and benefits into a closed-loop system model. It explains how a longer TTP may hamper organizational goals and why it is worth doing something about it.

CHAPTER 2
THE STUDY

THE RESEARCH STUDY ON TTP

This book is an expansion of the first-of-its-kind findings of an intensive 5-year research study titled *Modelling Accelerated Proficiency in Organisations: Practices and Strategies to Shorten Time-to-Proficiency of the Workforce* (the *TTP study*). I conducted this study as part of my doctoral work between 2014 and 2018, which addressed the larger question 'How to accelerate the TTP of the workforce in organizations?' (Attri 2018).

This chapter intends to summarize the study to set the context for readers and establish the credibility and generalizability of the TTP metrics discussed in the subsequent chapters. Readers may go through the participant distribution and general process to understand the rigor applied to conduct the research.

2.1 THE RESEARCH STUDY

2.1.1 Business challenge

The *TTP study* addresses one of the most critical challenges faced by modern organizations—the enormous amount of time taken by the workforce to reach full proficiency, irrespective of the job role. The enormous time taken creates both market and financial pressures on organizations.

In today's fast-paced world, most organizations are constantly struggling to bring their employees to the desired level on job-related skills in the shortest time possible. While organizations are focused on finding the strategies that can do the wonder and accelerate employee development, I observed that they

CH1 / INTRODUCTION

lack the comprehensive know-how on how to achieve this goal. Though there is plenty of research on various aspects of this topic, only a small portion of that has been transferred to the business world.

During the last decade, Hoffman[1] and Fadde[2] and other leading expertise researchers have conceptualized the constructs of *accelerated proficiency* and *accelerated expertise* in training and work settings. In their studies, Hoffman, Fadde and their and colleagues have identified the lack of a good understanding of the concept and process of accelerated proficiency, the need for accelerating proficiency, and the methods to accelerate proficiency in organizations. I aimed to understand the shortfall through the *TTP study*, that is, the way it plays out in the organizations. Through the study, I have explored the practices and strategies that have proven successful in reducing the TTP of the workforce.

2.1.2 Research objectives

The *TTP study*'s core research questions were: How do organizations view the business challenge of a long TTP of their workforce? How can organizations accelerate the TTP of their employees?

Part of these questions, the *TTP study* answered the four important aspects of the TTP metrics:

---

[1] Hoffman et al. 2008, 2009, 2014; Hoffman, Andrews & Feltovich 2012; Hoffman & Andrews 2012; Hoffman, Andrews, et al. 2010; Hoffman, Feltovich, et al. 2010

[2] Fadde & Klein 2010, 2012; Fadde 2007, 2009a, 2009b, 2009c, 2012, 2013, 2016

1. Meaning of accelerated proficiency, as seen by business leaders
2. Business factors driving the need for a shorter TTP
3. Business benefits accrued from shortening TTP
4. Practices and strategies to shorten the TTP of the workforce

This book builds a comprehensive, research-informed understanding of the first three aspects, while the fourth aspect is discussed in my other books[3]. The crux of these three aspects covered in this book is as follows: Despite the foundational understanding of the essence of time in business settings, organizational leaders still find it difficult to make a strong proposal or business case to convince their upper management to invest in projects or initiatives to accelerate performance (which involves reaching the desired output in a shorter time). This is mostly due to the lack of quantifiable data in that area. In the absence of initiatives focused on speeding up performance, most learning leaders and training organizations continue to emphasize improving the performance (which involves raising the level of output). The impediment is somewhat because of the gap in the contextual understanding among practitioners on how the TTP of the workforce drives business differentiation or affects the other operational metrics.

2.1.3 Research approach

I have used exploratory research, a qualitative research method, to conduct the *TTP study*, which is considered best to reveal '*how*

---

[3]Check section titled Author's relevant publications at the end of the book.

CH1/INTRODUCTION

things work in particular contexts' (Mason 2002). I have chosen this approach since accelerating proficiency in workplaces is a relatively new business challenge and needs to be understood in its natural settings. Also, the mechanisms and strategies adopted to accelerate proficiency of workforce are not the same across organizations. Incidentally, even within the same organization, different jobs may require different approaches. Therefore, it is important to understand why strategies work in some contexts and not in others.

2.1.4 Participants

I have been working in the learning industry for over two decades, specifically supporting business challenges of shortening time to proficiency. I knew that there were only a few experts around the world who possessed such know-how. Therefore, I targeted such experts using purposive sampling and criteria-driven sampling. From a range of databases such as LinkedIn and others, I spotted 371 potential experts who appeared to have evidence of leading at least one project to reduce the TTP of the workforce in their respective organizations. I used evidence from explicit mention written media (e.g., industry reports, interviews, newsletters, books, magazines, blogs, industry awards, affiliation, and success stories) and self-proclaimed sources (e.g., a LinkedIn, academic CVs, questionnaires, and personal communications). From the cluster of 371 experts, 85 project leaders took part in the study.

These participants (most of them being CEOs, consultants, or an equivalent and called 'project leaders' hereinafter) were some of the best-in-class experts, global training experts, and business leaders from 7 different countries. The mean number of years of experience was over 20 years. Most of the project leaders were highly educated, with 35% of them holding doctorate degrees and 39% master's degrees. Table 2-1 and Figure 2.1 shows the tabular distribution profile and the graphical distribution profile of the participants respectively.

Table 2-1 Distribution profile of the study participants

Participant's country		
USA	66	77%
Australia	5	6%
Netherlands	5	6%
UK	4	5%
Singapore	3	4%
UAE	1	1%
Philippines	1	1%
Total	85	100%

Participant's current industry (self-declared)		
Professional training & coaching	18	20%
Management consulting	13	15%
Education management	7	8%
Computer software	6	7%
Higher education	6	7%
Semiconductors	6	7%
Research	5	6%
E-learning	5	6%
Information technology & services	3	4%
Oil & energy	3	3%
Financial services	2	2%
Military	1	1%
Broadcast media	1	1%
Public relations & communications	1	1%
Electrical/Electronic manufacturing	1	1%
Education technology	1	1%
Banking	1	1%
Management consulting	1	1%
Internet	1	1%
Human resources	1	1%
Information services	1	1%
Unknown	1	1%
Total	85	100%

CH1 / INTRODUCTION

Participant's current position/title		
President/CEO/MD/Founder	27	32%
Researcher/Scientist/Academician/Author	13	15%
Consultant	12	13%
Program/Training manager	10	12%
Director/VP	9	11%
Trainer/Facilitator / Instructional designer	6	7%
CLO/CKO	5	6%
Leadership/HRD specialist	2	2%
Retired	1	1%
Total	85	100%

Participant's education		
Doctorate	29	35%
Masters	34	39%
Bachelors	16	19%
No information	6	7%
Total	85	100%

Participant's experience range (in years)		
0 to 10	3	4%
11 to 20	24	27%
21 to 30	22	26%
31 to 40	24	29%
41 to 50	7	8%
Unknown	5	6%
Total	85	100%

Figure 2.1 Graphical distribution profile of the study participants

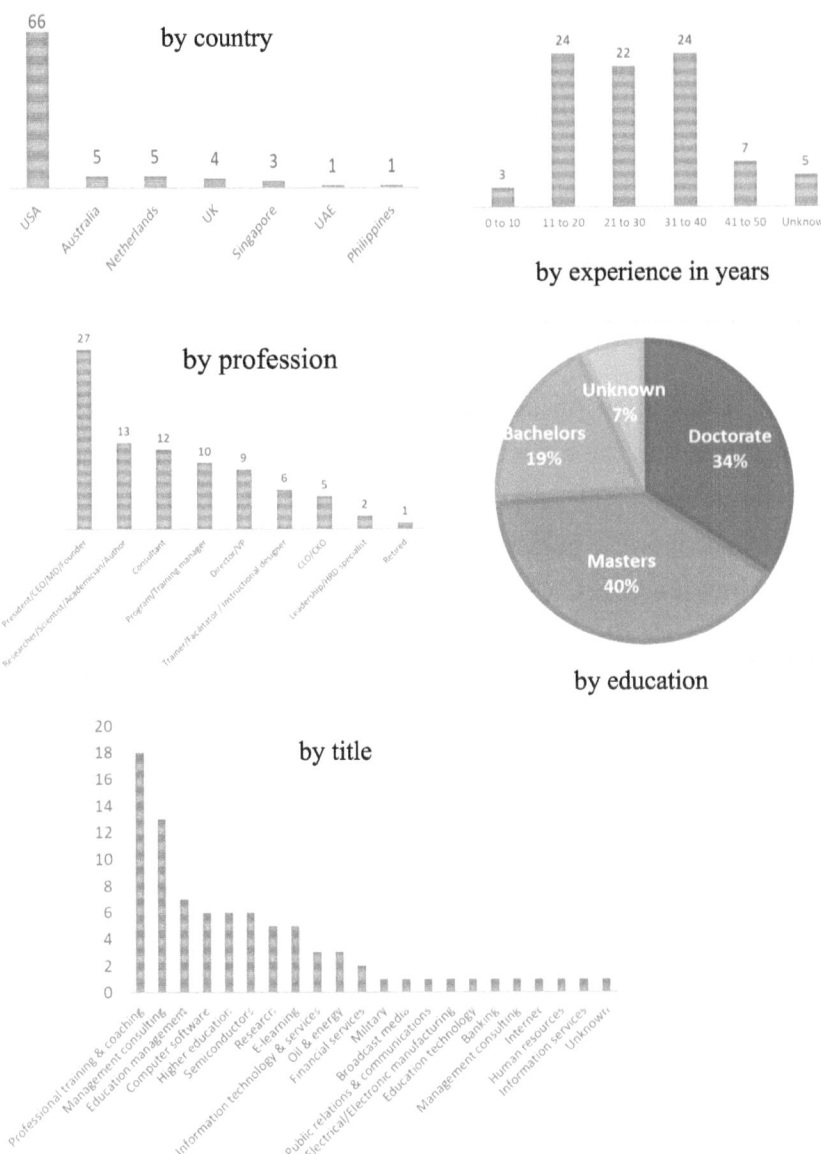

CH1/INTRODUCTION

2.1.5 Sampling unit

I used the *bounded project case* approach, wherein the bounded project case essentially was a success story with a defined start and end (i.e., a project), and was bounded (i.e., its boundaries are defined in terms of scope) (Merriam & Tisdell 2016; Miles, Huberman & Saldana 2014; Turner & Müller 2003). I gathered successful project cases to understand more clearly the need for shortening TTP, the methods that worked, and the results obtained.

I collected 66 successful project cases and 50 documents associated with the cases. I categorized the collected project cases into four broad categories based on the contextual variables: (1) sector—economic, business, or industry; (2) nature of job role; (3) critical-to-success (CTS) skills—primary skills required for the job; and (4) complexity level—the complexity of the skills required, the job role, or both.

I then subjected the 66 project cases through a criterion to ensure completeness of every project story, which had clear-cut evidence of shortening time to proficiency. Finally, I selected 60 projects which showed strong evidence or supported the results. These 60 project cases were seen to span across 10 economic sectors, 20 business sectors, and 28 industry groups, covering 14 different types of jobs, 15 different CTS skills involved in those jobs, and 5 levels of complexity. Table 2-2 shows the tabular distribution profile, and Figure 2.2 shows the graphical distribution profile of selected project cases. Therefore, it could be said that the study spanned across a reasonably wide spectrum. Table 2-3 presents a summary of project cases across all the contextual variables.

Table 2-2 Distribution profile of the project cases classified as per TR – Thomas-Reuters (TR) Business Classification System

Contextual variable	Value	No. of projects	%
Economic Sector (TR)	Technology	14	23%
	Financials	10	17%
	Healthcare	8	13%
	Industrials	7	12%
	Energy	7	12%
	Consumer non-cyclicals	5	8%
	Basic materials	3	5%
	Military/ government	3	5%
	Telecommunication services	2	3%
	Utility	1	2%
	Grand Total	**60**	**100%**
Business Sector (TR)	Technology Equipment	12	20%
	Energy - Fossil Fuels	7	12%
	Banking & Investment Services	6	10%
	Healthcare Services	4	7%
	Pharmaceuticals & Medical Research	4	7%
	Insurance	3	5%
	Industrial & Commercial Services	3	5%
	Government / Military	3	5%
	Industrial Goods	3	5%
	Telecommunications Services	2	3%
	Software & IT Services	2	3%
	Mineral Resources	2	3%
	Retailers	2	3%
	Real Estate	1	2%
	Transportation	1	2%
	Chemicals	1	2%
	Automobiles & Auto Parts	1	2%
	Utilities	1	2%
	Cyclical Consumer Services	1	2%
	Food & Beverages	1	2%
	Grand Total	**60**	**100%**

CH1 / INTRODUCTION

Contextual variable	Value	No. of projects	%
Industry Group (TR)	Semiconductors & Semiconductor Equipment	8	13%
	Oil & Gas	5	8%
	Investment Banking & Investment Services	4	7%
	Communications & Networking	3	5%
	Professional & Commercial Services	3	5%
	Healthcare Providers & Services	3	5%
	Insurance	3	5%
	Pharmaceuticals	2	3%
	Oil & Gas Related Equipment and Services	2	3%
	Telecommunications Services	2	3%
	Banking Services	2	3%
	Other Specialty Retailers	2	3%
	Biotechnology & Medical Research	2	3%
	Software & IT Services	2	3%
	Machinery, Equipment & Components	2	3%
	Metals & Mining	2	3%
	Military	2	3%
	Real Estate Operations	1	2%
	Electronic Equipment & Parts	1	2%
	Healthcare Equipment & Supplies	1	2%
	Chemicals -	1	2%
	Public Services	1	2%
	Hotels & Entertainment Services	1	2%
	Electrical Utilities & IPPs	1	2%
	Aerospace & Defense	1	2%
	Food & Tobacco	1	2%
	Freight & Logistics Services	1	2%
	Automobiles & Auto Parts	1	2%
	Grand Total	**60**	**100%**
Primary job Nature	Technical or Engineering	21	35%
	Sales - Non-Technical	8	13%
	Scientific or Development	5	8%
	Customer service helpdesk	4	7%
	Strategic Management, Leadership	4	7%
	Managerial	3	5%
	Sales - Technical	3	5%
	Medical, Healthcare	3	5%
	Production, Manufacturing	3	5%
	Financial services	2	3%
	Warehouse	1	2%
	Training or Education	1	2%
	Assembly	1	2%

Contextual variable	Value	No. of projects	%
	Management consulting	1	2%
	Grand Total	**60**	**100%**
Critical-to-success Skill	Complex troubleshooting	12	20%
	Sales and negotiation	11	18%
	Technical Problem solving	6	10%
	Innovation and design	5	8%
	Strategic thinking	4	7%
	Helpdesk support	4	7%
	Supervisory	3	5%
	Project execution	3	5%
	Precision machining	3	5%
	Medical and psychological care	3	5%
	Financial analysis	2	3%
	Business analysis	1	2%
	Teaching and training	1	2%
	Assembly	1	2%
	Data processing	1	2%
	Grand Total	**60**	**100%**
Complexity Rating	2. Medium-High	22	37%
	4. Medium-Low	14	23%
	1. High	9	15%
	3. Medium	9	15%
	5. Low	6	10%
	Grand Total	**60**	**100%**
Countries	USA	51	85%
	Netherlands	3	5%
	Singapore	3	5%
	Australia	2	3%
	Thailand	1	2%
	Total	**60**	**100%**

CH 1 / INTRODUCTION

Figure 2.2 Graphical distribution profile of selected project cases classified as per Thomas-Reuters (TR) Business Classification System

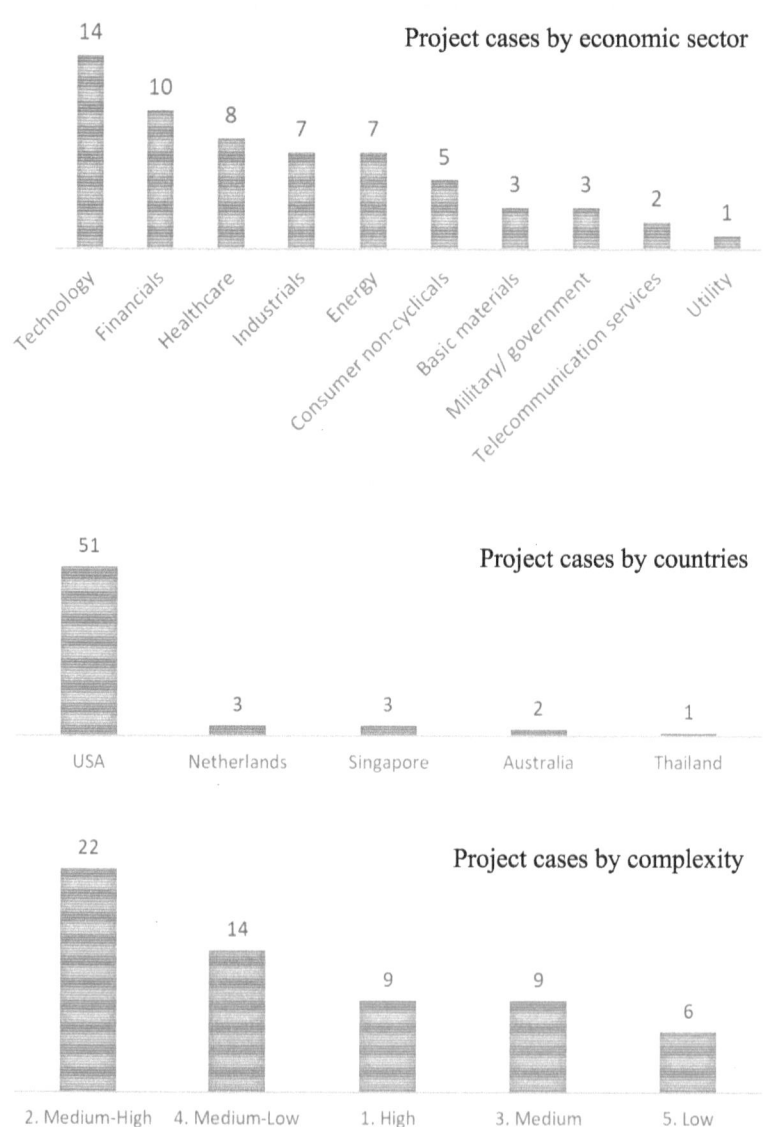

SPEED MATTERS

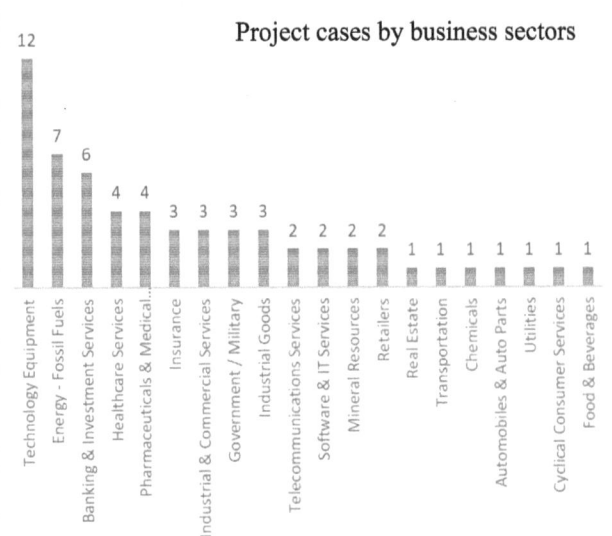

Project cases by business sectors

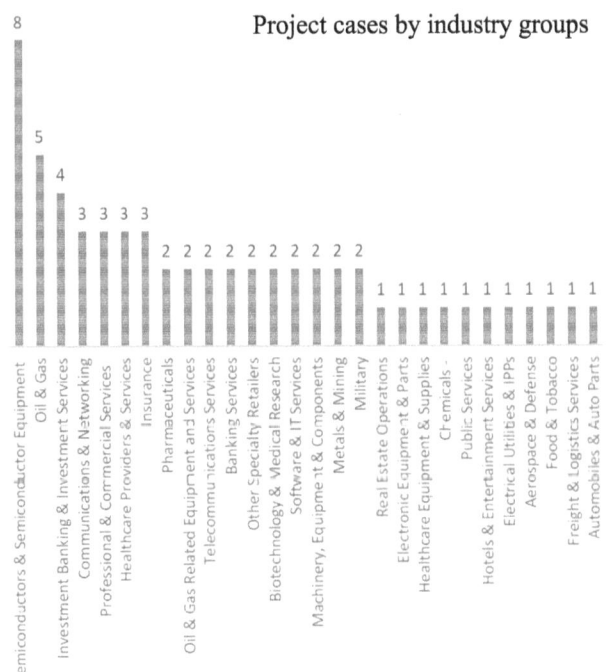

Project cases by industry groups

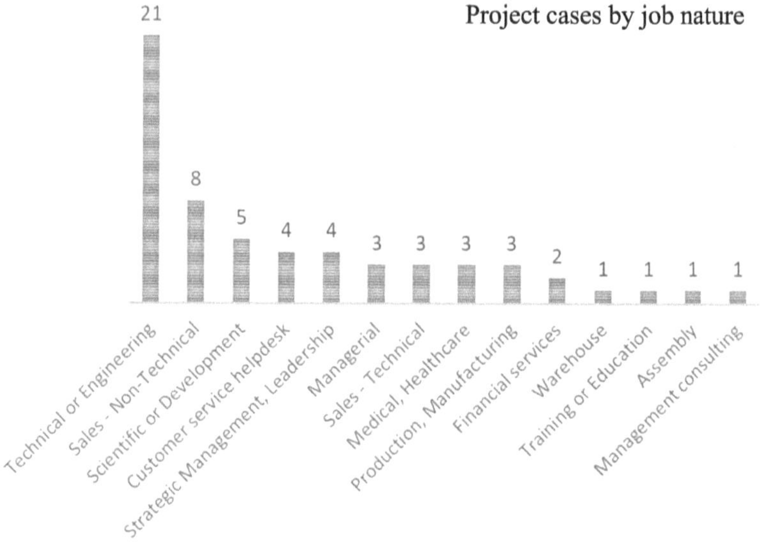

CH1 / INTRODUCTION

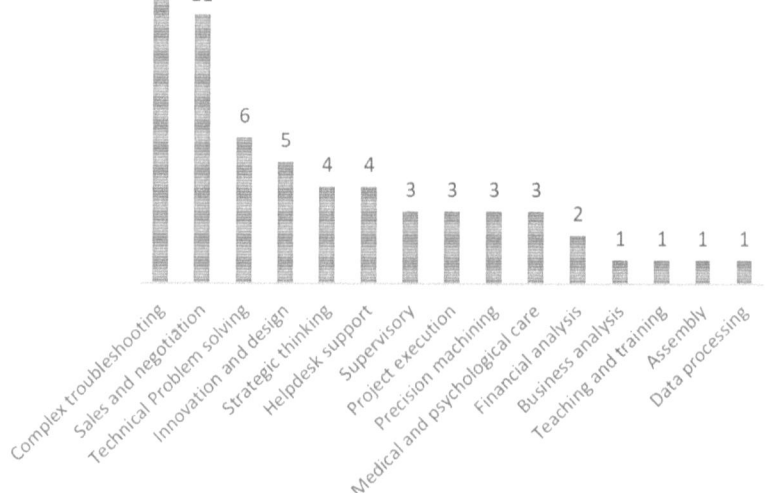

Table 2-3 Summary table of 60 project cases selected for analysis

Project case ID	Project case title	Location of project	Economic sector (TRBC)	Business Sector (TRBC)	Industry Group (TRBC)	Nature of primary job role	Critical-to-success Skill	Complexity Rating
1	Customer service engineers troubleshooting and repairing complex semiconductor equipment	Singapore	Technology	Technology Equipment	Semiconductors & Semiconductor Equipment	Technical or Engineering	Complex troubleshooting	2. Medium-High
2	Customer service helpdesk taking inbound calls for sales of investment products	USA	Financials	Banking & Investment Services	Investment Banking & Investment Services	Sales - Non-Technical	Sales and negotiation	4. Medium-Low
3	Technical trainers delivering food manufacturing process training	Philippines	Consumer non-cyclicals	Food & Beverages	Food & Tobacco	Training or Education	Teaching and training	4. Medium-Low
4	Software engineers developing large scale information applications (books)	US/ Thailand	Technology	Software & IT Services	Software & IT Services	Scientific or Development	Innovation and design	1. High
5	Cybersecurity analysts analyzing and identifying cyber-threats on client enterprise networks	USA	Technology	Technology Equipment	Communications & Networking	Technical or Engineering	Technical Problem Solving	2. Medium-High
6	Insurance agents selling insurance products	USA	Financials	Insurance	Insurance	Sales - Non-Technical	Sales and negotiation	4. Medium-Low
7	Customer service engineers troubleshooting and repairing complex semiconductor equipment	USA	Technology	Technology Equipment	Semiconductors & Semiconductor Equipment	Technical or Engineering	Complex troubleshooting	2. Medium-High
8	Console operators monitoring and controlling the processes at petrochemical plants	USA	Energy	Energy - Fossil Fuels	Oil & Gas	Technical or Engineering	Technical Problem Solving	2. Medium-High
9	Service engineers troubleshooting and repairing telecommunication network equipment	USA	Telecommunication services	Telecommunications Services	Telecommunications Services	Technical or Engineering	Complex troubleshooting	2. Medium-High
10	Console operators monitoring and controlling the processes at petrochemical plants	USA	Energy	Energy - Fossil Fuels	Oil & Gas	Technical or Engineering	Technical Problem Solving	2. Medium-High
11	Pharmaceutical biochemists manufacturing sophisticated cancer drugs	USA	Healthcare	Pharmaceuticals & Medical Research	Pharmaceuticals	Scientific or Development	Innovation and design	1. High
12	Managers managing retail donut baking stores	USA	Consumer non-cyclicals	Food & Beverages	Food & Tobacco	Managerial, Supervisory	Supervisory	3. Medium
13	Claim processing executives examining and processing health insurance claims	USA	Financials	Insurance	Insurance	Financial services	Financial analysis	4. Medium-Low
14	Sales representative selling pharmaceutical products	USA	Healthcare	Pharmaceuticals & Medical Research	Pharmaceuticals	Sales - Technical	Sales and negotiation	4. Medium-Low
15	Insurance agents selling insurance products	USA	Financials	Insurance	Insurance	Sales - Non-Technical	Sales and negotiation	4. Medium-Low

Project case ID	Project case title	Location of project	Economic sector (TRBC)	Business Sector (TRBC)	Industry Group (TRBC)	Nature of primary job role	Critical-to-success Skill	Complexity Rating
16	Console operators monitoring and controlling the processes at petrochemical plants	USA	Energy	Energy - Fossil Fuels	Oil & Gas	Technical or Engineering	Technical Problem Solving	2. Medium-High
17	Customer service helpdesk taking inbound calls for hotel and travel-related services	USA	Consumer non-cyclicals	Cyclical Consumer Services	Hotels & Entertainment Services	Customer service helpdesk	Helpdesk support	5. Low
18	Managers managing supermarket chains	USA	Consumer non-cyclicals	Retailers	Other Speciality Retailers	Managerial, Supervisory	Supervisory	3. Medium
19	Energy Corporation top executives transferring knowledge to successors	USA	Energy	Energy - Fossil Fuels	Oil & Gas	Strategic Management, Leadership	Strategic thinking	1. High
20	Hospital medical doctors and nursing staff providing pediatrics care services	USA	Healthcare	Healthcare Services	Healthcare Providers & Services	Medical, Healthcare	Medical and psychological care	3. Medium
21	Customer helpdesk taking inbound calls to remotely troubleshoot client computer and software issues	USA	Technology	Software & IT Services	Software & IT Services	Technical or Engineering	Complex troubleshooting	2. Medium-High
22	Customer service engineers troubleshooting and repairing complex semiconductor equipment	USA	Technology	Technology Equipment	Semiconductors & Semiconductor Equipment	Technical or Engineering	Complex troubleshooting	2. Medium-High
23	School administrator and teachers instituting school improvement programs	USA	Industrials	Industrial & Commercial Services	Professional & Commercial Services	Training or Education	Teaching and training	4. Medium-Low
24	Warehouse professionals adopting SAP for supply chain and logistics transactions	USA	Industrials	Transportation	Freight & Logistics Services	Warehouse	Data processing	5. Low
25	Console operators monitoring and controlling the processes at petrochemical plants	USA	Energy	Energy - Fossil Fuels	Oil & Gas	Technical or Engineering	Technical Problem Solving	2. Medium-High
26	Young military officers on the leadership pathway	USA	Military/government	Government / Military	Military	Strategic Management, Leadership	Strategic thinking	1. High
27	Military officers setting up a new command center to prevent cyberterrorism	USA	Military/government	Government / Military	Military	Strategic Management, Leadership	Strategic thinking	1. High
28	Biotechnology scientists strategizing business of brain implant technology for curing neurological diseases	USA	Healthcare	Pharmaceuticals & Medical Research	Biotechnology & Medical Research	Scientific or Development	Innovation and design	1. High
29	Machinists fabricating aircraft engine mechanical parts	USA	Industrials	Industrial Goods	Aerospace & Defense	Production, Manufacturing	Precision machining	3. Medium
30	Sales engineers selling hi-tech enterprise communication products	Netherlands	Technology	Technology Equipment	Communications & Networking	Technical or Engineering	Project execution	2. Medium-High
31	Electronics technicians to troubleshoot and repair of complex Navy electronics equipment	Netherlands	Technology	Technology Equipment	Electronic Equipment & Parts	Technical or Engineering	Complex troubleshooting	2. Medium-High
32	Benefit Evaluators examining eligibility for Govt. run benefits	USA	Military/government	Government / Military	Public Services	Financial services	Financial analysis	4. Medium-Low
33	Sales engineers selling hi-tech enterprise computer and server systems	USA	Technology	Technology Equipment	Communications & Networking	Technical or Engineering	Project execution	2. Medium-High
34	Customer service engineers troubleshooting and repairing complex semiconductor equipment	Netherlands	Technology	Technology Equipment	Semiconductors & Semiconductor Equipment	Technical or Engineering	Complex troubleshooting	2. Medium-High
35	Clinical staff and database administrators transitioning to new software for clinical trials data	USA	Healthcare	Pharmaceuticals & Medical Research	Biotechnology & Medical Research	Technical or Engineering	Project execution	2. Medium-High
36	Customer service helpdesk taking inbound calls for financial products	USA	Financials	Banking & Investment Services	Banking Services	Customer service helpdesk	Helpdesk support	5. Low

Project case ID	Project case title	Location of project	Economic sector (TRBC)	Business Sector (TRBC)	Industry Group (TRBC)	Nature of primary job role	Critical-to-success Skill	Complexity Rating
37	Healthcare professionals providing assisted living services for elders	USA	Healthcare	Healthcare Services	Healthcare Providers & Services	Medical, Healthcare	Medical and psychological care	3. Medium
38	Customer service engineers troubleshooting and repairing complex semiconductor equipment	USA	Technology	Technology Equipment	Semiconductors & Semiconductor Equipment	Technical or Engineering	Complex troubleshooting	2. Medium-High
39	Customer service engineers troubleshooting and repairing complex semiconductor equipment	Singapore	Technology	Technology Equipment	Semiconductors & Semiconductor Equipment	Technical or Engineering	Complex troubleshooting	2. Medium-High
40	Insurance agents selling insurance products	USA	Financials	Banking & Investment Services	Investment Banking & Investment Services	Sales - Non-Technical	Sales and negotiation	4. Medium-Low
41	Baseball players trying to recognize ball pitch	USA	Sports	Sports	Sports	Sports, Athletics	Perceptual and physical skills	2. Medium-High
64	Console operators monitoring and controlling the processes at petrochemical plants	UAE	Energy	Energy - Fossil Fuels	Oil & Gas	Technical or Engineering	Technical Problem Solving	2. Medium-High
42	Managers managing retail store chains	USA	Consumer non-cyclicals	Retailers	Other Speciality Retailers	Managerial, Supervisory	Supervisory	3. Medium
43	Plant maintenance engineers to troubleshoot production machine issues	USA	Industrials	Industrial Goods	Machinery, Equipment & Components	Technical or Engineering	Complex troubleshooting	2. Medium-High
44	Sales representatives upselling strategic service products	USA	Industrials	Industrial & Commercial Services	Professional & Commercial Services	Sales - Non-Technical	Sales and negotiation	4. Medium-Low
45	Reactor operators manufacturing chemical paints	USA	Basic materials	Chemicals	Chemicals -	Technical or Engineering	Technical Problem Solving	2. Medium-High
46	Customer service engineers troubleshooting and repairing complex semiconductor equipment	USA	Technology	Technology Equipment	Semiconductors & Semiconductor Equipment	Technical or Engineering	Complex troubleshooting	2. Medium-High
47	Real estate agents booking mortgages and listings	USA	Financials	Real Estate	Real Estate Operations	Sales - Non-Technical	Sales and negotiation	4. Medium-Low
48	Truck assemblers assembling and fabricating automobiles	USA	Consumer non-cyclicals	Automobiles & Auto Parts	Automobiles & Auto Parts	Assembly, Repair	Assembly	5. Low
49	Maintenance engineers repairing and maintaining petroleum pipeline feeds	USA	Energy	Energy - Fossil Fuels	Oil & Gas Related Equipment and Services	Technical or Engineering	Complex troubleshooting	2. Medium-High
50	Machine operators fabricating mechanical parts for petroleum exploration equipment	Singapore	Energy	Energy - Fossil Fuels	Oil & Gas Related Equipment and Services	Production, Manufacturing	Precision machining	3. Medium
51	Managers adopting new conversation and coaching tool with their employees	Australia	Consumer non-cyclicals	Cyclical Consumer Services	Media & Publishing	Managerial, Supervisory	Supervisory	3. Medium
52	Financial analysts assessing corporate insolvency cases	USA	Industrials	Industrial & Commercial Services	Professional & Commercial Services	Management consulting	Business analysis	2. Medium-High
65	Service personnel handling automobile service experience	USA	Consumer non-cyclicals	Automobiles & Auto Parts	Automobiles & Auto Parts	Sales - Non-Technical	Sales and negotiation	4. Medium-Low
53	Healthcare professionals providing residential care for severely disabled	USA	Healthcare	Healthcare Services	Healthcare Providers & Services	Medical, Healthcare	Medical and psychological care	3. Medium
54	Sales engineers selling construction products and equipment	USA	Industrials	Industrial Goods	Machinery, Equipment & Components	Sales - Technical	Sales and negotiation	4. Medium-Low
55	Customer service helpdesk taking inbound calls for internet phone service	USA	Telecommunication services	Telecommunications Services	Telecommunications Services	Customer service helpdesk	Helpdesk support	5. Low

Project case ID	Project case title	Location of project	Economic sector (TRBC)	Business Sector (TRBC)	Industry Group (TRBC)	Nature of primary job role	Critical-to-success Skill	Complexity Rating
56	Customer service helpdesk taking inbound calls for sales of financial products	USA	Financials	Banking & Investment Services	Banking Services	Sales - Non-Technical	Sales and negotiation	4. Medium-Low
57	Customer service helpdesk taking inbound calls for banking services	Australia	Financials	Banking & Investment Services	Investment Banking & Investment Services	Customer service helpdesk	Helpdesk support	5. Low
58	Design engineers developing complex semiconductor equipment	Netherlands	Technology	Technology Equipment	Semiconductors & Semiconductor Equipment	Scientific or Development	Innovation and design	1. High
59	Customer service helpdesk taking inbound calls for upselling of financial products	USA	Financials	Banking & Investment Services	Investment Banking & Investment Services	Sales - Non-Technical	Sales and negotiation	4. Medium-Low
60	Electrical engineers designing and repairing power plant equipment	USA	Utility	Utilities	Electrical Utilities & IPPs	Scientific or Development	Innovation and design	1. High
66	Computer programmers developing and testing general software	USA	Technology	Software & IT Services	Software & IT Services	Scientific or Development	Innovation and design	1. High
61	Sales engineers selling medical and surgical instruments	USA	Healthcare	Healthcare Services	Healthcare Equipment & Supplies	Sales - Technical	Sales and negotiation	4. Medium-Low
62	Business managers developing strategies for unforeseen drop in gold prices	USA	Basic materials	Mineral Resources	Metals & Mining	Strategic Management, Leadership	Strategic thinking	1. High
63	Underground miners preparing for unexpected underground fire during mining operations	USA	Basic materials	Mineral Resources	Metals & Mining	Production, Manufacturing	Precision machining	3. Medium

2.1.6 Data collection and interviews

I asked each of the selected project leaders to provide me with one successful project case. I structured the interviews based on five core elements of the project success stories, which were: (1) business challenge or the problem of TTP to be solved; (2) description of the solution in place (if any) to reduce TTP and the results arrived at (business metrics); (3) issues or challenges associated with the solution that was in place and the root cause of the problem; (4) description of the alternative solutions or strategies implemented to reduce TTP; and (5) the results (quantitative, qualitative, and anecdotal) in terms of the reduction in TTP.

I used three types of interviews to collect data from the project leaders: (1) in-depth qualitative, (2) questionnaire-based, and (3) e-mail-based. I conducted in-depth interviews with majority of participants over the phone or in person. A small percentage of participants opted for responding to questions via structured questionnaires or exchanges via e-mails. The interviews were structured around bounded project case descriptions in such a way that allowed a comparable and consistent structure of the final data. This approach ensured completeness of the required data as well as a higher level of data quality. The approach also favored cross-case analyses by comparing the bounded project cases across several variables, which enabled me to understand the commonalities, differences, transferability, and generalizability among the cases (Bower et al. 2015; Miles, Huberman & Saldana 2014; Stake 2006; Vohra 2014; Yin 2014).

2.1.7 Data analysis

I used two rigorous, widely used data analysis techniques in juxtaposition: (a) the thematic analysis approach by Boyatzis (1998) and Braun & Clarke (2006, 2013) and (b) the matrix analysis approach by Miles & Huberman (1994) and Miles, Huberman & Saldana (2014).

Using the thematic analysis approach, I identified new themes and patterns, and analyzed the association, relationship, and hierarchy among them. A number of themes, sub-themes, and overarching themes emerged during thematic analysis.

I arranged the new themes and patterns as matrices using the matrix analysis framework. Each matrix was basically a table of columns and rows to arrange the data for easy viewing in one place. Using this approach, I could arrange the themes and data of the bounded project cases as a multi-row, multi-column table. This enabled me to understand the dynamics of a single project case as well as that across project cases by stacking rows of data.

I used these matrices to compare the themes across the several variables in the project cases (Stake 2006; Yin 2014). I compared cases for similarities, patterns, and differences, and the relationship among the patterns was determined across different contextual variables such as business sectors, industry groups, nature of jobs, nature of skills involved, and complexity ratings.

First, I performed a within-case analysis in which I read one row of a given project case all the way across to all the columns. This enabled a thorough understanding of the dynamics of the project case, based on the characteristics, variables, and contexts, as well as the start-to-end success story of the project. The complete picture included a snapshot of business challenges; inefficiencies of previous models; factors and determinants; philosophical stands; proficiency measures; inputs; processes, methods, techniques, and practices used in each of the projects; and the project results. Using the within-case analysis, I first focused on one project in its entirety and then moved on to the next; by doing so, I got certain new insights with which I went back and reviewed my first project. In the light of new learning, I redefined and refined my understanding.

I then conducted a cross-case analysis of the project cases collected across a variety of contextual variables such as different organizations, industries, business environments, job types, complexity levels, and countries. I compared the themes among the different contexts. In the cross-case analysis, I picked variables or themes one-at-a-time and read vertically along the particular column through all the project cases. The variations in the key themes among project cases were noted. The themes were validated by a constant comparison among each other across all the project cases. Some themes were refined, collapsed, or expanded, while some were merged. Several display forms were constructed before reaching a useful view, which enabled meaningful conclusions to be drawn.

I then grouped the projects based on contextual variables such as the economic sector, business sector, generic job role, nature of primary skill, and complexity level. The sub-matrices were used to analyze the patterns of the themes across these contextual variables to identify their associations and relationships. The process was iterative, referring back repeatedly to data, codes, themes, concept maps, and matrices. This rigorous recursive process of reducing data, creating data display, and drawing conclusions led to the development of a conceptual model of accelerated proficiency based on six major practices and 24 strategies that prevailed across all project cases.

2.1.8 Expert focus group validation

I invited ten project leaders from diverse backgrounds and industries to participate in an expert focus group. I selected the experts based on their leadership, diversity of business sectors, and the probability of receiving responses. This focus group of experts aimed to review the research study's findings and the conceptual model developed during data analysis and provide me feedback on the validity, transferability, and utilization of the findings. I gave them a thirty-page document describing the strategies for accelerated proficiency and the model developed. I asked the experts specific questions and asked them to respond with their comments. The 'feed-forward' Delphi method round elicited inputs from them by 'presenting to respondents the information about emerging consensus derived from the prior interviews' (Gordon 1994, p. 5). I used their feedback to validate the model and the findings of the study, based on which necessary refinements were done in the analysis.

2.1.9 Generalizability and transferability

For any study, it is important to see how well the findings and observations apply across different settings. The sample size of 85 is already much larger when compared with the standards specified for a qualitative study. Also, the project cases spanned across 70 different organizational settings and were not constrained to a specific industry or business. The large sample size and the diverse selection of organizational settings support the fact that my study covers a wide range and that the findings and inferences can be applied in various other settings as well.

I used the frameworks and techniques specified by Lincoln & Guba (1985) and Miles, Huberman & Saldana (2014) to ensure and test the objectivity, dependability, and credibility of the data, data analysis, and the findings. As part of the process, I used data triangulation methods that involved gathering data not only from in-depth interviews but also cross-checking them with the documentation gathered from various sources like write-ups, case studies, presentations, blog posts, white papers, and magazine articles related to the project case under discussion.

For data analysis, I used multiple supplementary techniques, which included matrix analysis, thematic analysis, concept maps, thematic maps, thematic networks, template analysis, and within-case and cross-case comparative analyses. All of these techniques collectively enhanced the accuracy of the data analysis and improved the representation of participants' experience.

I then conducted a prevalence analysis to test for generalizability and transferability. The analysis verified that all the themes and strategies included in the final model were indeed strongly prevalent across the majority of the project cases. I also engaged highly experienced professionals to conduct peer reviews of the findings, which were then thoroughly reviewed by the experts of the focus group.

Collectively, with the application of the above rigorous reliability and validation best practices, I established that the findings of this study exhibited a high level of generalizability, transferability, applicability, and fittingness across a wide range of contexts. The model generated in this study was found to be generalizable across several contexts.

2.2 RESEARCH OUTCOMES

The research study revealed the following outcomes:

- The concept, meaning, and measurement of accelerated proficiency.
- The three business drivers that trigger a reduction in TTP.
- The business benefits of shortening TTP.
- The model including six business practices and 24 strategies to reduce TTP.

As mentioned previously, in this book, I shall focus only on the first three outcomes. I highly encourage you to read my forthcoming book (tentatively titled *Get There Faster*) that covers the fourth outcome in regard to the strategies and models.

CHAPTER 3
THE PROFICIENCY

THE ROLE OF PROFICIENT
PERFORMANCE IN
WORKPLACES

Before we dive into the metrics of TTP, let us understand the nature of proficiency or proficient performance at work. In this chapter, I intend to describe the different aspects of proficiency. I have often noticed that direct managers and leaders rarely use proficiency-related language in their daily discussions or measurements. This, I strongly believe, is the primary reason why organizations never get to shorten the point of the desired proficiency. This chapter delves into previous research studies that dealt with proficiency in workplaces. This chapter aims to provide readers with a sound conceptual and business acumen as it focuses on developing workforce to the desired proficiency level. In this chapter, I first discuss the nature of performance before qualifying the need for proficiency in workplaces. I then establish the relevance between the stages of proficient performance and how its progression happens from one stage to the next. Finally, I describe certain essential characteristics of proficient performance that managers and leaders should know.

3.1 NATURE OF WORKPLACE PERFORMANCE

Effective performance from employees is a key business expectation that fuels the operations, profit, and competitive advantage of a business (Sonnentag & Frese 2002). Poor performance of employees in their jobs is sure to have far-reaching consequences on their team's performance and, eventually, their organization's performance.

Performance in workplace has been explained through several perspectives: task vs. contextual performance (Borman &

Motowidlo 1993); behavioral vs. outcome performance (Campbell et al. 1993); task vs. job performance (Kanfer & Kantrowitz 2002); individual vs. team performance (Sonnentag & Frese 2002); and job vs. organizational performance (Griffin, Neal & Parker 2007; Sudnickas 2016).

There are two primary views on individual performance: behavioral and outcome.

3.1.1 Behavioral performance

Behavioral performance was one of the key dimensions found in the classic studies of Campbell (1990) and Murphy (1989). Murphy (1989) believed that task performance is about the accomplishment of duties and tasks written in job descriptions. He theorized that work performance has four dimensions: (1) task behaviors; (2) interpersonal behaviors; (3) downtime behaviors (related to work avoidance); and (4) destructive/hazardous behaviors (related to noncompliance, violence, etc.).

Taking it further, Campbell (1990) considered not only task-related behaviors but also performance behaviors not directly related to the task. He acknowledged that performance is not just about job-specific task proficiency. Rather, an individual's proficiency in several non-job-specific tasks as well, such as perseverance and discipline that is required to get reasonable performance. Campbell et al. (1993) and Campbell & Wiernik (2015, p. 48) defined performance as behaviors or actions that people do that contribute to the organization's goals. This view implied that the outcome of the work, such as the number of parts made, the number of sales made, among other metrics, resulted from individual behavior. Campbell (1990) included eight dimensions to the work performance: (1) job-specific task proficiency; (2) non-job-specific task proficiency; (3) written and oral communications; (4) demonstrating effort; (5) maintaining personal discipline; (6) facilitating peer and team performance; (7) supervision; and (8) management and administration

However, this view maintained that measuring an individual's performance in terms of job outcomes was problematic. Motowidlo, Borman & Schmit (1997) strongly argued that a performance model should not include results but should focus on behaviors only. They reasoned that results are a function of not only an individual's performance but also several other factors. Unless these factors are isolated, results do not represent an individual's contribution to the organization's goals (Motowidlo, Borman & Schmit 1997, p. 73).

3.1.2   Outcome performance

Individual performance based on outcomes suggests that the outcomes and results of the behaviors are equally important indicators of work performance. Supporters of this school of thought have positioned a contradictory view that business organizations value performance in terms of accomplishments (e.g., Gilbert 2013). Accomplishments can be job outputs (such as decisions made and strategies identified) or end results (such as sales improvement). Binder (2017, p. 20) stated that 'the value delivered by human performance is in the *accomplishments* it produces and that the behavior needed for producing those accomplishments is costly, not valuable for its own sake.'

Reconciling these views, Viswesvaran & Ones (2000) suggested a middle ground based on their analysis of over 400 different dimensions found by them from their studies on work performance in the last several decades. They defined work performance as a combination of actions, behavior, and outcomes, which are linked to organizational goals.

3.1.3 Task performance

From the meta-analysis of 107 studies published until 2010 in four major databases, Koopmans et al. (2011) observed task performance or task proficiency to be one of the prominent trends in measuring individual job performance. However, task performance is just one of the dimensions of the overall job performance: 'There is not one outcome, one factor, or one anything that can be pointed to and labelled as job performance. Job performance really is multidimensional' (Campbell, McHenry & Wise 1990, p. 314).

It is vital to measure performance to figure out how well an employee has met the standards set for his tasks, actions, behaviors, results, or accomplishments to meet the organizational goals. Irrespective of how performance is measured, each employee's job performance is a critical determinant of an organization's performance and competitiveness. In this book, the term *performance* refers to the job performance an employee must demonstrate to meet the organizational goals. Performance could be task performance, outcome performance, or job performance, depending upon what is being measured to determine proficiency.

3.2 PROFICIENCY AND PERFORMANCE

The concept of performance has an essential dimension of proficiency (Griffin, Neal & Parker 2007; Koopmans et al. 2011). If performance is defined in terms of actions and behaviors, managers need to know how "proficiently" an employee demonstrates those actions or behaviors. More commonly, proficiency represents the mastery of skills, tasks, knowledge, or job function by an employee as a result of his/her experience, that is, how good someone is in that domain (Enos, Kehrhahn & Bell 2003, p. 371).

Proficiency has also been used as a measure of performance. The *Business Dictionary* defines proficiency as the 'Mastery of a specific behavior or skill demonstrated by consistently superior performance, measured against established or popular standards.'[4]

In most studies, performance was considered as the final outcome of the level of proficiency exhibited by an employee. The higher the proficiency, the higher is the performance. Performance, in this context, could be task performance, outcome performance, or job performance, depending upon what is being measured for proficiency.

---

[4]http://www.businessdictionary.com/definition/proficiency.html

CH3/THE PROFICIENCY

3.2.1 Task proficiency as a measure of performance

Campbell (1990, 1999) was one of the first researchers to use proficiency as a measure of performance, though it was in the context of the performance of specific tasks. He proposed *job-specific task proficiency* as a vital determinant of an employee's performance, which communicated his/her ability to do a particular task. Campbell & Wiernik (2015, p. 48) highlighted the importance of proficiency: 'For those [actions and behaviors] that are relevant, the level of proficiency with which the individual performs them must be scaled.' Most commonly, an individual's proficiency indicates the level of his/her performance.

In the context of job performance, Kanfer & Kantrowitz (2002, p. 30) observed that 'job proficiency is generally more narrowly defined as a task-relevant outcome.' They indicated that in some studies, performance was measured with regard to a cognitive ability, which, in turn, was measured in terms of task proficiency. However, these instances limited the reference to proficiency in the context of job-specific tasks. Several performance-related studies use the term *proficiency* in the context of task performance in a job (Borman & Motowidlo 1993, 1997; Campbell & Wiernik 2015; Koopmans et al. 2011; Motowidlo, Borman & Schmit 1997; Motowidlo & Van Scotter 1994; Viswesvaran & Ones 2000; Viswesvaran 1993).

3.2.2 Proficiency as a stage of performance

Some models suggest viewing proficiency as a specific stage of performance, characterized by the behaviors shown by an individual. One of the common models that supports this view is the *Dreyfus and Dreyfus model*. According to Dreyfus (2004), a proficient performer is deeply involved with the task and has the ability to identify the important aspects of the task(s) assigned to him/her and pay requisite attention to complete them. A proficient person views the situations holistically in terms of various elements: 'With holistic understanding, decision-making is less labored since the professional has a perspective on which of the many attributes and aspects present are the important ones' (Benner 1984, pp. 13–34). As the situation changes, his/her deliberation, plan, and assessment may change. With changing situations, s/he is able to see new patterns which deviate from normal. Decision-making is very quick and fluid because of his/her experience of a similar situation in the past. 'Action becomes easier and less stressful as the learner simply sees what needs to be done rather than using a calculative procedure to select one of several possible alternatives' (Dreyfus & Dreyfus 2005, p. 786). A proficient performer considers fewer options and focuses on the correct aspect of the problem (Benner 1984). For example, Benner (2004) noted that nurses who have reached the proficiency stage exhibit a situated understanding of their patients' responses: 'The nurse feels increasingly at home in the situation and can now recognise when she or he has a good sense of the situation' (id. 195). Dreyfus & Dreyfus (2005, p. 787) further clarified that 'the *proficient performer*, immersed in the world of skillful activity, *sees* what needs to be done, but *decides* how to do it.'

Alexander (2003a) describes proficiency as one of the stages of the three-stage progression. She explained it from the angle of the different strategies adopted by various proficient performers. She described a three-stage model of learning based on the studies conducted in educational settings, and characterized proficiency as an interplay of knowledge, strategies, and motivations. She observed that at the proficiency/expertise stage, performers demonstrated the use of a broad and deep knowledge base on the topic or domain, along with in-depth processing strategies. They displayed high individual interest and engagement in the task, which was similar to the observation made by Dreyfus and Dreyfus (1986, 2004, 2005). The research suggested the role of reasoning skills as a differentiator in proficiency measurement as: 'Proficiency is defined not just in terms of knowledge but also in terms of reasoning strategies and skills' (Hoffman, Feltovich, et al. 2010).

3.2.3 Proficiency as the quality of job performance

Mainstream literature continues to emphasize proficiency in terms of the knowledge, skills, behaviors, and competencies to perform the desired function (Dixon 2015). However, proficiency, from a business perspective, appears to be beyond simply the measurement of knowledge, skills, and tasks.

Proficiency in a given job means a state of someone being fully productive and not requiring much supervision. A performer is said to be proficient when s/he meets this standard. 'Proficiency is when a new employee achieves a predetermined level of performance on a consistent basis' (Rosenbaum & Williams 2004, p. 14).

In the *TTP study* that I conducted, the project leaders described how they viewed, defined, and measured proficiency in workplaces. The leaders viewed proficiency as the state at which an individual achieves the required performance, while consistently meeting and maintaining the predefined standards of the job role. Most of the leaders measured proficiency in terms of business outcomes or the observable actions that closely represented or led to business outcomes. However, achieving business outcomes rather than performing tasks or activities was regarded as the hallmark of the state of proficiency. Project leaders also differentiated that proficiency was not just about learning an isolated skill, task, or activity in a job.

To do a job to satisfaction, an employee needs to have a minimal level of proficiency. This minimum level is referred to as the *desired or target proficiency* in this book. The definition of desired or target proficiency varies from organization to organization and from job to job. It takes time for an employee to acquire the desired proficiency in any given role.

Therefore, it is imperative that any kind of learning goals in workplaces and outside, including employee development endeavors, should be intended to produce highly proficient employees in the assigned work or job role. If not, organizations should not invest in such programs. Enos, Kehrhahn & Bell (2003, p. 371) emphasize this aspect and position proficiency as 'the primary objective of both formal and informal learning undertakings in organisations.'

Nevertheless, workforce proficiency appears to be an important determinant of how successfully organizations handle business challenges daily (Hoffman, Feltovich, et al. 2010). Having employees with high levels of proficiency is crucial to organizations:

> Domain practitioners who achieve high levels of proficiency provide technical judgment to speed decision-making in time-critical events. They provide resilience to operations by resolving tough problems, anticipating future demands and re-planning, and acting prudently by judgment rather than by rule. (Hoffman et al. 2014, p. 2)

3.3 NOVICE-TO-EXPERT PROGRESSION

Performance development literature emphasizes heavily on the process and nature of novice-to-expert transition. This transition is basically how a novice develops and progresses toward becoming an expert (Benner 2001; 2005; 2004; 2020). Researchers have maintained that expertise is not an end state; rather, it is a journey that is characterized by progressively upgrading one's skills, experience, and intuition (Benner 2001; 2005; 2004; 2020).

3.3.1 Stages of novice-to-expert progression

Novice-to-expert transition is generally viewed as a staged progression. The view reports the level-like shifts in the qualitative characteristics of employees, indicating the stages they pass through in an attempt toward achieving a higher level of skill mastery or performance. While the basic idea of such a transition is that experts are relative to the novice, the goal of such an approach is 'to understand how we can enable less skilled or experienced persons to become more skilled...' (Chi 2006, p. 23).

Classical studies have defined progression toward the automaticity of skills as a series of stages (Ackerman 1988; Anderson 1982; Fitts & Posner 1967). Several researchers have developed more refined details on the stages toward proficiency. Among them, Shuell (1986, p. 364) noticed that 'as an individual acquires knowledge, his or her knowledge structure gradually evolves in qualitative as well as quantitative ways.' Classical studies indicated a qualitative shift in traits as novice learners moved toward higher proficiency (Benner 1984; Dreyfus & Dreyfus 1986). The qualitative shifts were supported by Hoffman (1998, p. 84) as: 'The distinction between "novice" versus "expert" implies that development can involve both qualitative shifts and stabilizations in knowledge and performance.' These observations imply that we can view the novice-to-expert transition as comprising several stages.

Hoffman, Feltovich et al. (2010, p. 28) proposed the continuum view of progression in terms of proficiency, which was similar to the views by other researchers, but it was charactcristically grounded on different criteria: 'We are considering a concept of expertise referred to as "high proficiency."' They viewed proficiency as an indicator of an employee's level of experience or expertise in his/her job role. They proposed that was a need for some mechanism to scale proficiency. They further stated that 'The analysis of proficiency and proficiency scaling can usefully commence by distinguishing experts (high and very high proficiency) from novices (very low proficiency)' (id. 32). Employees, on this continuum, progress toward higher proficiency through stages like naïve, novice, initiator, apprentice, journeyman, expert, and master (Hoffman 1998). In this view, a novice is a person who has low or very low proficiency, while an expert is someone with very high proficiency in that particular aspect (skill, task, function, or job).

Theorists have used different development parameters for qualifying level-like shifts, for example, the transformation of skills as second nature (automaticity) and implicit knowledge (Alexander 2003b; Spiro et al. 2003). Some studies have established that it is possible to define proficiency levels qualitatively in terms of skills and knowledge exhibited by professionals on the job.

Dreyfus and Dreyfus (1986, 2004, 2005) carried out the most significant studies on progression. They produced a model popularly known as the Dreyfus and Dreyfus model. Dreyfus & Dreyfus (2004, 2005) suggested a progression in terms of how a performer handles a situation. They suggested that an employee acquires an intuitive grasp on the situations and problems while passing through the five stages of proficiency—novice, advanced beginner, competent, proficient, and expert. As one progresses through the stages, s/he becomes more intuitive toward solving problems. This staged model could explain the progression toward expertise reasonably well in nursing and medical professions (Benner 2004). Benner (2004) attempted to define the levels of proficiency of the Dreyfus and Dreyfus model in terms of certain attributes of expected performance at each level in the context of the nursing and medical professions. Peña (2010) and Khan & Ramachandran (2012) applied the Dreyfus and Dreyfus model in the context of clinical practice and healthcare jobs and asserted that there is a level-like progression which can be demarcated qualitatively in terms of job attributes.

Some researchers asserted that task performance could be an indicator of different stages (Chi 2006; Merrill 2006; Schreiber et al. 2009). According to this premise, a novice completes simple versions of his/her tasks during training and moves to more complex tasks as his/her skill levels increase. Progressively, s/he becomes skillful at relatively more complex tasks, and starts addressing several cues at the same time. Literature shows that measurement of task performance must reflect this gradual acquisition of skill. Merrill (2006, p. 269) stated that proficiency measurement requires one to 'detect increments in performance demonstrating gradually increased skill in completing a whole complex task or solving a problem.'

Another group of researchers took a measurement approach to define proficiency levels in terms of the measurable attributes of jobs. For example, Chi (2006) proposed that proficiency levels could be roughly measured using inputs such as academic qualification, years of experience in performing the task, peer feedback, and profession-related tests. Schreiber et al. (2009) developed metrics for the measurement of pilot proficiency using simulators and postulated that it is possible to develop an objective measurement of performance in complex jobs that require a range of judgment and meta-skills. Kim (2012, 2015) proposed a different approach: measurement in terms of knowledge structures across different levels of the learning progress. Kim defined a set of measures corresponding to the levels of the features of knowledge structure. The relationship between the measures and the features of knowledge structures was determined based on theoretical assumptions as well as empirical evidence. A similar approach was suggested by Dörfler, Baracskai & Velencei (2009), who used knowledge as the demarcation for levels to explain the stages or levels of expertise.

3.3.2 Novice-to-expert progression as a process

The concept of stages conveys the idea of progression being a process. Both foundational and more recent research studies support the idea that developing a higher level of performance to proficiency and expertise can be viewed as a process. Studies by Lajoie (2003) focused on transitions and trajectories to increase expertise. In characterizing this progression, Lajoie (2003, p. 22) noted that 'becoming an expert is a transitional process.' At the same time, researchers have also opined that expertise is not the ultimate goal; rather, it is a 'nonlinear process state' (Moon, Kim & You 2013, p. 228). Possessing a certain amount of knowledge, skills, or behavior does not mean expertise. Bransford et al. (2004) also maintained that expertise is not a finished product; rather, it is a continuous process. Expertise is not a defined stage; rather, expertise grows from the interactions with the environment. Literature has viewed expertise as a continuous process of adjusting to knowledge, relearning, and changing his/her mental representation as s/he interacts with situations, reflects upon them, and uses pattern recognition to correct his/her way of thinking (Alexander 2003b). In terms of the continuous process toward making adjustments, Sternberg (1999, p.

359) contended that developing expertise involves 'the ongoing process of the acquisition and consolidation of a set of skills needed for a high level of mastery in one or more domains of life performance.' In a dynamic world, abilities are not always static. Alexander (2003a, p. 12) asserted that 'the journey toward expertise is unceasing. Even those who have attained the knowledge, strategic abilities, and interests indicative of expertise cannot sit idly by as the domain shifts under their feet.' Thus, it is reasonable to infer that expertise involves a constant evaluation of one's progress toward mastery.

While the staged model largely provided a theoretical framework on the progression toward expertise, it did not explain the actual mechanisms or methods of developing an employee to the next level of performance (Dall'Alba & Sandberg 2006; Peña 2010). The issue is that the actual mechanism of acquiring proficiency has not been dealt with elaborately in the currently available literature on expertise in a way that could be applied or used in organizations. Moon, Kim & You (2013, p. 226) stated the limitation of the literature on expertise: 'Most studies can't explain how the expertise reaches to a specific level or stage by multiple mechanisms. Accordingly we have to develop specific and realistic model for how expertise develops [sic].' Therefore, the fundamental challenge is the lack of understanding of the concept and the process of proficiency in organizations.

3.3.3 Stages of novice-to-expert progression

The Dreyfus and Dreyfus model has seen its place in several classical studies on proficiency acquisition. Dreyfus & Dreyfus (1986) observed numerous performers, mostly aircrew emergency staff and jet pilots, to understand how they tackle direct problems. They proposed a model that was based on the premise that skill acquisition is a continuous process in which skills are transformed into performance by experience and mastery (proficiency). Dreyfus & Dreyfus (1986) observed that experience with real-time situations alone produced higher levels of performance. They discovered that during skill acquisition, a learner passed through the five levels of proficiency.

Dreyfus and Dreyfus identified the characteristics of the employees that varied gradually when they moved from one stage to the next, how they perceived the elements of the situations (components), how they recognized which part of the situation to pay attention to (perspective), how they made decisions to act in a particular way (decision-making), and, finally, how much they were committed or involved with the task (commitment) (Dreyfus & Dreyfus 1986, 2004, 2005). They observed that the perception shifted from context-free understanding of facts to more of situational understanding. The knowledge began to be treated in the context of the situation by employees when they moved up from the novice stage. Further, with experience, an individual became more selective with the elements of the situation that were considered more important. In the beginning, novices were not able to recognize the relevance of their knowledge of the skill, but started doing so as they moved to the next stage. The context was analyzed analytically to begin with and the analysis developed into a more holistic assessment at higher stages. Dreyfus and Dreyfus contend that there was an observable shift from analytical approaches to intuition-based approaches while making decisions. Decision-making was rational in all learners except in experts who made decisions intuitively. The degree of involvement increased from a detached commitment to highly involved, along with the understanding of the task, decision-making, and the outcomes (Dreyfus & Dreyfus 1986, 2004, 2005).

Based on these shifts, Dreyfus and Dreyfus developed the characteristics of the five stages of proficiency. A general description of the five stages based on the characteristics suggested not only by Dreyfus & Dreyfus (1986) but also by later researchers who applied the model in various professions, for example, clinical practice (Peña 2010), healthcare (Khan & Ramachandran 2012), correctional services (Scobey 2006), education (Bedi 2003), and nursing (Ramsburg 2010) is as follows:

Novice: Novices are those who do not know much about the task or domain. The only mechanism they usually have to perform their task is some form of training. Novices are typically placed in training where they learn some facts about the skills and the rules to apply the skills. While applying these skills, novices view everything context-free. For every new thing, they require rules and maxims to solve, and are usually trained to follow them without exceptions. At this stage, they do not have a contextual understanding of how to evaluate a situation and how to decide whether a given rule will be applicable in that situation. Therefore, novices cannot discriminate between situations (Dreyfus & Dreyfus 1986, 2004, 2005).

Advanced beginner: Novices move up as advanced beginners as they start gaining experience in real situations. Advanced beginners start grasping the concepts underlying the situations and start comprehending the facts about situations. As they gain more experience, they start comparing and discriminating the situations. While they reach the ability to apply the rules in a structured setting, they do not have the experience to tackle real world situations. When they encounter a new situation, they tend to identify the unrecognized aspects of the situation, tend to apply the previously learned rules, and try to relate to the situation. They do develop situational perceptions, but these are still very limited. Task involvement increases, at which point their performance improves marginally (Dreyfus & Dreyfus 1986, 2004, 2005).

Competent: As advanced beginners start gaining experience, they start handling more and more situations. Employees at this stage start developing an understanding of both context-free and situational elements. They can now recognize the various aspects of a problem and can set goals. They may not apply rules all the time, depending on the situation, but they definitely try to tackle situations in novel ways. At this point, they have a better contextual understanding of whether a rule should be applied in a given situation or not. However, decision-making is still analytical. A competent performer is highly involved with the task, as well as the outcome of the task (Dreyfus & Dreyfus 1986, 2004, 2005). The term "competent" has seen the appeal in training and instruction design for a long time as an indication of an employee's ability.

However, Eraut (1994, p. 126) clarified that 'the Dreyfus definition of competence is based on how people approach their work, not on whether they should be judged as qualified to do it.'

Proficient: At this stage, the involvement of the performers with the task, as well as its outcome, is very high. The context is considered holistically, and proficient performers are able to make situational discriminations and pay attention to what is important and what is not. Pattern recognition is strengthened whereby performers are able to recognize new (previously unrecognized) elements of a novel situation. While they have very little dependence on the rules of familiar situations, they tend to use maxims in novel situations. At this stage, the decision-making is very quick, and the performance improves drastically. For example, in the context of clinical practice, Khan & Ramachandran (2012, p. 5) observed a proficient performer as the one who was able to handle complex routine work unsupervised but required supervision for nonroutine complex tasks; the performance was usually based on experience. Benner (2004, p. 198) observed that there was a change in perception regarding situations in proficient performers. At this stage, they were deliberate about changing the strategies based on understanding the new situation.

Expert: This last stage in skill progression was seen to be acquired with concrete experience. Thorough involvement and an understanding of the situations, tasks, and outcomes resulted in highly contextual experiences. Learners developed deep tacit knowledge and an intuitive grasp of the situations. Thus, the decision-making became intuitive rather than analytical. At this stage, performers also developed higher-order skills to make subtle discriminations between situations and were able to ascertain the type of knowledge used in different situations. Experts adopt a contextual approach to problem-solving to understand the relative, non-absolute nature of knowledge. Based on their experience, they could even work out the solutions for novel and never-seen-before problems (DiBello & Missildine 2011). Reflection comes naturally, and experts solve problems almost effortlessly. At this point, the skills of experts become automatic to the point that they are not even aware of it (Dreyfus & Dreyfus 1986, 2004, 2005).

3.3.4 Implications of the "stages" concept

Researchers like Eraut (1994) recognized that the strength of the Dreyfus and Dreyfus model was in 'the case it makes for tacit knowledge and intuition as critical features of professional expertise in "unstructured problem areas."' The model also emphasizes the process view, which positions progression toward the expertise stage as 'the way in which experts solve problems, rather than simply by [sic] the amount of knowledge that experts possess' (Ge & Hardré 2010, p. 24). It has proven to be an extremely useful model for depicting the levels of expertise in any profession. The most significant research on the Dreyfus and Dreyfus model is the work by Benner (2004, p. 194), who tested the applicability of the model by conducting nine studies spanning over 21 years. Benner found that the model was 'predictive and descriptive of distinct stages of skill acquisition in nursing practice.' She described the nature of expertise at each stage of proficiency which enriched the description of stages initially specified by the Dreyfus and Dreyfus model.

Lately, researchers have expanded and characterized each stage of proficiency.

Despite the fact that the Dreyfus and Dreyfus model is simple and easy to apply to any setting, another school of thought questioned the validity of the model. For example, Day (2002) noted that it is difficult to apply the five stages model in professional settings because practitioners perform a range of tasks in their jobs, and, therefore, will not fit into one particular stage for all the tasks they do. Thus, the most common objection raised was a representation that proficiency acquisition is a linear process, independent of the influence of external factors and domain expertise (Grenier & Kehrhahn 2008).

Another objection to the Dreyfus and Dreyfus model was 'its failure to explain how someone becomes an expert and its stress on the importance of experience and not of its impact' (Farrington-Darby & Wilson 2006, p. 29). Other concerns included the absence of a social structure in knowledge and skill acquisition, lack of objective quantification on how to measure the attainment of each stage or where a particular stage ends, and the lack of operational definitions of intuition (Peña 2010). Even though these staged skill acquisition models conceptually explain how an individual learns, 'one cannot accurately predict where people are in the skill-acquisition process' (Langan-Fox et al. 2002, p. 106).

Though studies have either detected or forced-fit the characteristics of individual proficiency to the description of stages found in such models, it is not clear from those studies if there was any business benefit to the organization or any development benefit to the individual (Benner 2004; Beta & Lidaka 2015; Ramsburg 2010; Scobey 2006). Dall'Alba & Sandberg (2006) observed that experience and understanding of practice were the major determinants of any professional skill development, and that it may not have level-like stages. In the *TTP study,* I raised the question on the usefulness of the meaning or representation of stages of skill/proficiency acquisition in workplaces. I also raised a question of whether proficiency tracking in workplaces should rely on staged-transition models (Attri 2018).

The major implication of the Dreyfus and Dreyfus model was the evolution of the concept of scaling proficiency as stages so that suitable instructional designs could be put in place for learning at different stages. Researchers have translated the stages into appropriate instructional methods to be used at each stage to move a novice through to higher stages of proficiency (Benner 2001; Clavarelli, Platte & Powers 2009). Despite its limitations, the Dreyfus and Dreyfus model appears to be a starting point in identifying the methods and strategies to develop the proficiency of learners.

3.4 PROFICIENCY SCALING

The Dreyfus and Dreyfus model explained the novice-to-expert transition in terms of stages on the basis of how employees approach work. Another school of thought treats proficiency as a progression rather than a static stage. Whether an employee reaches the desired or target proficiency in a job or how soon s\he reaches there is based on how the measures of proficiency are defined. One may be less proficient or highly proficient in a specific set of tasks (or skills). This calls upon the concept of 'proficiency scaling,' according to which if the proficiency level of an employee can be quantified, it may be possible to plot it on the proficiency scale to see where s/he is in the progression toward high proficiency (Hoffman 1998). Hoffman et al. (2014) considered proficiency scaling as the fundamental action that needs to be taken in any accelerated proficiency study 'to forge a domain—and organisationally [*sic*] appropriate scale for distinguishing levels of proficiency.'

3.4.1 The Hoffman proficiency scaling

Instead of differentiating between the confusing constructs, competence, proficiency, and expertise, Hoffman, Feltovich, et al. (2010) viewed proficiency as an indicator of an employee's level of experience or expertise in the skills, which created a need for a mechanism to scale proficiency. Hoffman et al. (2014, p. 26) contended that it was important to develop 'a scale that is both domain and organisationally appropriate, and that considers the full range of proficiency.' They believed that it was possible to scale proficiency by using various inputs such as interviews, age, seniority, experience, education, training, professional certifications, performance measures, and social standing.

Hoffman (1998) recognized the challenges in defining expertise and posited that the differentiation between novices and experts itself suggested the presence of qualitative shifts of knowledge and performance between the two extremes of the development continuum. He commented, 'If one acknowledges that expertise develops, and that qualitative changes occur over the developmental period, then one must make some attempt at stage-like categorization, if only to motivate research' (Hoffman 1998, p. 84).

If novices and experts can be defined in terms of characteristics, knowledge, and performance, it will be possible for us to retrieve the remaining stages in the continuum of development from the literature. Hoffman, Feltovich, et al. (2010) stated, 'The analysis of proficiency and proficiency scaling can usefully commence by distinguishing experts (high and very high proficiency) from novices (very low proficiency)' (p. 32). In this view, experts were believed to possess a large body of knowledge. Novices, on the other hand, were believed to have not reached as high a proficiency level as an expert, even though they could be highly experienced individuals in their respective domains. Hoffman, Feltovich, et al. (2010, p. 28) viewed all such levels in terms of proficiency in which expertise is referred to as 'high proficiency.' However, the notion of high proficiency was akin to the stage of expertise in the Dreyfus and Dreyfus (1986, 2004, 2005) model. Researchers also viewed proficiency as a qualitative indication of expertise or mastery (Scobey 2006). Chi (2006, p. 22) supported a similar position of using the term *proficiency* to mean mastery in skills as 'expertise is a level of proficiency that novices can achieve.'

Hoffman et al.'s (2014) concept of proficiency is expressed as a continuum of mastery in knowledge, skill, function, or job in which a novice is someone who has low or very low proficiency, while an expert is someone with very high proficiency in a particular aspect, that is, skill, task, function, or job. On this continuum, an employee progresses toward higher proficiency through stages such as naïve, novice, initiate, apprentice, journeyman, expert, and master (Hoffman 1998). Based on the middle ages craft guilds in Europe, Hoffman (1998) proposed that we could represent the novice-to-expert transition through seven stages, similar to gaining mastery in a craft, as shown in Table 3-1.

Table 3-1 Proficiency scaling proposed by Hoffman (1998)

Stage	Characteristics
Naïve	Completely ignorant about the domain.
Novice	A member in the domain who has minimal exposure to the domain.
Initiate	A novice who has started on the profession.
Apprentice	Someone who is taking up instructions beyond introductory level. S/he is working with and assisting an experienced person.
Journeyman	One who is executing orders and performs a day's work and duties unsupervised. S/he has achieved some level of competence, has become experienced and is a reliable worker.
Expert	A distinguished journeyman regarded for his/her accurate judgements, is efficient and delivers reliable performance. Special skills attained due to extensive experience and can deal effectively with rare or "tough" cases.
Master	A journeyman or expert who is also qualified to teach those at a lower level. Highly experienced experts whose judgments establish regulations, standards, or ideals. Equally regarded by other experts as the "real" expert in certain subdomains.

Source: adapted from Hoffman (1998)

Hoffman's (1998) progression was based on changing knowledge and skills that are associated with experience. Macmillan (2015, p. 36) explained this approach as:

> Hoffman's Scheme, on the other hand, presumes a progression of knowledge and capabilities associated with different amounts of instruction and domain-specific experience. It describes relative levels of expertise or proficiency within a single knowledge domain. In doing so, it fulfils its traditional function as a means of describing the progression of increasing knowledge and skills as one moves, over many years, from the status of novice to a master in a specific field.

Some researchers criticized the lack of scientific rigor in the Hoffman (1998) framework. For example, Farrington-Darby & Wilson (2006, p. 29) commented, '[w]hat this classification does not provide is the process that has to occur to move between the classifications.' Hoffman (1998) suggested this model in order to advance the research thinking in the absence of any scientifically validated model.

3.4.2 The Jacobs taxonomy of human competence

On similar lines, Jacobs (1997) proposed a 'taxonomy of human competence,' which suggested that human competence could be scaled with designations such as novice, specialist, experienced specialist, expert, and master. The distinction was based on an individual's ability to produce outcomes. At the same time, it was recognized that '*master*, *expert*, a *specialist*, or a *novice* are usually relative notions' (Jacobs 2003, p. 7). While novices are those whose 'outcomes are less valuable or who produce no outcomes can [*sic*] have lower of competence' (Jacobs 2003, p. 5), experts are those who 'achieve the most valuable outcomes in organisations.' Masters are considered the 'experts of the highest order' (Jacobs 2003, p. 5). The taxonomy of human competence (Jacobs 2001, 1997, 2003; Jacobs & Washington 2003) specified the definitions of novice, expert, and master, which were almost similar to those by Hoffman (1998); however, the definitions of *specialist* and *experienced specialist* specified by Jacobs closely aligned with the definitions of *apprentice* and *journeyman* levels of Hoffman (1998).

3.4.3 Implications of proficiency scaling

The major implication of proficiency scaling was that it envisioned a full spectrum of proficiency and suggested that individuals at different stages of their career may possess different levels of proficiency (Hoffman 1998) or competence (Jacobs 2001, 1997, 2003; Jacobs & Washington 2003). Thus, the scaling taxonomies (Jacobs and Hoffman) did not propose proficiency as a specific stage as suggested by the Dreyfus and Dreyfus (1986, 2005, 2006) model. Rather, these taxonomies explain that even a competent person has a certain level of proficiency in his/her skills, tasks, or job functions, though qualitatively and quantitatively (if measurable) may be less than that of a proficient performer. Moreover, the stage of journeyman (Hoffman 1998) or experienced specialist (Jacobs 1997, 2001, 2003) corresponds to the competent or proficient stage suggested by Dreyfus and Dreyfus (1986, 2004, 2005).

While proficiency scaling in terms of stages is a generally accepted method, there is a clear lack of methods to quantify proficiency by distinguishing one stage from another objectively or in measurable terms. Even among researchers, there is less agreement on performance measures in regards to whether to measure job performance in terms of tasks, behaviors, or outcomes (Koopmans et al. 2011). Literature does not provide much guidance on the nature of proficiency for each stage in any of the staged models. In particular, organizations need to understand the mid-range proficiency levels, such as journeyman (Hoffman 1998) or an experienced specialist (Jacobs 1997). Hoffman et al. (2014, p. 3) clarified about journeyman that 'they have practiced to the point where they can perform their duties unsupervised (literally, they can go on a journey).' They further point out that:

> While there may be some requirements for more senior experts in select areas, there is more profound and continuing need for journeyman and senior journeymen to carry out the complex cognitive work effectively to ensure current and future success. (Hoffman et al. (2014, p. 3)

It should be noted that the implication of stages is not really to create another staged view of proficiency; rather, it is to introduce the concept of scaling of proficiency at each stage of the progression, whether using the model suggested by Dreyfus and Dreyfus (1986, 2004, 2005) or any other researcher.

3.5 PROFICIENT PERFORMANCE IN ORGANIZATIONS

Proficiency in workplaces, which signifies the overall work performance, is a much larger construct (Griffin, Neal & Parker

2007). Studies in human resource development acknowledge that such overall job or work proficiency includes aspects of behavioral performance, task performance, contextual performance, team performance, and organizational performance. It also recognizes the challenges associated with developing individuals to such levels (Campbell & Wiernik 2015; Dumas & Hanchane 2010; Houger 2006; Kanfer & Kantrowitz 2002; Khan, Khan & Khan 2011; Quartey 2012; Wallace 2006).

In the *TTP study*, the project leaders described how they view and define proficiency in the workplace. It revealed four key characteristics of proficiency in various job roles across 20 business sectors. I explain these four characteristics in the following sections.

3.5.1 Meeting the established performance thresholds

Leading thought leaders on *Learning Paths* defined proficiency as: 'Being able to perform a given task or function up to a predetermined standard. Proficiency and independently productive are often used as synonyms' (Rosenbaum & Williams 2004, p. 5). They further iterated: 'This is the point in time when you are left totally on your own and that you can do your job without asking questions or making mistakes' (Rosenbaum & Williams 2004, p. 13). For a given job, a predefined level of performance is expected from the employees, which can be expressed in terms of customer satisfaction scores, revenue generated, the number of transactions conducted, or defect rates (Rosenbaum & Williams 2004, p. 14). A performer is said to be proficient when his or her performance meets these predefined levels or standards for that job. Supporting this view, Jacobs (2003) indicated that '[p]eople whose outcomes are less valuable or who produce no outcomes can have lower levels of competence [or proficiency].'

The *TTP study* suggested that most of the project leaders viewed proficiency as a state in which an employee displayed a performance that met the threshold performance set by the organization for a given job role:

> A performer who meets certain thresholds of business metrics was identified by the business as having achieved proficiency. (Sam, Project leader 56)
>
> Proficiency is defined as a required level of performance in terms of measurable result and observable actions. (Stephen, Project leader 53)

Project leaders viewed proficiency as a non-negotiable state—the performer was either above the set level or s/he was not. They also suggested that there was no other in-between state important enough for a business to track. This point was clear from the comments of some of the project leaders:

> You either did it right and got checked off, or you did it wrong and did not get checked off. (Diana, Project leader 11)
>
> It is simply whether they achieve the specification for the task? And, it is kind of you have to do it through the 100% standard; it has to be 100% correct. If you are less than 100%, then you did not do it. (Johnson, Project leader 22)

The job role was an anchor in the concept of defining proficiency in workplaces. A job role is a specific set of responsibilities or expectations and more coherent than simply the title of a job, which may encompass several other things as well. However, most of the practitioners viewed proficiency more in terms of how a given job role was performed as a whole (i.e., all the employees performing the same job role collectively) rather than how an individual employee performed a task or activity in that job role. Thus, the high investment efforts on the initiatives/projects to speed up proficiency were focused on accelerating the outcomes at the job role level rather than at the employee level. Recently, there is more focus by organizations on job role-based performance tracking. Bersin (2013) stated on his blog that 'in today's high performing companies, people now take on "roles" not "jobs."' It has been contended that 'job roles better encapsulated the totality of performance' (Baker 2016). Every job role in an organization is designed for a purpose. Therefore, it has defined and specific expectations in terms of outcomes, results, and deliverables, which all are measured with some metrics. A performer justifies being in a job role by producing these outputs to the established standards.

Business leaders set proficiency as a business metric, that is, proficiency in a job role is a key performance indicator (KPI) and needs to be measured. A white paper from Alorica (2017, p. 7) defines: 'To be truly proficient, an agent must master not only the required skills for the position, but be able to work independently while meeting all KPIs.' Charles Fred coined and defined "proficiency" as 'use of knowledge in action for the purpose of producing value for a customer' (Fred 2002, p. 43). As we can see, he specified proficiency in terms of business metrics about which organizations care.

CH3 / THE PROFICIENCY

Practitioners refer to proficiency as a state in which an employee is 'independently productive' and is fully contributing (Rosenbaum & Williams 2004, p. 13). An employee's productivity is measured with reference to the standards of performance defined for a given job role. Scholarly literature expresses this stage as the 'journeyman' stage at which 'an individual can handle day-to-day job independently, is experienced and reliable' (Hoffman 1998, p. 85).

In the *TTP study*, I found that most of the 85 project leaders viewed proficiency in terms of how well an employee performs a job or function as opposed to his/her skills/knowledge, which, of course, are virtues that form the proficiency but do not reflect it completely. The project leaders emphasized business metrics as a means to define proficiency. They differentiated proficiency from being good in a few skills, knowledge, or behaviors, or the ability to perform some activities, steps, or tasks. Thus, proficiency is about results rather than about demonstrating a skill, task, or activity. Certainly, without knowledge, skills, and behaviors and without the ability to perform the required tasks, procedures, or activities, it is not feasible to produce the desired outcomes. Fred (2002, p. 43) perhaps suggested the closest relationship between knowledge and outcome, and valued the outcomes that come out of acquiring knowledge: 'The proficiency threshold, therefore, is the exact moment when a worker can convert knowledge through action into the promised value for the customer.' However, being able to produce the designated results independently ultimately determines whether or not an employee is proficient, and, if not there yet, how soon s/he could reach that state.

As mentioned before, a vast amount of literature emphasizes the progression toward proficiency as several stages in which each stage is described with a qualitatively different proficiency in skills (Alexander 2003a; Benner 2004; Dreyfus & Dreyfus 2005, 2009; Hoffman 1998). On the contrary, in this study, organizations did not appear to get any advantage by putting labels on their employee's development or progression in the journey toward proficiency. None of the project leaders expressed any inclination toward characterizing or labeling an in-between stage before proficiency. This finding also raises the question of how well stage representation useful to drive discussions in workplaces. The main question surrounding managers appeared to be whether an employee was operating in a state of proficiency or not.

3.5.2 Consistency as the hallmark of proficiency

In the *TTP study,* I identified consistency in producing business outcomes or deliverables as the hallmark of the state of proficiency. This was also the key differentiator between a proficient and a non-proficient performer. Practitioners like Rosenbaum & Williams (2004, p. 14) posited that proficiency is attained when a new employee achieves a predetermined level of performance on a consistent basis. In the *TTP study*, meeting standards consistently and repeatedly was recognized as proficiency (or proficient performance), and merely achieving the set standards once was not considered as proficiency. A project leader commented:

> Because they can hit those performance objectives one time, we would not consider that proficiency. We want to see a pattern [of consistency]. Again, there are three times

that they are evaluated against those metrics, and if they consistently hit those thresholds, then we would say that they are proficient. (Sam, Project leader 56)

An important characteristics of consistency measurement is that it must be demonstrated over a fairly long period of time. Thus, maintenance of performance, that is, consistently being at a particular performance level, is proficiency in a job role.

Though not many studies investigated the role of consistency, it is an expected attribute of proficiency in high-risk or life-saving jobs. For instance, in a study involving 200 patients who underwent thoracoscopic lobectomy by two different surgeons, Li, Wang & Ferguson (2014, p. 1154) noticed that efficiency and consistency defined the surgeons' proficiency. Efficiency meant being fast enough while being effective and consistent meant being reliably accurate each time. They found that while the personal experience of over 100 cases made a surgeon efficient, 'attaining consistency requires 200 or more cases' (id. 1154). Also, in the sports arena, consistency is valued quite heavily to determine pay-for-consistency in the performance of the players (Deutscher et al. 2017).

The idea of consistency implied that proficiency is a level or a non-negotiable state. Irrespective of the mastery of the constituent skills, the primary concern of the project leaders in the *TTP study* was whether a given employee was operating at or below the desired proficiency (i.e., producing the desired business outcomes).

3.5.3 Proficiency measurement by outcomes

According to Charles Fred, the father of the term "speed to proficiency," 'the proficiency threshold is reached when sales and marketing team can sell and advertise value to customers with confidence, when orders are filled on time, when services meet customer expectations, and when management team is leading as envisioned' (Fred 2002, p. 44). Thus, proficiency is best expressed as results or actions that represent achieving the results.

An analysis of the *TTP study* suggested that organizations typically used 15 proficiency indicators which can be grouped into three types of proficiency measures (summarized in Table 3-2):

(1) measurable business outcomes;

(2) observable actions; and

(3) controlled performance.

Most project leaders (95%) defined and measured proficiency of a job role in terms of measurable business outcomes (such as meeting customer satisfaction) or in terms of the observable actions (such as work–output meeting the specifications) that closely represented the business outcomes. Some project leaders expressed this observation as:

> A performer who meets certain thresholds of business metrics was identified by the business as having achieved proficiency. (Sam, Project leader 56)

> Proficiency is defined as a required level of performance in terms of measurable results and observable actions. (Stephen, Project leader 53)

CH3 / THE PROFICIENCY

> The measurable results and observable actions define proficiency (the ability to perform independently to an appropriate level of quality for the position). (Stephen, Project leader 53)

The key is meeting the expectations of the job role consistently. More than half (53%) of the project cases primarily measured proficiency in a job role in terms of measurable business outcomes, for example, business results, customer satisfaction scores, KPIs, work performance specifications, individual productivity, or work quality score. I observed these measurement methods being used in project cases where measurable business outcomes were feasible or were the norms. Some project leaders expressed:

> People have to get to this level of performance—they have to produce this much [outputs] with this much [inputs] with this reject rate [specifications]. (Stephen, Project leader 53)

> We have to focus on things that matter—metrics that matter for the organizations. (Matt, Project leader 33)

> People have to be at this level of performance in order for them to be here [proficient] and to be working and productive, and that's how we'll define proficiency. It's a level of performance. (Stephen, Project leader 53)

A project leader further explained with an example:

> For a chemical manufacturer, synthesizing the right products in the right quantity with minimum wastage and in a timely fashion is the most important, so that the products can be delivered to the customers according to their expectations. Therefore, it is important to check whether the chemist/operator is at full proficiency. In order to check this, a sample from a batch is taken and a quality assurance test is done; if the sample met the

required criteria at every step, it can be taken that the batch also meets the required specifications. From this, the manufacturer will be able to get the confidence that the chemist/operator was demonstrating full proficiency. (Richardson, Project leader 45)

This insight supports the premise of using accomplishments, results, or work outcomes as a measure of human performance in the human performance technology (HPT) framework (Binder 2017; Gander 2006). On the same lines, using an outcome-based view, leading practitioners stated that 'Proficiency can be defined in numbers of transactions, dollars sold, defect rates, customer satisfaction scores, or anything else that is measurable and related to results' (Rosenbaum & Williams 2004, p. 14).

However, there are instances when it is not possible to measure the end business results or outcomes (e.g., strategy-related jobs). In such situations, they measured proficiency in terms of observable actions (i.e., quality and quantity of activities, comparison with experienced peers, number of repetitions, verifiable and observable behaviors, and evidence from authentic work). For example, evidence from authentic work would mean producing a business report. Such observable behaviors can be translated into outcomes. Pollock, Wick & Jefferson (2015) emphasized that only those actions, which lead to the outcome as "good performance," have value to the business. Such actions or activities produce high-value outcomes at relatively low input cost. 42% of the project leaders utilized observable actions, which closely represented the business outcomes as the measure of proficiency. They expressed proficiency estimation as a measurement of activities, comparison with experienced peers doing the same work,

CH3 / THE PROFICIENCY

evidence of authentic work, the number of repetitions performed on a task, and verifiable and observable behaviors or actions. This method appeared to apply to project cases where some sort of benchmark existed or where activities represented the outcomes that would be achieved by performing those activities. Some project leaders expressed the intent of such measures as:

> We can describe what that looks like and what's going on and that really is proficiency for that particular role. (Stephen, Project leader 53)

For example, a comparison of the performance of a technical support executive responsible for troubleshooting computer software with that of his peers revealed:

> [The goal was to] be proficient enough that they're performing at the same level as someone who's already been doing the job for a number of months. (Jason, Project leader 21)

I observed that a small percentage of project leaders (5%) used performance in a controlled representative environment as the only indicator of proficiency, particularly when it was not feasible for them to measure the results or when the results were not available immediately (e.g., business strategy role).

Data analysis also suggested that there was not always one single indicator of proficiency. On average, an analysis of the project cases in this *TTP study* showed that proficiency was measured using two or three different indicators. Among those, business outcome-related indicators were invariably the primary source. For example, the proficiency of customer service executives selling investment products over phone was measured using three different indicators, productivity, customer satisfaction scores, and comparison with experienced performers:

> Productivity was measured by calls per hour... 9.6 calls per hour (productivity measures); how well the phone calls met the criteria set by the team (customer satisfaction scores); at the end of the 4 weeks, the employee had to be at the same performance level as the current average of the performance level of experienced people on the floor (comparison with experienced performers). (Billy, Project leader 2)

In a nutshell, the success of any job role was mainly assessed based on the business outcomes (e.g., business results, KPIs, productivity, performance specifications, customer satisfaction scores, etc.). Thus, key characteristics of proficient performance is that it is measured in terms of business outcomes or by observable actions representative of (or leading to) business outcomes. For the rest of the book, any reference to *producing desired business outcomes* will connote referring to the state of proficiency.

Table 3-2 Three categories of indicators of proficiency measures

Sub-themes for proficiency measures	% of project cases	Indicator of proficiency	Representative quotes
Measurable business outcomes	53%	Business results	Deliver every machine at the expected date at the customer. (Teresa, Project leader 58) The number of actual sales made and the commissions generated. (Rodridge, Project Leader 47)
		Customer satisfaction scores	A 90% or higher customer satisfaction score. (Mike, Project leader 36)
		Key performance indicators (KPIs) improvements	Reduce downtime and get outages corrected more quickly. (Mayer, Project leader 9)

CH3 / THE PROFICIENCY

		Performance specs	Meet the color specifications and meet the customers' needs. (Richardson, Project Leader 45)
		Productivity	Complete at least 20 parts to desired proficiency as rated by their trainer. (Hogdan, Project Leader 29)
Observable actions	42%	Quality and quantity of activities	How many referrals did you get, number of contacts and then your success to get new appointments with that referral, the number of fact find meetings you're doing, your discovery meetings, the number of points in the analysis that you've completed, then making your recommendations. (Christen, Project Leader 6)
		Comparison to experienced performers	Comparing new agent to an agent who we consider proficient, they would be at 80% of what those metrics were. (Hallmark, Project Leader 17)
		Evidence from authentic work	Quality assurance auditors would review the work to determine if those claims have been processed accurately enough. (Liza, Project Leader 13)
		Number of repetitions	They will need to have 10 repetitions of completing this task. (Richardson, Project Leader 45)
		Verifiable observable behaviors	To stand up and actually discuss the action plan, how they look at the data or what they want to do next. (Mohammad, Project Leader 39)
Controlled performance	5%	% of skill mastered	It was defined through the use of a skills matrix for tasks that were desired. (Mille, Project Leader 38)
		Pre- and post-performance in training	We try to do pre- and post-testing with our clients that they could work on their own. (Bella, Project Leader 28)
		Proficiency scores	Accumulate enough points to be at an acceptable level of sales performance. (Matt, Project Leader 33)
		Simulated performance	How long did it take them time one versus time two versus time three? (White, Project Leader 63)
		Testing at regular intervals	We also looked a year down the road and how rapidly they were able to be able to take on far more complex

> and challenging situations than they were with people who have been through a situation. (Aloha, Project Leader 19)

However, this characteristics (of measuring proficiency in terms of business outcomes) is contrary to the school of thought, which maintains that individual performance should be measured in terms of behaviors and not results (Campbell & Wiernik 2015). Some authors and researchers have created the divide between behaviors and outcomes to ease the measurement of individual performance from the measurement of work performance, which, in fact, is the sum of several other factors (Baker 2016, p. 2). An outcome-based view, as emphasized by this theme, also suggests that proficiency is a true measure of the ability of an employee to produce the desired outcomes in his/her workplace, amidst all the unknowns, environmental influence, and the enabling or constraining factors surrounding a job role. Thus, proficiency in the workplace is a much larger construct which signifies the overall work performance (Griffin, Neal & Parker 2007).

3.5.4   Proficiency is not just about learning

Business articles and academic papers continue to emphasize the composition of proficiency in terms of knowledge, skills, and competencies to perform the desired functions in a job role. For example, Dixon (2015), in her article, provided a more straightforward view: 'Proficiency is the quality of having great facility and competence.' Every job requires its employees to demonstrate certain job competencies to a certain level of proficiency. Competencies are 'a set of observable behaviors that provide a structured guide to help identify, evaluate and develop key knowledge, skills, and attitudes to perform the job effectively.'[5] In the *TTP study,* project leaders also differentiated the related term 'competency' from 'proficiency':

> We're saying competencies are not the same thing [as proficiency]. Competencies are skills, knowledge, and attitude kind of stuff. (Stephen, Project leader 53)

> Proficiency definitions include key business measures which are usually left out of competency statements. This makes them far easier to measure. (Stephen, Project leader 53)

Proficiency is specified in terms of business metrics about which organizations care, rather than in terms of skills or competencies. In the *TTP study*, I observed that proficiency was more about results rather than about demonstrating a skill, task, or activity. Fred (2002, p. 43) considered proficiency as converting knowledge into useful value to the business or customers. Producing such outcomes in a job role required the orchestration of many skills, tasks, and activities at the same time among the complex influence of several other conditions. Thus, it was not a few isolated skills or tasks in which proficiency mattered to project leaders. As opposed to the popular view of proficiency as being good in some skills, knowledge or attitude or ability to perform some activities, steps, or tasks, the project leaders emphasized that proficiency suggests a specific performance level. One project leader supported this view by stating:

---

[5]https://talentculture.com/time-to-proficiency-orientation-and-onboarding/

> People have to be at this level of performance in order for them to be [proficient] here and to be working and productive. And that's how we'll define proficiency. It's a level of performance as opposed to I've got to know something... It's not about acquiring skills, knowledge, and attitudes, rather about how these building blocks are successfully used on the job to produce the required results. (Stephen, Project leader 53)

Another project leader used an analogy to differentiate proficiency from the steps and activities involved in performing a task:

> If proficiency is [to] make a delicious sandwich, then the steps in the process would be to get the bread, meat, and the condiments; spread the right quantity of condiments on the bread; and lay out the right quantity of meat, cheese, and lettuce. So, those are steps and not the proficiencies. Proficiency is making a delicious sandwich. (Richardson, Project leader 45)

In some studies, performance researchers considered job-specific task proficiency to be the most common outcome measure, and, thus, the central factor of an employee's job performance (Koopmans et al. 2011). Studies in HRD have used task performance as an outcome measure to determine competence or proficiency levels of employees (Borman & Motowidlo 1993; Campbell 1990; Jacobs 1997, 2001, 2003; Viswesvaran & Ones 2000). In contrast, proficiency researchers considered over-reliance on the concept of task performance as a roadblock to accelerating proficiency, calling it a 'paradox of tasks' which created an 'artificial sense of linearity and separability' (Hoffman et al. 2014, p. 178). Task domains are probably still important for expertise building in closed domains (e.g., sports and music) or where there is a limited set of well-defined static tasks (Shanteau 2015).

Admittedly, without knowledge, skills, and behaviors and without the ability to perform the required tasks, procedures, or activities, it is not feasible to produce the desired outcomes. However, being able to produce the designated results independently determines whether an employee is proficient, and, if not there yet, how soon could s/he reach that state. This observation supports the viewpoint of the performance paradigm in HRD to enhance total individual performance not just by training interventions but also by other interventions (Clark 2008; Swanson & Holton III 2001).

Project leaders focused more on expressing performance in terms of business metrics and stayed focused on when an employee attained that performance consistently, instead of labeling the stage where s/he was at a given point of time. Still, the study findings indicated that proficiency and competence in organizations were viewed as markedly different constructs. Project leaders viewed competence as a combination of knowledge, skills, and attitudes necessary to do the task or job, but it did not convey an employee's ability to produce consistent business outcomes. Achieving consistent business outcomes was considered the hallmark of being at the state of proficiency, while competence merely suggested possession of needed skills. Here are the comments from those project leaders who supported this distinction:

> Competence is much more related to the knowledge and skills and to some extent the attitude of the person that we're talking about, but just because people are

competent doesn't mean they can do the job when they're given it at their desk. (Connan, Practice Leader 5G)

With a lesser direct focus on isolated skills, tasks, or activities, project leaders were not much concerned about a terminological divide between a competent vs. proficient performer, which is generally a key concern of training designers discussed widely in literature (Khan & Ramachandran 2012). Project leaders just considered terms like *competence* and *competency* as training-specific terms and ruled out considering them because their basic assumption was that training only plays a minor role in the overall goal of shortening TTP. While the *TTP study* neither confirms nor refutes the usefulness of such constructs (or differentiation among such constructs) in workplaces, they might still hold value in describing the progression of development in studies focused on training curriculum (Alexander 2003a; Jacobs 2003; Kim 2015; Scobey 2006; Teodorescu 2006).

3.5.5 Job-role proficiency

Beta & Lidaka (2015, p. 1961) indicated that the state of proficiency has 'no clear-cut explanation of the word, which allows the use of different interpretations according to the application.' Supporting that, Kim (2015, p. 2) stated that 'missing accounts of the middle stages [of proficiency] leave the developmental process somewhat unclear.' However, the role theory enables us to define job-role proficiency: 'It is possible to assess proficiency when the requirements of a work role are formalized because there is a clear standard against which these judgments can be made' (Griffin, Neal & Parker 2007, p. 329). The four characteristics of proficiency revealed in the *TTP study* suggested a construct of *job-role proficiency* that explained the characteristics and nature of performance at the 'state of proficiency.'

> Job-role proficiency is [*sic*] state of performance at which performers produce business outcomes or deliverables consistently to the set performance thresholds expected from a given job role. It refers to achieving and maintaining one pre-established performance level and does not imply progression through different stages or levels of performance. It refers to the business performance of the job role and does not convey an individual's performance demonstrated on a task or skill' (Attri 2018, p. 236).

Table 3-3 summarizes the construct to show what proficiency is and what it is not.

Table 3-3 Job-role proficiency

What it is	What it is not
Job role level	Individual's task performance
State of performance	Learning a task or skill
Threshold performance standards	One-time performance
Consistency of performance	Implied progression of stages
Measured by business outcomes	
Measured by actions leading to outcomes	

As we can see, job-role proficiency is characteristically different from other definitions of proficiency used in task and skill domains, such as job-specific task proficiency (Campbell et al. 1993), task performance (Borman & Motowidlo 1993), technical proficiency (Griffin, Neal & Parker 2007), human competence (Jacobs 1997, 2001, 2003), stage of proficiency (Dreyfus & Dreyfus 2005), and proficiency as a continuum (Hoffman 1998). Thus, proficiency for a job role is much more than an individual's performance.

3.6 EXPERT PERFORMANCE

It is imperative to differentiate proficient performance from expert performance. One stream of literature is almost entirely devoted to novice–expert differences. The pioneering research by De Groot (1965; 1966) on the differences in performance of novices and experts in the game of chess has motivated the other studies on this subject (Chi, Glaser & Farr 1988). Subsequently, several studies revealed how experts were different from novices, and a few researchers have attempted to explain the general nature of expertise (Chi, Glaser & Rees 1981; Farrington-Darby & Wilson 2006; Schraagen 1993). Expertise is best understood by understanding what an expert does. In the proficiency scale, Hoffman (1998, p. 85) considered an expert as a person who has special skills, extensive experience, and the ability to crack tough problems. From that perspective, expertise has been defined as 'the possession of a large body of knowledge and procedural skills' (Chi, Glaser & Rees 1982, p. 8). In their seminal work, Glaser & Chi (1988) pointed out that knowledge structures, processing capability, and problem-solving are the collective elements to develop expertise. An argument on expertise being acquired and hence an outcome or goal of skill acquisition was posited by Chi (2006, p. 23) as 'presumably the more skilled person became expert-like from having acquired knowledge about a domain, that is, from learning and studying' and 'from deliberate practice.' Moreover, experts within their respective domains are considered skilled, competent, and able to think in qualitatively different ways than novices (Anderson 2000; Chi, Glaser & Farr 1988).

Among the classical theories, the Fitts & Posner (1967) model asserted the value of practice in developing automaticity during skill acquisition. However, Ericsson (2009a) believed that practice, as described by Fitt and Posner (1967), helped achieve automaticity only in everyday skills and was no way a mechanism to attain superior or expert performance. While classical expertise studies characterized experts and expertise, Ericsson et al. (1993) suggested a mechanism of achieving *expert perform*ance based on several studies in domains such as music, chess, and physical sports. They maintained that the construct of expert performance was special. Ericsson & Charness (1994, p. 731) described expert-level performance (or expert performance) as 'if someone is performing at least two standard deviations above the mean level in the population, that individual can be said to be performing at an expert level.' Such superior performance is achieved with a combination of high skill levels, domain-specific knowledge, and skilled memory (Charness & Tuffiash 2008).

In studies in the domains such as music and chess, the findings indicated that individuals normally used extensive training, deliberately and carefully designed professional practice, and extended domain-related activities, which improved their performance incrementally (Ericsson et al. 1993). The deliberate efforts included constant engagement in similar domain activities, exposure to new issues in their respective domains, and subjecting themselves to a certain special type of practice called *deliberate practice*. Deliberate practice is not just practice or any other domain-related activity such as work or on-the-job training events (Ericsson & Charness 1994). Rather, it is a highly individualized training on tasks selected by a qualified teacher to build expertise in an individual. Deliberate practice is based on the premise that 'expert performance requires the opportunity to find suitable training tasks that the performer can master sequentially... typically monitored by a teacher or coach' (Ericsson 2006, p. 692). The feedback from a designated coach is considered an important factor in deliberate practice. With such efforts, the individual may be able to gain expertise.

In several studies, Ericsson emphasized and characterized the nature of deliberate practice (Ericsson, Prietula & Cokely 2007; Ericsson 2000, 2002, 2003, 2004, 2006, 2007, 2008, 2009b). In their studies, Ericsson et al. identified four components in the deliberate practice model: (1) focused goals which are determined by a teacher in order to improve a specific aspect of performance; (2) concentration and effort; (3) feedback from a teacher comparing actual to desired performance; and (4) further opportunities for practice (Ericsson 2007, 2008, 2009b). Deliberate practice activities are designed to include repeated experience that allows learners to observe the various critical aspects of tasks. Constant stretching and correcting of mistakes were central to the expert performance model because 'attempts for mastery require that the performer always try [*sic*], by stretching performance beyond its current capabilities, to correct some specific weakness while preserving other successful aspects of function' (Ericsson 2006, p. 700). Such stretching of skills results in gradual changes in cognitive mechanisms leading to long-term skill retention. Ericsson (2014, p. 81) suggested that 'new cognitive mechanisms are gradually acquired during the extended period, and they mediate the superior performance, thus leading to qualitative differences in structure compared to untrained performance.' Ericsson (2000, 2002, 2003, 2004, 2006a, 2007, 2008, 2009c) further hypothesized that the dramatic difference in the performance between experts and nonexperts could be attributed to the amount of deliberate practice. Thus, the acquired performance of an individual is a direct function of the time engaged in deliberate practice activities.

In their earlier studies, Ericsson et al. (1993) confirmed that it takes 10,000 hours or 10 years of intense training and deliberate practice to become an expert in almost anything. Since then, researchers have applied the concept of deliberate practice in domains such as science, weather forecasting, engineering, military command and control, surgery, and sports and have seen that the framework reasonably explained or supported the development of expertise (Ericsson & Ward 2007; Kirkman 2013; Roth 2009; Ward et al. 2007; van de Wiel & Van den Bossche 2013). Ericsson et al. (1993) hypothesized that the true measurement of expert performance could happen only in laboratory settings by studying the reproducibility of superior performance on representative tasks. Expert performance, as suggested by the deliberate practice mechanism, is defined and measured on the representative and specific set of tasks on which reproducibility and superiority of performance could be verified in a laboratory (Ericsson 2014).

Though organizations are continuously striving to develop the skills of their employees to the next level of proficiency, expert performance is seen to be drastically different from proficient performance because the business challenges are new and competition is fierce. Developing employees to the desired proficiency is not the same as developing expertise. Expertise is considered an elite status bestowed on few domain specialists. Not everyone may need to be developed to that level in an organization or a particular job role. For example, for critical functions or roles in organizations such as the CEO's, there may be a need to develop a few employees to a high level of proficiency, based on the challenges to be faced. Such brilliant, hand-picked employees are most likely to be experts in their respective domains. However, not all employees need to be or can be experts of that order. Hoffman, Andrews & Feltovich (2012, p. 8) supported this with the following:

> We do not assume that every organisation needs to have every employee be expert at every task. Instead, we are recognizing that for the majority of employees achieving a degree of competence to become journeymen is just fine. Hence our general reference is to accelerated proficiency.

The notion of expertise specifies deliberate practice in a specific set of non-changing tasks. However, in workplaces, professionals hardly get to work on the same set of tasks for a long time. For these reasons, Fadde & Klein (2010) contended that deliberate practice, and, hence, the achievement of expert performance, is not even a realizable goal in any job for any organization.

At ground level, proficiency and expertise are not the same virtues. Project leaders in the *TTP study* indicated that developing an employee to be proficient is not the same as making someone an expert in something. Some project leaders stated:

> I think that, in most organizations, while there could still be some experts that are required, not everybody has to be an expert, but they should be proficient. (Andrew, Practice leader 2G)

> Developing people to be experts is a much different thing than developing people to be proficient at something. (Ron, Project leader 48)

Literature has revealed an increasing trend that several researchers opine that employees should be prepared to reach the proficient level or journeyman level as a minimum in organizations (Hoffman et al. 2014; Jung, Kim & Reigeluth 2016; Moon, Kim & You 2013). For instance, Hoffman et al. (2014) believed that the skills of most employees needed to be developed at least at the journeyman level, that is, one who can do his/her job productively and independently. Lately, the organizations expect a minimum journeyman level of proficiency from their employees while they would still develop a few selected employees as experts.

3.7 WHAT IT MEANS TO YOU

☞ **Thinking in terms of job-role proficiency:** Job-role proficiency is a state of performance at which performers produce business outcomes or deliverables consistently to the set performance thresholds expected from a given job role. It does not imply different stages or levels of performance; rather, it refers to achieving a pre-established performance level. It does not convey an employee's task-level performance, his/her learning/demonstrating a skill, or meeting specified thresholds at one time.

👉 **Develop a clear definition of proficiency:** The foremost recommendation I have for practitioners is to develop a definition of proficiency for a given role with as much clarity as possible. A clear definition of proficiency leads to goal orientation while aligning all the other elements of the organization toward that goal.

👉 **Organization-wide alignment on proficiency definition:** I suggest that an organization-wide alignment and agreement be sought from various stakeholders so that everyone knows what is being targeted. One agreed definition of proficiency across the stakeholders will help align the resources and efforts in the same direction.

👉 **Outcomes, rather than activities:** I encourage practitioners to avoid the tendency to define performance in terms of activities and tasks. Rather, proficiency should be defined and measured in terms of business outcomes as much as possible. For example, suppose that the success of a salesperson

CH3 / THE PROFICIENCY

is measured in terms of the number of cold calls s/he made in a month. In that case, the metrics for success (the desired state of proficiency) will be measured in terms of the number of calls made, which is an incorrect measure of his/her proficiency. Instead, suppose the success metrics are specified in terms of the revenue generated in a month. In that case, proficiency is likely to be measured for indications when an individual consistently produces the desired revenue for the company.

CHAPTER 4
THE METRICS

IMPORTANCE OF THE TTP METRICS IN ORGANIZATIONS

We expect employees in organizations to meet the minimum standards of performance set by the employers. Developing employees to the desired level of proficiency is a key goal of organizations for their sustainability (Bruck 2015). 'Proficiency is critical to performance in complex work contexts' (Hoffman, Feltovich, et al. 2010, p. 250). In the context of jobs, proficiency is the level at which practitioners reach the ability to perform like journeymen (Kuchenbrod 2016). Hoffman et al. (2014, p. 24) defined a journeyman as 'a person who can perform a day's labor unsupervised, although working under orders ... An experienced and reliable worker, or one who has achieved a level of competence.' Therefore, organizations expect a minimum of journeyman level proficiency from their employees. However, reaching that point takes time. Business enterprises have responded to the challenges of increased competition and keeping pace with the changes in the business world by developing new metrics tied to 'time' and 'speed' for tracking the performance of the workforce. Some of the recently developed, widely used metrics tied to 'time' and 'speed' include *time to proficiency*, *speed to proficiency*, *time to competence* or *time to full productivity*, and *accelerated proficiency*.

4.1   TIME TO PROFICIENCY (TTP)

Business leaders consider that it is very important to identify the stage at which an employee starts operating at or above the desired or expected proficiency (Fred 2002). Rosenbaum & Williams (2004), leading *Learning Paths* gurus, stressed the importance of identifying the stage at which the desired performance is delivered: 'You need to know the *level of performance* required to do the job and *how long* it takes to get there... when you can get employees up-to speed in far less time, productivity rises at far less expense.'

Employees, irrespective of their job role, require a certain amount of time to reach the level of proficiency desired by the organization they are associated with. This time is referred to as the *time to proficiency* (TTP). Practitioners define TTP as: 'the time it takes to reach a predetermined level of proficiency. In other words, the time from day one to [sic] independently productive' (Rosenbaum & Williams 2004, p. 5). On these lines, Bachlechner et al. (2010, p. 378) defined TTP as 'the amount of time an individual spends in a new job environment before it [sic] is able to fulfil most tasks without help from colleagues or supervisors.'

Studies on TTP date back to the late 1980s. Carpenter et al. (1989) and Faneuff et al. (1990) were the first to develop a TTP model in a military context for recording the proficiency of aviators. In their study involving avionics communication specialists, Carpenter et al. (1989) measured TTP in terms of performance in a selected set of tasks. They defined TTP as 'the length of time it takes to bring people with different attributes (especially mental aptitude) to targeted levels of task performance' (Carpenter et al. 1989, p. 1). They established a relationship between productivity, attrition, cost, and aptitude in their model using the TTP study. Based on the model, they found that the TTP metrics were viable performance measurement methods in a job which 'provides sufficient information for the modeling of productivity' (Carpenter et al. 1989, p. i).

In a different application of the same concept, Pinder & Schroeder (1987) conducted a TTP study that involved 354 managers from 8 companies in Canada who were surveyed regarding their TTP after job transfers. They conceived TTP as 'the length of time that elapses between the individual's movement into a new job and ascendancy of that individual to a level of performance at which a balance between inducements and contributions exists' (id. 337). The inducements were the investments made in an employee when s/he started on a new job, while contributions were his/her productivity from the new job. In their study, TTP was expressed in terms of productivity and contributions to the job instead of a certain set of tasks. This definition reveals the key implication that while an employee is working toward achieving the desired proficiency and trying to be productive in a new job, his/her performance has a financial impact on the business, thus making it a compelling reason to monitor the TTP values in a given job.

Hoffman et al. (2014, p. 169), renowned academic researchers on *accelerated proficiency,* have described TTP in terms of career stages as the time taken by an employee to reach a desired level of proficiency. The career stages that were most frequently referred to by them were the journeyman and the senior journeyman. The "journeyman" stage is characterized by virtues such as being reliable, experienced, able to work unsupervised, and having achieved a certain level of competence. The senior journeymen possess more experience and competence.

However, more often, the concept of TTP is viewed from the lens of a task domain, which means expressing it to mean achieving certain level of performance or skills or knowledge in a specific task. For instance, *Training Industry*'s glossary pitches TTP as: 'Time to proficiency refers to the time needed or taken by an individual to acquire the skills and knowledge necessary to reach an acceptable level of performance.'[6]

Some business leaders prefer to use terms such as time to full productivity or time to competence (or competency). Cornerstone, a leading software provider, places time to productivity as 'a metric that measures how long it takes a new hire to contribute to an organization.'[7] Millington (2018) states:

> Time-to-full productivity can mean one of two things. It can refer to the time it takes a new recruit to ably complete every aspect of their job role as measured by their manager. Alternatively, it can refer to the time it takes a recruit to reach an equivalent level of performance as their closest colleagues. Essentially, it means how long it takes a newcomer to be proficient in their job.

In a survey, i4cp (2011)[8] observed:

> Time-to-full-productivity is a metric few organizations use, but which many acknowledge they should be tracking. Just 16% of respondents to an i4cp survey stated that they use the time-to-full-productivity metric to a high or very high extent, but 64% say they should be using it to manage talent more effectively.

Knowledge Powered Solutions, an IT support and solutions provider, considers time to competency as 'the time to achieve the

---

[6] https://trainingindustry.com/glossary/time-to-proficiency/
[7] https://www.cornerstoneondemand.com/glossary/time-productivity
[8] https://www.i4cp.com/productivity-blog/2011/09/14/why-you-should-measure-time-to-full-productivity

target performance level.'[9] Nevertheless, these different terms essentially mean the same thing (or similar things) as the term 'time to proficiency.' These time-based metrics are becoming important business metrics for fast-paced technological organizations.

4.2 SPEED TO PROFICIENCY

Jay Cross, a leading workplace learning expert, has stated that 'the faster a worker becomes proficient, the more profitable the firm' (Cross 2013). Such a concept of being fast is usually referred to as 'speed to proficiency.' The earliest usage of the term "speed to proficiency" was in the book *Breakaway: Deliver value to your customer—Fast!!!* in which Fred (2002, p. 16) defined:

> Proficient workers speed things up: organizational change, operational improvement, problem solving, and delivery of service all happen faster. When you shorten the time it takes for workers to become proficient, the capital and resources required to introduce a new product, maintain operations and infrastructure, and perform a service are also proportionally reduced. I call this *speed to proficiency*.

In the last decade, the term 'speed to proficiency' became a common buzzword. Of late, organizations have started realizing that speed with which employees learn new skills and attain required performance, in turn, drives speed with which they can meet customer expectations, meet business needs or develop solutions (Attri & Wu 2015; Attri 2014). Bruck (2007) identified the value of

---

[9]https://www.kpsol.com/speed-to-competency-service-agents-measurement-action/

'speed to proficiency' as: 'In any business arena where the demonstrated mastery of new knowledge and skills is critical to the success of the business speed to proficiency is the name of the game'[10]. Cedar Interactive, a training solutions provider, positioned it as: '"Speed to Proficiency" refers to the time required to bring a person up to a proficient level of performance at a job or task.'[11] In a white paper, Alorica (2017, p. 7) defines:

> To be truly proficient, an agent must master not only the required skills for the position, but be able to work independently while meeting all KPIs. How long an individual or team takes to reach this level of competence is the speed to proficiency.

Organizations constantly face a pressing need to accelerate the speed to proficiency of their employees in almost every job. Fred (2002, p. 16) makes an interesting argument:

> Speed to proficiency is more than a theoretical advantage: It is the most devastating competitive weapon in the world where the competitive forces of scale, automation, and capital are subordinate to the power of proficient workforce.

Time is money, and a reduction in the time taken should be the first goal of any training program or other employee development interventions, keeping in mind not to lose focus on the effectiveness and quality of training, though. Organizations worldwide are striving to figure out interventions, systems, and strategies to shorten the TTP of employees (Fred 2002).

---

[10]http://www.q2learning.com/docs/WP-S2P.pdf
[11]http://cedarinteractive.com/serv-speedtopro.htm

4.3 ACCELERATED PROFICIENCY

Speed to proficiency is also called *accelerated proficiency* in mainstream academic literature. Organizations are short of time (Fadde & Klein 2010). Therefore, Fadde et al. and Hoffman et al.[12] have appealed to hasten the process of acquiring expertise or at least acquiring a certain level of mastery in skills.

Hoffman, Andrews & Feltovich (2012, p. 9) pointed out that the fact that it takes a long time to achieve proficiency is the basis of accelerating the same. Hoffman, Feltovich, et al. (2010, p. 9) called this concept *accelerated proficiency* and defined it as the 'phenomenon of achieving higher levels of proficiency in less time' (p. 9) and dealt with 'how to train and train quickly to higher levels of proficiency' (p. 8). Hoffman et al. (2014, p. 13) further qualified accelerated proficiency as 'getting individuals to achieve high levels of proficiency at a rate faster than ordinary.'

Hoffman et al. (2014, p. 169) expressed accelerated proficiency in terms of TTP. The TTP, in turn, is expressed in terms of career stages as the time taken by an individual to reach a desired level of proficiency. The career stages they most frequently referred to were journeyman and senior journeyman. The journeyman career stage exhibited characteristics like being reliable, experienced, able to work unsupervised, and having achieved a certain level of competence. These characteristics, in general, though not entirely,

---

[12]Fadde & Klein 2010, 2012; Fadde 2007, 2009a, 2009b, 2009c, 2012, 2013, 2016; Hoffman et al. 2008, 2009, 2014; Hoffman, Andrews & Feltovich 2012; Hoffman & Andrews 2012; Hoffman, Andrews, et al. 2010; Hoffman, Feltovich, et al. 2010

lined up well with the proficiency stage of Dreyfus & Dreyfus (2005) model.

Hoffman et al. (2014, p. 169) explained reducing TTP in terms of an S-curve of proficiency acquisition, as shown in Figure 4.1. The proficiency axis shows the stages such as initiate, apprentice, journeyman, and expert. Hoffman et al. have split the journeyman and expert stages into three different levels (junior, middle and senior) to indicate seniority based on tenure in the career.

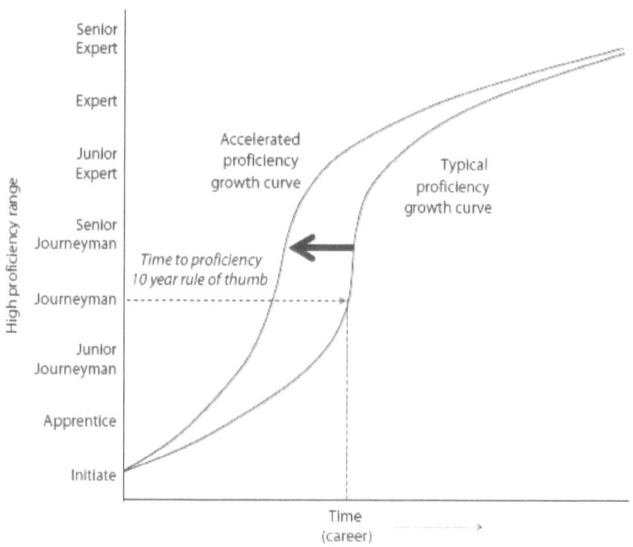

Figure 4.1: Accelerated proficiency growth curve and TTP (Adapted from Hoffman et al. (2014)).

Accelerated proficiency, thus, is the deliberate and conscious effort of shortening the time an employee takes to reach the desired proficiency.

SPEED MATTERS

Lately, organizations have made some conscientious efforts to institute focused projects to accelerate proficiency. Such projects entail the goal of achieving a shorter TTP in a given job role. In general, we refer to such efforts as *accelerating speed to proficiency* and *reducing time to proficiency,* all of which mean the same as *accelerated proficiency* (Bruck 2015; Fadde & Klein 2010; Fred 2002; Hoffman et al. 2014; Rosenbaum & Williams 2004).

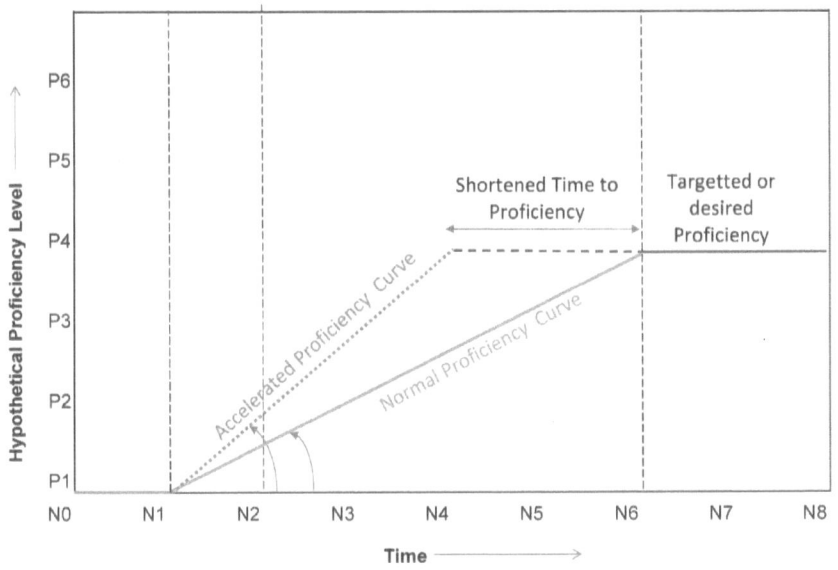

Figure 4.2: The concept of accelerating time to proficiency.

From a practical standpoint, organizations' foremost business challenge is how to bring their employees up to a certain level of proficiency to do their jobs to the desired standards. I depict the concept of accelerating TTP in Figure 4.2. This is a simplistic representation in terms of time intervals N0 to N8 on the horizontal axis and hypothetical proficiency P1 to P6 on the vertical axis. The idea is to put in focused efforts to change the trajectory of employees from the *normal proficiency curve* to the *accelerated proficiency curve* with a higher rate of proficiency acquisition. By applying focused efforts, the desired proficiency P4 can be achieved in a shorter time N4 as compared to the earlier N6.

Business enterprises worldwide have shifted their focus (or started including the focus) on the necessity for acceleration and speed to develop their workforce at a faster rate, increase the rate of skill acquisition, and reduce the time with which their workforce become ready to do their jobs. Market pressure, particularly during the last decade, has warranted accelerating the expertise cycle as a necessity (Clark 2013). Wray & Wallace (2011, p. 243) appealed, 'A more realistic aspiration is to create conditions encouraging all individuals to proceed at the maximum pace possible for them, both in training settings and workplace practice.'

However, the existing literature does not fully describe or characterize the concept of accelerated proficiency, even though the need for the acceleration of proficiency is universal in the business world. Hoffman & Andrews (2012) have raised the concern that understanding of the concept of accelerated proficiency remains crystallized. Hoffman et al. (2014) contended that there was no unified theory yet that could explain the concept, nature, and process of accelerated proficiency. They implied that potentially two theories—cognitive flexibility theory (Spiro & Jehng 1990) and cognitive transformation theory (Klein & Baxter 2009), could be merged to form a new theory for accelerated proficiency: 'Both tap into same general empirical base about the phenomenon of proficiency, expertise, and high-end learning' (Hoffman et al. 2014, p. 136).

While research and synthesis by Hoffman et al. (2014) advanced the understanding of the nature of accelerated proficiency, a unified theory remains elusive, more so in natural settings of organizations.

4.4 DEFINING TTP METRICS

In the *TTP study*, I attempted to study the views and experiences of 85 world-renowned leaders on how they viewed the TTP metrics and the phenomenon of accelerated proficiency. The study revealed two characteristics of accelerated proficiency metrics as it plays out in organizations. The first one is measuring improvement in TTP and the second one is creating a clearer definition of proficiency. These two characteristics are foundational to managers and leaders attempting to define or measure TTP in their organizations.

4.4.1 Measure TTP improvement

Organizations measure the acceleration in proficiency based on TTP measurement. In the *TTP study,* project leaders monitored the proficiency measures to track TTP. The measurement started from the date of his/her hiring or transfer to a new role to the point in time when they reach the state of desired performance:

> We define TTP as the time at which the performance of an employee meets all the thresholds of performance identified by the business. (Sam, Project leader 56)

> And so the time to competence (or TTP) is from the time the employees start their on-the-job training... until the step four is signed off on, all the steps have been signed off on by their trainer and their production leader and the learner. (Hogdan, Project leader 29)

> We typically talk about TTP as how long it takes for people to become 80% proficient. (Reese, Practice leader 14G)

As noted above, TTP did not always mean the onboarding time and did not apply only to newly hired employees (Rosenbaum 2014). It equally applied to employees who were transferred from one job role to another. TTP is not measured based on just a single activity; rather, it involves the collective time required for several activities such as onboarding, formal training, informal training and on-the-job training, projects and other activities to gain experience on specific tasks or skills required to do the job (Attri & Wu 2015).

Further, project leaders in the *TTP study* did not measure the TTP of just one employee; rather, they measured the TTP for the entire job role and usually averaged the values across all employees serving the job role (Borton 2007).

As seen in the *TTP study*, the term TTP appears to have a very clear meaning to business people, although they always did not know how to shorten it. The definition of *proficiency* was mostly used to track TTP. Some project leaders commented:

> I had a very clear definition of TTP, and, that was, how long would it take for someone to be able to do 9.6 calls per hour. (Billy, Project leader 2)

> TTP was determined by business leaders using the same criteria they used in evaluating incumbent performers. The criteria consisted of 11 key metrics and measures. A

performer who meets certain thresholds was identified by the business as having achieved proficiency. (Sam, Project leader 56)

I noticed that, though the metric is very clear, it may not always be feasible to measure TTP accurately, or some job roles simply do not offer any measurable metrics for proficiency; for example, jobs related to fire control, enforcement officers, and business strategy.

4.4.2 Clearer definition of proficiency

In the first place, defining proficiency is a key requirement to accelerate it. Project leaders in the *TTP study* mentioned that the lack of a clear and crisp definition of proficiency is the biggest hindrance to accelerating proficiency. Thus, a clear definition of proficiency for a job role is the most critical requirement to baseline, monitor, and shorten TTP. A clearer internal definition of proficiency leads to identifying that point in the historical data to baseline TTP and also allows managers to track that point in the future. This definition served as a way to drive an agreement across the teams and tools to track proficiency. For instance:

> You have to really be careful to define what those results are... That number one is: you have to define what the results look like. (Dickenson, Project leader 12)

> First of all, we have to define what we mean by proficiency... What do you need to be able to do to show that you're proficient and able to do this? So, that was the first step. And, actually, that in itself became very valuable because it became a great set of expectations of what employees should be able to do. (McDonalds, Project leader 32)

> The concept of proficiency also served as an ongoing assessment tool. (Stephen, Project leader 53)

> We then took those same metrics and started applying them to the graduates of the new program to see if we were able to get them to achieve the required TTP at a faster pace. (Sam, Project leader 56)

Performance improvement tools, such as the HPT model, typically advocate conducting comprehensive performance analysis and defining performance measures upfront in any performance improvement endeavor (Kang 2017). More than anything else, a clear definition supports managers in planning the path to the proficiency of a set of individuals performing a job role (Rosenbaum 2014).

While acknowledging the importance of the definition of proficiency, the project leaders also pointed out that business leaders in organizations struggle to define proficiency clearly. However, without an undebated definition agreed upon by all stakeholders, it is not feasible to dedicate efforts and investments and drive alignment among managers about what needs to be achieved. In the absence of a clear definition, organizations did not know if their employees in a given role had attained proficiency or not. Some project leaders emphasized this issue:

> Most organizations can't actually tell you what they mean by proficiency, and they only have a very general idea of on average, how long does it take?... So, if you're serious about reducing the TTP, then you have to get clear about what that means and then you have to start tracking it so that you can apply process improvement principles. (Reynold, Project leader 49)

People have such a poor understanding of what proficiency was, is that [sic] they didn't even agree on that. So, it is hard to find TTP if you don't agree on what proficiency is. (Stephen, Project leader 53)

A training project needs to start out by describing in behavioral terms exactly what proficiency looks like, and there is the problem. A lot of people don't take the time to really describe what proficiency looks like in behavioral terms. Once you do that, you have to have a plan to measure to make sure when you've gotten people to proficiency. I think most people fail on those two counts. (Dickenson, Project leader 12)

4.5 DRAWING THE BOUNDARIES

An analysis in the *TTP study* led to identifying the core characteristics of the term accelerated proficiency:

> *Accelerating proficiency* means shortening the time someone takes in a given job role to reach to a state of consistent performance that meets the set thresholds. This is measured in time-to-proficiency. A clearer definition of job-role proficiency and its measures are the foremost critical requirement to the acceleration of proficiency. Accelerated proficiency is not about learning a body of content faster or shortening the training duration because the solution to a shorter time-to-proficiency lies beyond training interventions (Attri 2018, p. 236).

This definition is foundational to how we define, measure, and track the TTP metrics in organizations. At the same time, the definition establishes some important distinctions every manager and leader must know when s/he works on employee development plans. The first distinction is understanding how accelerating proficiency (or shortening TTP) differs from similarly sounding phrases such as accelerating learning, accelerating training, and accelerating expertise. The second distinction is to understand whether accelerating proficiency means shortening the training period or the employees' overall journey. However, the term "accelerating proficiency" can confuse managers who are not from the learning profession. The one thing that probably differentiated successful project leaders from traditional managers is how "accelerating proficiency" was clear to the former group.

I discuss some inferences drawn from these conversations in the following subsections.

4.5.1 It is not about accelerating learning

I observed, based on my conversations with successful project leaders, that accelerated proficiency was a characteristically different construct from the traditional concept of "accelerated learning," which meant speeding up the learning curve of an employee, that is, making him/her learn a given content in a shorter time or more content in the same time (Imel 2002; Patchan et al. 2015; Radler & Bocianu 2017; Trekles & Sims 2013). The reality in workplaces is that employees (even in the same job profile) learn at different rates and using different styles. However, controlling an individual's learning curve is not feasible, and that is not the intent of accelerated proficiency. Learning something quickly does not necessarily mean an individual would start producing consistent business results quickly too.

The project leaders in the *TTP study* suggested that accelerated proficiency is not about speeding up the learning curve of a certain individual, or it is not learning or training a given content in a shorter time. It is about enabling people to reach the same level of mastery in attaining business performance, irrespective of their speed of learning. One of the project leaders commented:

> We might have to put in a coach, we might have to let the person repeat some things, we might let that employee do a remedial loop, but s/he can achieve only the same level of mastery. That is where TTP could mislead people sometimes. Sometimes, not all human beings can learn quickly. (Dickenson, Project leader 12)

For example, if a sales engineer's monthly quota was $1M, learning the details of the product features, sales processes, and sales techniques is not a guarantee that s/he will certainly produce $1M consistently month after month. Such outcomes require more than just learning content, knowledge, or skills. Thus, learning more content in a short time may or may not always contribute toward a shorter TTP. S/he would have to develop relationships, connections, and leads and gain experience in all aspects of the job role to achieve the quota of the sale worth $1M every month in a shorter time.

In the context of accelerating proficiency, the value or contribution of accelerated learning aligns with 'faster attainment of skill and knowledge, and an increase in on-the-job performance with better retention of learning,' as conceptualized by Andrews & Fitzgerald (2010, p. 2).

Accelerated proficiency refers to the performance of a job role as a whole and a group of people serving that role as a whole. Thus, it is not about one employee's learning and is more about the achievement collectively for the entire group in a job role (Bologa & Lupu 2007). Though overlapping in meaning, accelerated learning and accelerated proficiency represent different intents for business.

4.5.2 It is not about shortening training

The concept of accelerated proficiency is differentiated from the intent of the traditional concept of accelerated training or shortened training duration. In the *TTP study*, I observed that accelerated proficiency projects are generally not carried out with an intent to shorten training duration or *rapidize training,* that is, 'the idea of training individuals to achieve some *minimal level of proficiency* at a rate faster than usual' (Hoffman et al. 2014, p. 13).

In the *TTP study*, I observed the goal of accelerated proficiency as reducing the total time taken to reach the state of proficiency, rather than reducing the training duration alone. Project leaders indicated that reducing the training duration was not the goal of their accelerated proficiency projects, though the shorter duration of training came out as a by-product in most of the project cases. In most project cases, achieving the state of proficiency took several times more time than the duration of the training interventions used. For example, one of the project leaders stated:

> Do the week's program in a day and that is not we are talking about...we are talking about moving the 18 months target down to 12 months. (Stephen, Project leader 53)

Several organizations do use structured on-the-job training (S-OJT) methods. The S-OJT methodology does result in a reduction in the training duration while preparing the employees for initial readiness. For instance, S-OJT methods have shown up to 10 times reduction in the training time compared to unstructured OJT methods in the development of initial readiness for a given job (Jacobs & Bu-Rahmah 2012; Jacobs 2014). However, attaining such initial operating readiness (Duguay & Korbut 2002) to put an employee on the job to do the basic duties is also not the goal of accelerated proficiency, though some project cases paid attention to this goal as well.

In some project cases, it was noted that if proficiency to initial operating readiness was important, shorter training duration was used as a strategy to have the employees start producing business-specific outcomes sooner:

> 'How quickly can I teach you [to be ready for basic job role]?'...what we found was, we could do an initial program that would at least get you the basics, to get in front of the computer within roughly about 2–4 weeks. (Christian, Project leader 5)

However, in a majority of project cases, the true goal of accelerated proficiency was seen to be to make an employee fully productive and fully functioning in his or her job so that outcomes designated for the job role may be produced (Rosenbaum & Williams 2004). Thus, shortening the training duration is not an explicit goal of accelerated proficiency projects in organizations, though in almost every case, it was attained as a by-product.

4.5.3 It is not about increasing work speed

The goal of accelerated proficiency is not to shorten the transaction time or activity time to appear to be doing work faster. For example, it is not about how soon a sales employee makes a sale to a given customer or how fast s/he closes the sales cycle; rather, it is about how soon the employee reaches the mark where s/he produces the set sales targets consistently. For instance:

> [Proficiency is that] I should be able to do 80% of my job... It may take me longer to do them right, but I can still get it done. (Kieve, Project leader 24)

4.5.4 It is not about accelerating expertise

Expertise is considered an elite status bestowed upon few domain specialists, and not all of the workforce may need to be developed to that level. Development of expertise takes a long time, sometimes even as long as 10 years, as noted in Section 3.6. Thus, the efforts required to speed up the journey toward proficiency and that toward expertise are significantly different. As a manager or leader, you might need to keep this distinction clear that accelerating TTP refers to speeding up the stage of proficiency and in any manner does not convey speeding up development towards the stage of expertise.

4.5.5 It is not about improving training

I came from a traditional training background. It was quite a surprise for me to take in in the first place. Almost all the project leaders unanimously opined that training alone rarely accelerates proficient performance and that it requires solutions beyond training. I observed that the overall role of formal training interventions in accelerating proficiency was relatively small. The journey toward proficiency was much more than training events or learning interventions. One of the project leaders commented:

> The real answer to compressing time to competence is that one has to look outside of the training—look at what is wrapped around it. (Charlie, Project leader 4)

Training interventions were seen as one of the several potential solutions to accelerate proficiency, rather than the total solution in itself. Almost all the participants asserted that training alone was not the solution to accelerate proficiency. However, typical managers tend to consider training as a magic wand and trainers as magicians who would transform their novice employees into fully productive machines overnight. On the other hand, the successful project leaders in my study viewed training as one of the many solutions. They used a range of non-training solutions as well to reduce TTP. Several project leaders commented:

> Training is not the answer in every situation, and for many situations, you need a very different strategy as the main approach to getting people to the point when they are competent. (Todd, Project leader 57)
>
> Training is usually one of the more insignificant ones [solutions]. (Dickenson, Project leader 12)
>
> Training very rarely will result in the desired performance; that it takes a number of different interventions, all woven together to produce an outcome. (Harry, Project leader 18)
>
> When you think about really learning to do something to a level of performance or a level of proficiency, it takes a lot more than that [training] and that is what people kind of fall short... (Stephen, Project leader 53)

Performance improvement practitioners have maintained this stance for a much longer time that training is one of the several performance interventions (Stolovitch & Keeps 1999).

CH4/THE METRICS

Leading practitioners Pollock, Wick & Jefferson (2015, p. 41) asserted that performance results from the interaction of the worker, work, and workplace, but the '[t]raining impacts worker only.' Training is useful only if it focuses on developing performers to produce business results. However, most of the time, training is just an event with the specific purpose of delivering necessary skills or behaviors. It usually has a specific assessment checkpoint that signals its end. Usually, the goal of training interventions is not to produce the desired results immediately or to wait for it. In fact, such a wait is certainly not feasible.

Admittedly, training is a critical part of most performance improvement interventions (Clark 2008; Kraiger 2014). There are cases in which the employees attained the desired proficiency in training settings, or that training is the only viable, practical option; for example, job roles in which life and safety matter (e.g., military officers, pilots, surgeons, and firefighters) and failure is no option in real situations (Hintze 2008; Jenkins et al. 2016; Klein & Borders 2016; Kuchenbrod 2016). Alternatively, training may be a more feasible solution in job roles that are not readily evaluated in terms of immediate on-the-job outcomes (e.g., roles related to business strategy) or job roles that are governed by licensing or other regulatory norms (e.g., jobs in the oil & gas industry). Such situations may necessitate training as a fail-safe mechanism or even a mandatory requirement (Crichton & Flin 2004).

In the *TTP study,* I found that training was a continuous process, mostly on-the-job, as opposed to a formal event. Thus, it continued until employees achieved the desired proficiency. A similar approach is taken with the proficiency-based curriculum

(Angelo et al. 2015; Lee 2011; Rosenthal et al. 2009; Wilcox et al. 2014), focused on mastery learning (Guskey 2009), which is the practice on a given task until proficiency is achieved, instead of 'seat time,' which is spending predefined time on a given task (Nagel 2011).

In the *TTP study*, in the instances where training was designed, the focus was on making performers produce the desired business outcomes that mattered most to the organization. Training did not seem to end until that state was achieved. It appears that their focus was not so much on making the performers learn something:

> You really need to be clear about what is the business point, not what people need to learn, but what needs to happen for the business or how do they need to perform. (Reynold, Project leader 49)

> Completion of [traditional] training is specifically the moment that the trainer conveys all the information. But, in this model [of accelerated proficiency], training is complete only when the learner has achieved proficiency...It was less about how much time we have covered and how many PowerPoint slides have been involved—and much more focused on how to help the learners become proficient in their job as quickly as possible so that they are contributing to the overall roles of the organization...It was not that the training was content-free by any means, but it was all focused on whether the chemist/operator was performing at the level I needed, as measured by making batches quickly and efficiently without errors and making sellable products. (Richardson, Project leader 45)

It might be a bit surprising for instructional designers that the traditional instructional design processes actually come on the way to improve TTP. In several cases, I observed that training generated

CH4 / THE METRICS

outcomes that were not required or not immediately useful. In fact, in some instances, the training design even caused a slower rate of proficiency. One of the project leaders shared an insightful reflection of how organizations care less about traditional training modalities if the goal is shortening TTP:

> [It was] liberating [for me] in some way, not to have to abide by those sorts of cultural norms or [traditional] training development and instructional design that I was so familiar with. All that really mattered was for the employee [to] make the product within specification in a timely fashion to meet the customers' needs. At no point in the process was any stakeholder interested really in what instructional design methodologies are used or any of those things that we often in our field use to judge ourselves about. That just was not of importance to the stakeholders in this case. It was 'I want to get the product out of the door to our customers.' It has their specifications and that is really what matters. That is what drives our organization and that is what we care about. I had to learn to let go of many things that I held dear as just not what was important to the project... While I am willing to consider that as technical language from a training or learning and development standpoint, I do not wish to introduce that type of language or those constructs to my team. There was no explicit attempt to link what we were doing for developing task analysis to what I would call those academic constructs that you just named. Just the language would not have been familiar to the members of the team and I do not think it would have helped them arrive more quickly at the set of proficiency statements...And, no one really was interested in a lot of the metrics we had developed for ourselves in the training industry because that was not why the paint company was in business. (Richardson, Project leader 45)

Project leaders in the *TTP study* appeared to believe that the dynamics of a training intervention was not a true representation of workplace challenges and complexities in the real world in terms of pressure, consequences, goals, and experience:

> Retention happens when there is a good emotional loading on it... Now, it is difficult to get that emotional loading onto something in a training room... most things that happen in a training room are fairly ordinary. People are sitting there, absorbing stuff, and talking about stuff... but it is not an emotional rollercoaster, let's put it that way. (Mathews, Practice leader 16G)

Some researchers also shared similar views. Chevalier (2004; 2015), Soderstrom & Bjork (2015), and Stolovitch (2000) argued that performance during training interventions could be a misleading indicator of proficiency and long-term learning of behaviors that should persist in workplaces. Unless such interventions prepare the performers to produce business outcomes in a shorter time, training may not contribute toward accelerating proficiency. Project leaders strongly iterated that performance during a training event was a false indicator of an employee's proficiency. They also recognized that not all of the performance seen in any training event would transfer to the job toward accelerating proficiency. Some project leaders supported this by stating that:

> Performance during the acquisition process is misleading, and in many situations, is the only thing that people [responsible for training] are going to see. (Robert, Practice leader 4G)

> In traditional training, what people do is to go inside a competency [list] and then start saying, 'how do we train each of these competencies?' I am going to use a competency, let us do a training session... (Stephen, Project leader 53)

While modern studies emphasize aligning training objectives with business needs and goals (Hughes 2003; Saks, Haccoun & Belcourt 2010; Salas et al. 2012), preparing performers toward achieving proficiency in a shorter time appears to be beyond the reach of any instructional design models; this is because instructional design models tend to focus on knowledge, skills, and behaviors. Baker (2017) argued that, in modern organizations, the assumption, that a technically superior workforce is the key to organizational performance, has geared all solutions to being skill-focused or training-focused. As seen in previous themes, achieving business outcomes to pre-established standards consistently within the complexity of workplaces requires not only skills, knowledge, and behaviors but also several other support mechanisms and interventions. This closely aligns with the HPT practices (Kang 2017; Marker et al. 2014; Pershing 2006; Van Tiem, Moseley & Dessinger 2012; Wallace 2006). This theme also confirms observations made by Swanson & Holton III (2001) and (Dean 2016) with regard to the need to use several non-linear interventions in addition to learning interventions to attain desired performance.

However, the value of training in skill acquisition and knowledge acquisition was not undermined by any project leader. Some of them even believed that the primary goal of a training intervention should be to reduce TTP. Otherwise, it may not be useful:

> Training has only one value, and that is to improve skills and knowledge. That is all it does. (Harry, Project leader 18)

> If training is not shortening the time, then, maybe they should not be doing it. It should always shorten the time. (Diana, Project leader 11)

The goals of accelerated proficiency are not described in terms of learning knowledge or skill. However, neither theme undermines nor negates the critical value that learning and training play in acquiring knowledge, skills, and proficiency. There is no doubt that learning is an underlying process in all the endeavors undertaken by an individual in the workplace (Saks, Haccoun & Belcourt 2010; Salas et al. 2012). Nevertheless, what is being measured and how success is being reported are matters of perspective.

4.6 WHAT IT MEANS TO YOU

☞ **TTP measurement depends upon the definition of proficiency:** Managers or leaders usually either do not measure TTP for critical roles or they cannot do because proficiency for those roles is not defined clearly.

☞ **Differentiate between accelerating proficiency versus accelerating learning:** Typically, leaders think that by learning fast, the employees would become proficient soon too. However, the assumption would lead to strategies more geared toward learning and training rather than the entire ecosystem that surrounds the job. Therefore, do not confuse or interchange

CH4 / THE METRICS

the intent of accelerated proficiency to mean as accelerated learning.

☛ **Baseline TTP for each job role:** Employ various objective data sources and data analytics to the extent possible to measure the baseline TTP of a given job role. Remember that TTP is measured across an entire job role (all the employees in that role) rather than at an individual level. Further, the baseline measurement can be established either based on backward-looking historical data or forward-looking future data. TTP should be averaged across all employees in a given role with the min-to-max range identified.

☛ **Identify the TTP values of your best-performing folks:** By the law of averages, there are usually some exemplary performers in each team and in each job role who may be demonstrating shorter TTP values when compared with the rest of the workforce. The TTP values of such exemplary performers should be benchmarked.

CHAPTER 5
THE TRIGGERS

THE MAGNITUDE AND SCALE OF TTP

SPEED MATTERS

Few classical studies on expertise or expert performance have focused on the time taken by employees to reach high proficiency (expertise). Ericsson & Charness (1994) proposed, '[t]o measure the duration of the acquisition process, we analyze the length of time it takes for best individuals to attain the highest levels of performance within a domain.'

The measurement of the time taken to gain high proficiency has intrigued researchers for long. Chase & Simon (1973) found that several other domains exhibit the patterns of achieving high proficiency in 10 years, similar to the observations made in the domain of chess. Since then, the 10-year rule of achieving expertise has been empirically tested by researchers (Hayes 1989; Simonton 1997). The most extensive work on this aspect was carried out by Ericsson et al. (1993), who analyzed the effect of deliberate practice by comparing 30 under-training violinists with 24 expert and amateur pianists. Through extensive modeling and measurements, Ericsson et al. (1993) concluded that it requires about 10,000 hours or 10 years of intensive training and deliberate practice activities to attain expertise in any field.

In a study involving 215 modern writers, researchers measure the time to their best works since the time they published their first work (Kaufman & Kaufman 2007). They found that it required at least 10 years for several famous writers to reach the point of publishing their work in a reputed publication, which required, in addition, an even longer preparation time. Nevertheless, they also stated that 'it takes 10 years to become not just an "expert" but a "world-class" expert' (id. 115). However, this estimate of 10 years was for attaining notable expertise or an elite performance on a specific set of representative tasks or skills, mainly in a closed domain (such as chess, music, sports), where the standards of performance have been well established (Ericsson & Towne 2010; Ericsson 2002, 2003).

Hoffman, Feltovich, et al. (2010, p. 61) criticized the 10-year deliberate practice as a rule to gain a high level of proficiency: 'Our reason for calling out the ostensive limitations of the "approach" is that if expertise is achieved only after deliberate practice (the 10-year rule of thumb), then acceleration would not be possible.'

In the present context, TTP refers to the time taken by an employee to reach the point where s/he can do his or her job reliably and can produce consistent results. By nature of the measurement, this time is expected to be much shorter than the one suggested by expert performance studies (i.e., 10 years). Still, the overall TTP could be in months or years, depending on the nature of the job.

The specific estimates are scarce in the literature available currently. There are only a handful of estimates in the form of a few reports and books (Accenture 2013; Borton 2007; Fred 2002; Pollock, Wick & Jefferson 2015, p. 285; Thompson 2017, p. 169). For example, the TTP of new bankers was estimated to be between 11 and 14 months in one of the studies (Thompson 2017, p. 173). According to an estimate, a pilot takes a minimum of 1500 hours (the equivalent of flying for 2 hours every day for 2 years) to be certified to fly a commercial plane (Government Publishing Office 2013). Similarly, the TTP of air force communication specialists was observed to be in the range of 18–36 months, depending upon their aptitude scores (Carpenter et al. 1989). In a study by Borton

(2007) involving 300 call center agents, the TTP of the agents was found to be in close proximity of 6 months. More recently, a survey conducted among the chief sales officers of 1200 companies worldwide by Accenture (2013) indicated that the TTP of 73% of the new sales representative workforce was approximately one year or more.

Apart from the above studies, there has been no comprehensive data on the size of TTP in any job role. In the *TTP study*, I found the actual TTP across various job roles. However, it turned out to be alarmingly large.

5.1 MEASURING TTP

It was for the first time that TTP figures were studied in the *TTP study*. What I found was that the magnitude of TTP may be as large as 3 years in certain job roles, which encompassed becoming productive enough to deliver the required performance metrics. When this magnitude is multiplied across the total number of individuals serving the same job role, it becomes a business problem of such a huge scale that organizations simply cannot afford to ignore its impacts.

In the *TTP study*, all 60 project cases were analyzed through a comparative analysis with each other to understand what worked in one context versus the other contexts and categorized based on two important factors:

1. First, the ones that characterize the job itself—complexity, job type, and primary skills.

2. Second, the ones that describe the space in which the job role operates—economic sector, business sector, and the industry group (categorized per Thomson Reuters Business Classification System).

The analysis revealed an exceptionally alarming understanding of the TTP numbers in different contexts. Two parameters emerged that allowed recognizing the seriousness of the problem and the extent of TTP numbers in various settings:

- **Magnitude**—the absolute length of TTP in a given job role
- **Scale**—the minimum and maximum lengths of TTP and their impact across all the employees in a given job role

5.2 THE MAGNITUDE OF TTP

The measurement of the length of TTP sets a compelling reason that drives organizations to attend to the business problem of long TTP in any job role. Here is my analysis of the TTP data across various dimensions.

5.2.1 By job type

I arranged the project cases by job nature, as shown in Table 5-1. As one can see, the magnitude of TTP is significantly large across the job role types. I summarize below my major observations:

- Employees in sales-related jobs (technical as well as non-technical such as equipment sales engineers, medical and pharmaceutical sales engineers, sales agents, insurance agents, real estate agents, and sales representatives) require about 1.5 months to 1.5 years to reach the desired proficiency, as seen in 8 project cases.

- Employees in relatively certain managerial jobs (such as managers of the retail industry, supermarkets, and bakeries shops) require about 3 months to 1.5 years to reach the desired proficiency, as seen in 3 project cases. The training required for the initial readiness of managers itself ranged from 4 to 13 weeks. Despite these managerial jobs perceived as relatively simpler, the TTP was still quite large. On the other hand, the TTP was much longer for the managers in strategic roles or those working in technology, scientific or similar complex industries. Ironically, the TTP of management staff does not get noticed enough by organizational leaders as they typically require managers and expect them to learn quickly by jumping into the fire. The large TTP numbers for the managerial jobs suggest that senior leaders should worry equally about their management staff when the goal is to make them adapt readily to new technologies. How often are managers given systematic ecosystems and tools to work toward acquiring proficiency quickly?

- Strategic management or leadership-related roles (such as business managers, top executives, and military officers) displayed TTP numbers in the tune of 1 year to several years. Due to their long tenures, it is hard to measure or obtain TTP

CH5/THE TRIGGERS

values in such job roles. Similarly, for some strategic roles, the TTP values are extremely long. It was mainly because, in such roles, employees were required to handle some events which happened once in 10-20 years. For example, an unforeseen drop in gold prices, underground mining fire, or retirement of senior folks in the energy sector, all of which do not happen too often to acquire proficiency at an accelerated rate.

- Employees in technical or engineering-related jobs (such as database administrators, plant console operators/maintenance engineers, remote client troubleshooting specialists, equipment or plant service/repair engineers, cybersecurity analysts, electronic technicians, and non-technical sales engineers) require about 2 months to several years to reach the desired proficiency, as seen in 16 project cases.

- Employees in scientific or development-related jobs (such as biotechnology/biochemistry researchers, design engineers, equipment engineers, plant engineers, and software developers) require about 6 months to 3 years to reach the desired proficiency, as observed in 4 project cases.

- Employees in assembly and production-related jobs (such as machine operators, machinists, miners, and assemblers) took lesser time, about 1 week to 5 months, to reach the desired proficiency, as observed in 4 project cases.

A point to note is that the training programs alone typically took as low as 1 week to as high as 18 weeks of classroom time across different job types.

Table 5-1 Magnitude of TTP across different primary job types

Primary Job Nature	No. of Project Cases	Time to Proficiency	Time to Training
Technical or engineering	16	2 months to several years	5 to 18 weeks
Sales - non-technical	5	3 months to 1.5 years	1 to 10 weeks
Scientific or development	4	6 months to 3 years	No data
Customer service helpdesk	4	1.5 months to 1 year	4 to 12 weeks
Sales – technical	3	Unknown to 1.5 years	No data
Managerial, supervisory	3	1 month to 14 months	4 to 13 weeks
Strategic management, leadership	3	1 year to very long#	No data
Medical, healthcare	3	3 months to 1 year	
Production, manufacturing	3	1 month to 5 months*	
Financial services	2	5 months to 3 years	15 weeks
Training or education	1	1-2 years	No data
Assembly, repair	1	1 week	

Exceptions: Some rare events that happen once in 10-20 years (e.g., managers having to handle declining gold prices)
*Exceptions: Some rare events that happen once in 8–10 years events (e.g., miners dealing with underground fires)

5.2.2 By complexity

Complexity is associated either with the job nature, the skills involved, or a combination of both. For example, both scientific development and strategic leadership are highly complex despite their different nature and skills involved. Similarly, engineering jobs involving problem-solving or management consulting jobs involving analytical skills may both be medium-high in complexity.

CH5 / THE TRIGGERS

I arranged the project cases by complexity, as summarized in Table 5-2. Some major observations from the table are as under:

- The TTP of employees involved in highly complex jobs or in jobs requiring higher-order problem-solving skills varies from as little as 6 months to as high as 3 years. Some highly complex jobs (such as those involving business strategies for never-seen-before events) may not even have enough event frequency for their employees to attain proficiency. In such cases, proficiency may be acquired in as large a time as 10–20 years.

- Most of the cases analyzed fell in the medium-high range of complexity; the TTP numbers in these jobs were found to be anywhere between 2 months to several years. Training programs for such job roles varied from 5 to 18 weeks.

Table 5-2 Magnitude of TTP across complexity ratings

Complexity Rating	No. of Project Cases	Time to Proficiency	Time to Training
1. High	9	6 months to 3 years#	No data
2. Medium-High	22	2 months to several years	5 weeks to 18 weeks
3. Medium	9	1 month to 14 months*	4 weeks to 13 weeks
4. Medium-Low	14	3 months to 3 years	1 week to 15 weeks
5. Low	6	1 week to 1 year	4 weeks to 12 weeks

\# Exceptions: Some rare events that happen once in 10-20 years (e.g., managers having to handle declining gold prices)
*Exceptions: Some rare events that happen once in 8–10 years events (e.g., miners dealing with underground fires)

5.2.3 By critical skills

Although a job role requires a combination of several different skills and in different proportions, there is always one primary or the most underlying core skill that is the most important and determines the individual's overall success in that job. In this study, I mapped each project case to one of the 15 core or primary critical skills. I summarize the TTP magnitudes against these critical skills in Table 5-3. Some inferences that can be drawn from the mapping are:

- An employee required anywhere between 2 months and anywhere between 3 years, depending upon the context and product/process, to become proficient in the most advanced skills such as complex troubleshooting and problem-solving.

- The TTP in innovation and design skills is about 2 years. However, it must be noted that such jobs typically leverage the previous experience, and, thus, the TTP referred to that of experienced engineers working on a new project or technology.

- An employee in the supervisory or managerial role typically required 1–14 months to become proficient. The lower side is in jobs in smaller retail stores, and the higher side in jobs with more complex responsibilities in the retail segment.

One must note that there may not be a direct correlation between TTP and the complexity of the skills. For example, an employee requires between 5 months and 3 years to gain proficiency in financial analysis, which is actually categorized under the low–medium complex job role. Proficiency is a direct function of the

CH5 / THE TRIGGERS

number of exposures and event frequency seen. Thus, employees in relatively less complex jobs, like helpdesk handling, may even take up to 1 year to become proficient, subject to the number of exposures available to them.

Table 5-3 Magnitude of TTP across critical skills

Critical-to-success Skill	No. of Project Cases	Time to Proficiency	Time to Training
Complex troubleshooting	11	2 months to 3 years	5 weeks to 18 weeks
Sales and negotiation	11	3 months to 1.5 years	1 week to 10 weeks
Technical Problem solving	6	6 months to several years	No data
Innovation and design	5	6 months to 2 years	No data
Strategic thinking	4	1 year to very long#	No data
Helpdesk support	4	3 months to 1 year	4 weeks to 12 weeks
Supervisory	3	1 month to 14 months	4 weeks to 13 weeks
Project execution	3	6 months to 1 year	No data
Precision machining	3	1 month to 5 months*	No data
Medical and psychological care	3	3 months to 1 year	No data
Financial analysis	2	5 months to 3 years	15 weeks
Business analysis	1	No data	No data
Teaching and training	1	In years	No data
Assembly	1	1 week	No data
Data processing	1	No data	No data

\# Exceptions: Some rare events that happen once in 10-20 years (e.g., managers having to handle declining gold prices)
*Exceptions: Some rare events that happen once in 8–10 years events (e.g., miners dealing with underground fires)

5.2.4 By economic sector

I then arranged the project cases by economic sectors (per Thomson Reuters Business Classification System), as summarized in Table 5-4. The table provides the following significant insights into the trends in various sectors/industries:

- The technology sector (13 project cases) shows a TTP between 2 months and 3 years.

- The basic materials sector (3 project cases) appeared to have a very long cycle to proficiency because it deals with low-frequency events such as underground mine fires and declining gold prices.

- The training duration was as short as 1 week in the financial and consumer sectors, and as long as 18 weeks in the technology, financial, energy, and industrial sectors.

Table 5-4 Magnitude of TTP across economic sectors

Economic Sectors	No. of Project Cases	Time to Proficiency	Time to Training
Technology	13	2 months to 3 years	5 to 13 weeks
Financials	9	1.5 months to 1 year	1 to 15 weeks
Healthcare	7	Unknown to 2 years	No data
Consumer non-cyclicals	5	1 week to 14 months	4 to 13 weeks
Energy	4	1 month to several years	No data
Industrials	4	5 months to 1.5 years	18 weeks
Basic materials	3	1.5 to 2 years*	No data
Telecommunication services	2	3 months to 1 year	
Military/ government	2	1 to 3 years	

Utilities	2 years

* Exceptions: Some rare events that happen once in 10-20 years (e.g., managers having to handle declining gold prices) or once in 8–10 years (e.g., miners dealing with underground fires)

5.2.5 By business sector

Following the economic sector-wise classification, I arranged the project cases by business sectors (per Thomson Reuters Business Classification System), as summarized in Table 5-5. The table provides the following significant insights:

- Technology equipment business sector (such as semiconductor equipment, cybersecurity platforms, radar equipment, communication products, and servers) displayed TTP values up to 3 years, which was one of the highest TTP values by business sector.

- For most of the other business sectors, while the lower side of TTP was 1 month, the upper side was on an average up to 2 years.

- Services sectors like software and IT services, telecom, and food and beverage exhibited very short TTP values in the tune of a few months.

- Some business sectors that rely on high technical know-how (such as the pharmaceutical, medical, chemicals, energy, and healthcare industries) exhibited TTP values in the order of 1–2 years.

Table 5-5 Magnitude of TTP across business sectors

Business Sector (TR)	No. of Project Cases	Time to Proficiency	Time to Training
Technology Equipment	12	6 months to 3 years	6 weeks to 13 weeks
Energy - Fossil Fuels	7	1 month to several years	
Banking & Investment Services	6	1.5 month to 1 year	1 week to 12 weeks
Healthcare Services	4	3 months to 1 year	
Pharmaceuticals & Medical Research	4	6 months to 2 years	
Government / Military	3	1-3 years	
Industrial & Commercial Services	3	X years	
Industrial Goods	3	5 months to 1.5 years	18 weeks
Insurance	3	5 months to 1.5 years	15 weeks
Mineral Resources	2	In some exceptions 8-20 years event frequency	
Retailers	2	14 months	8 weeks to 13 weeks
Software & IT Services	2	2 months	5 weeks
Telecommunications Services	2	3 months	
Automobiles & Auto Parts	1	1 week	
Chemicals	1	1.5 -2 years	
Cyclical Consumer Services	1		4 weeks
Food & Beverages	1	1 month	4 weeks
Real Estate	1		
Transportation	1		
Utilities	1	2 years	

5.2.6   By industry group

I segregated project cases by industry group (per Thomson Reuters Business Classification System), as shown in Table 5-6. The categorization allowed an analysis by industry:

CH5 / THE TRIGGERS

- The semiconductor equipment, biotechnology & research, and the oil & gas industries exhibited the longest TTP.
- The banking and finance industry (such as investment banking, insurance, and banking) exhibited TTP values of 1 year or below.

Table 5-6 Magnitude of TTP across industry groups

Industry Group (TR)	No. of Project Cases	Time to Proficiency	Time to Training
Semiconductors & Semiconductor Equipment	8	6 months to 3 years	6 weeks to 13 weeks
Oil & Gas	5	Up to several years	
Investment Banking & Investment Services	4	1.5 month to 3 months	1 week to 12 weeks
Communications & Networking	3	6 months to 1 year	
Professional & Commercial Services	3	X years	
Healthcare Providers & Services	3	3 months to 1 year	
Insurance	3	5 months to 1.5 years	15 weeks
Pharmaceuticals	2	6 months	
Oil & Gas Related Equipment and Services	2	1 month to 1 year	
Telecommunications Services	2	3 months	
Banking Services	2	1 year	10 weeks
Other Specialty Retailers	2	14 months	8 to 13 weeks
Biotechnology & Medical Research	2	2 years	
Software & IT Services	2	2 months	5 weeks
Machinery, Equipment & Components	2	1.5 years	18 weeks
Metals & Mining	2	Very long*	

*Exceptions: once in 8–20 years events (miners dealing with underground fires).

If you see Table 5.1 to 5.6, you will notice that the TTP of most jobs across several economic sectors is not in days; rather, it is as long as 3 years in some project cases. Also, you would conclude that the duration of training programs to develop proficiency to a reasonable level ranges up to 18 weeks.

The question arises as to why there is so much deviation in the TTP numbers across project cases within a given industry, business sector, or job type. I attribute the variations in the TTP to the difference in the job goals, contexts, organizational work cultures, team compositions, and factors that are not necessarily the same, even for the same job nature across organizations.

Table 5-7 summarizes the range of TTP across project cases classified based on the economic sector, business sector, industry group, primary job nature, and CTS skills.

Table 5-7 TTP range across project cases

Economic Sector (TR)	Business Sector (TR)	Industry Group (TR)	Primary Job Nature	Critical-to-success Skill	Time to Proficiency	Time to Training	Project Cases
BASIC MATERIALS	Chemicals	Chemicals	Technical or Engineering	Technical Problem solving	1.5- 2 years		1
	Mineral Resources	Metals & Mining	Strategic Management, Leadership	Strategic thinking	10-20 years event frequency		1
			Production, Manufacturing	Precision machining	8-10 years event frequency		1
CONSUMER NON-CYCLICALS	Automobiles & Auto Parts	Automobiles & Auto Parts	Assembly, Repair	Assembly	1 week		1
	Cyclical Consumer Services	Hotels & Entertainment Services	Customer service helpdesk	Helpdesk support		4 weeks	1
	Food & Beverages	Food & Tobacco	Managerial, Supervisory	Supervisory	1 month	4 weeks	1
	Retailers	Other Specialty Retailers	Managerial, Supervisory	Supervisory	14 months	8-13 weeks	2
ENERGY	Energy - Fossil Fuels	Oil & Gas	Technical or Engineering	Technical Problem solving	Several years		4
			Strategic Management, Leadership	Strategic thinking	very long		1

Economic Sector (TR)	Business Sector (TR)	Industry Group (TR)	Primary Job Nature	Critical-to-success Skill	Time to Proficiency	Time to Training	Project Cases
		Oil & Gas Related Equipment and Services	Technical or Engineering	Complex troubleshooting	1 year		1
			Production, Manufacturing	Precision machining	1 month		1
FINANCIALS	Banking & Investment Services	Investment Banking & Investment Services	Sales - Non-Technical	Sales and negotiation	3 months	1-4 weeks	3
			Customer service helpdesk	Helpdesk support	1.5 month	12 weeks	1
		Banking Services	Sales - Non-Technical	Sales and negotiation		10 weeks	1
			Customer service helpdesk	Helpdesk support	1 year		1
	Insurance	Insurance	Sales - Non-Technical	Sales and negotiation	1.5 years		2
			Financial services	Financial analysis	5 months	15 weeks	1
	Real Estate	Real Estate Operations	Sales - Non-Technical	Sales and negotiation			1
HEALTHCARE	Healthcare Services	Healthcare Providers & Services	Medical, Healthcare	Medical and psychological care	3 months to 1 year		3
		Healthcare Equipment & Supplies	Sales - Technical	Sales and negotiation			1
	Pharmaceuticals & Medical Research	Pharmaceuticals	Scientific or Development	Innovation and design	6 months		1

Economic Sector (TR)	Business Sector (TR)	Industry Group (TR)	Primary Job Nature	Critical-to-success Skill	Time to Proficiency	Time to Training	Project Cases
			Sales - Technical	Sales and negotiation	6 months		1
		Biotechnology & Medical Research	Technical or Engineering	Project execution			1
			Scientific or Development	Innovation and design	2 years		1
INDUSTRIALS	Industrial & Commercial Services	Professional & Commercial Services	Management consulting	Business analysis			1
			Training or Education	Teaching and training	X years		1
			Sales - Non-Technical	Sales and negotiation			1
	Industrial Goods	Machinery, Equipment & Components	Technical or Engineering	Complex troubleshooting		18 weeks	1
			Sales - Technical	Sales and negotiation	1.5 years		1
		Aerospace & Defense	Production, Manufacturing	Precision machining	5 months		1
	Transportation	Freight & Logistics Services	Warehouse	Data processing			1
MILITARY/ GOVERNMENT	Government / Military	Military	Strategic Management, Leadership	Strategic thinking	1 year		2
		Public Services	Financial services	Financial analysis	1-3 years		1
TECHNOLOGY	Software & IT Services	Software & IT Services	Technical or Engineering	Complex troubleshooting	2 months	5 weeks	1

Economic Sector (TR)	Business Sector (TR)	Industry Group (TR)	Primary Job Nature	Critical-to-success Skill	Time to Proficiency	Time to Training	Project Cases
			Scientific or Development	Innovation and design			1
	Technology Equipment	Semiconductors & Semiconductor Equipment	Technical or Engineering	Complex troubleshooting	6 months to 13 years	6 weeks to 13 weeks	7
			Scientific or Development	Innovation and design	3 years		1
		Communications & Networking	Technical or Engineering	Project execution	6 months to 1 year		2
				Technical Problem solving	6 months		1
		Electronic Equipment & Parts	Technical or Engineering	Complex troubleshooting		7 weeks	1
TELECOMMUNICATION SERVICES	Telecommunications Services	Telecommunications Services	Technical or Engineering	Complex troubleshooting			1
			Customer service helpdesk	Helpdesk support	3 months		1
UTILITY	Utilities	Electrical Utilities & IPPs	Scientific or Development	Innovation and design	2 years		1
Grand Total							60

CH5/THE TRIGGERS

5.3 COMPARATIVE ANALYSIS OF TTP

5.3.1 Technology

The study involved 7 project cases from semiconductor equipment manufacturing companies that involved customer service engineers troubleshooting and repairing complex semiconductor equipment. These cases were located in different countries in the technology equipment sector. The TTP varied from 2 to 3 years, as shown in Table 5-8.

Table 5-8 Magnitude of TTP for Hi-Tech project cases

Case Title	Time to Proficiency	Time to Training
Customer service engineers troubleshooting and repairing complex semiconductor equipment	53 weeks	13 weeks
Customer service engineers troubleshooting and repairing complex semiconductor equipment	several months	-
Customer service engineers troubleshooting and repairing complex semiconductor equipment	2-3 years	-
Customer service engineers troubleshooting and repairing complex semiconductor equipment	1-2 years	-
Customer service engineers troubleshooting and repairing complex semiconductor equipment	1-2 years	-
Customer service engineers troubleshooting and repairing complex semiconductor equipment	1-2 years	-
Customer service engineers troubleshooting and repairing complex semiconductor equipment	6 months	6 weeks

5.3.2 Sales

Job roles involving sales representatives or sales engineers, technical and non-technical, showed a TTP of 12 weeks to 18 months in various sectors, as shown in Table 5-9.

Table 5-9 Magnitude of TTP for sales-related project cases

Case Title	Time to Proficiency	Time to Training
Sales representative selling pharmaceutical products	24 weeks	-
Sales engineers selling hi-tech enterprise communication products	1 year	-
Sales engineers selling hi-tech enterprise computer and server systems	12 weeks for new hires and 6 weeks for experienced sellers	-
Sales engineers selling construction products and equipment	18 months	-

5.3.3 Plant maintenance

Job roles requiring plant maintenance such as navy equipment, production floors, petroleum pipeline feeds, and electrical utility plant in different industrial sectors required a TTP of 1–2 years while the training duration was 7–8 weeks, as shown in Table 5-10.

Table 5-10 Magnitude of TTP for plant maintenance-related projects

Case Title	Time to Proficiency	Time to Training
Electronics technicians to troubleshoot and repair of complex navy electronics equipment	-	7 weeks

Plant maintenance engineers to troubleshooting production machine issues	-	8 weeks
Maintenance engineers repairing and maintaining petroleum pipeline feeds	1 year to 18 months	-
Electrical engineers designing and repairing power plant equipment	2 years	-

5.4 THE SCALE OF TTP

We find the magnitude of TTP to be so large that it will not be possible for organizations to ignore its scale, particularly when its effect is multiplied across the entire workforce.

I figured that while the magnitude conveyed that the TTP problem could be very large in certain industries or job roles, it did not entirely communicate the severity of its impact. For example, the TTP magnitude of 16 weeks is far less in scale for a given job role with 10 people compared with the same magnitude of 16 weeks for 100 people performing the same job role. Thus, the TTP problem may become larger in scale, even to the tune of hundreds of "person-years" because a given role may be served by hundreds or thousands of people globally based on the size of the organization. The fact that it is not one employee's TTP; instead, it multiplies across a job role, and, hence, is a significantly sized business problem.

Thus, the "scale" of TTP conveys the true severity of the problem. The magnitude (how long is the TTP of one employee in a given job role) and scale (how much is the TTP of the overall staff serving the same job role) collectively present an alarming figure for organizations to understand the severity of the problem and its impact on the business.

SPEED MATTERS

Case in point 5.1

In one of the project cases involving 3000 design engineers developing complex semiconductor equipment at a large semiconductor equipment manufacturer in the Netherlands, the project leader commented:

> They [the organization] have something like 3000 people in development and engineering, and they knew they had to grow with 1200 more within a year. They knew that it took approximately 3 years for people to reach the desired speed but they wanted it down to approximately 1 year... (Teresa, Project leader 58)

Case in point 5.2

In another project case involving 600 customer service helpdesk executives taking inbound calls for financial products at a large business process outsourcing company in the US, the magnitude of TTP was found to be 1 year. Scaling to the entire group of employees led to 600 person-years worth of time, indicating compelling reasons to address the problem. The project leader commented:

> It was probably about close to 3 months of training before they were able to get on the phone... Three months is a long, long time... So, there were 3 months in sort of training and then it was taking them an additional 9 months to reach that score... So then, it would take them about a year to basically start reaching

CH5/THE TRIGGERS

> those high scores. It was too long! The financial institution would grade the business process outsourcer them on those scores. If in two-quarters you are below these numbers, we have the right to cancel the contract. (Mike, Project leader 36)

Case in point 5.3

In yet another project case, 20 customer service engineers involved in troubleshooting and repairing complex semiconductor equipment at customer sites for a large semiconductor equipment company in Singapore were required to undergo a certification program every year in which the magnitude of the time-to-certification was a minimum of 53 weeks. Scaled to the total number of engineers per year, it amounted to 20 person-years worth of time or 100 person-years in 5 years. The project leader commented:

> In my current program, training takes 13 weeks [total] for five different modules [courses], and each module has 10 weeks of an average waiting time [in-between modules]. I have five modules, so it totals around 53 weeks or basically a year for the engineer to get certified. (Benny, Project leader 1)

Table 5-11 provides a quick glimpse on the scale of TTP across employees serving a targeted job role for 60 project cases.

Table 5-11 Scale of baseline TTP across project cases

*Note: project ID 3, 41, 51, 64, 65, and 66 did not qualify for final selection. Total 60 project cases selected for analysis are listed here.

Project case ID	Case Title	Estimated employees	Primary Job Nature	Industry Group (TR)	Magnitude of TTP	Scale of TTP in person-years
1	Customer service engineers troubleshooting and repairing complex semiconductor equipment	200	Technical or Engineering	Semiconductors & Semiconductor Equipment	1 year	200
2	Customer service helpdesk taking inbound calls for sales of investment products	4100	Sales - Non-Technical	Investment Banking & Investment Services	3 months	350
4	Software engineers developing large scale information applications	1800	Scientific or Development	Software & IT Services	-	900 to 1800
5	Cybersecurity analysts analyzing and identifying cyber-threats on client enterprise networks	900	Technical or Engineering	Communications & Networking	6 months	450
6	Insurance agents selling insurance products	10000	Sales - Non-Technical	Insurance	1.5 years	10000
7	Customer service engineers troubleshooting and repairing complex semiconductor equipment	3000	Technical or Engineering	Semiconductors & Semiconductor Equipment	several months	Up to 1500
8	Console operators monitoring and controlling the processes at petrochemical plants	Unknown	Technical or Engineering	Oil & Gas	Several years	-

147

Project case ID	Case Title	Estimated employees	Primary Job Nature	Industry Group (TR)	Magnitude of TTP	Scale of TTP in person-years
9	Service engineers troubleshooting and repairing telecommunication network equipment	Unknown	Technical or Engineering	Telecommunications Services	-	-
10	Console operators monitoring and controlling the processes at petrochemical plants	Unknown	Technical or Engineering	Oil & Gas	-	-
11	Pharmaceutical biochemists manufacturing sophisticated cancer drugs	500	Scientific or Development	Pharmaceuticals	6 months	250
12	Managers managing retail donut baking stores	100	Managerial, Supervisory	Food & Tobacco	1 month	8
13	Claim processing executives examining and processing health insurance claims	500	Financial services	Insurance	5 months	125
14	Sales representative selling pharmaceutical products	100	Sales - Technical	Pharmaceuticals	6 months	50
15	Insurance agents selling insurance products	10000	Sales - Non-Technical	Insurance	-	Unknown
16	Console operators monitoring and controlling the processes at petrochemical plants	100	Technical or Engineering	Oil & Gas	-	Unknown
17	Customer service helpdesk taking inbound calls for hotel and travel-related services	3000	Customer service helpdesk	Hotels & Entertainment Services	-	Unknown
18	Managers managing supermarket chains	100	Managerial, Supervisory	Other Specialty Retailers	14 months	100
19	Energy corporation top executives transferring knowledge to successors	100	Strategic Management, Leadership	Oil & Gas	very long	100
20	Hospital medical doctors and nursing staff providing pediatrics care services	500	Medical, Healthcare	Healthcare Providers & Services	1 year	500

Project case ID	Case Title	Estimated employees	Primary job Nature	Industry Group (TR)	Magnitude of TTP	Scale of TTP in person-years
21	Customer helpdesk taking inbound calls to remotely troubleshoot client computer and software issues	1000	Technical or Engineering	Software & IT Services	2 months	166
22	Customer service engineers troubleshooting and repairing complex semiconductor equipment	3000	Technical or Engineering	Semiconductors & Semiconductor Equipment	2-3 years	6000
23	School administrator and teachers instituting school improvement programs	500	Training or Education	Professional & Commercial Services	X years	500
24	Warehouse professionals adopting SAP for supply chain and logistics transactions	10000	Warehouse	Freight & Logistics Services	-	5000
25	Console operators monitoring and controlling the processes at petrochemical plants	3000	Technical or Engineering	Oil & Gas	-	Unknown
26	Young military officers on leadership pathway	300	Strategic Management, Leadership	Military	-	Unknown
27	Military officers setting up a new command center to prevent cyberterrorism	300	Strategic Management, Leadership	Military	1 year	300
28	Biotechnology scientists strategizing business of brain implant technology for curing neurological diseases	100	Scientific or Development	Biotechnology & Medical Research	2 years	200
29	Machinists fabricating aircraft engine mechanical parts	500	Production, Manufacturing	Aerospace & Defense	5 months	250
30	Sales engineers selling hi-tech enterprise communication products	500	Technical or Engineering	Communications & Networking	1 year	500
31	Electronics technicians to troubleshoot and repair of complex navy electronics equipment	200	Technical or Engineering	Electronic Equipment & Parts	-	Unknown

Project case ID	Case Title	Estimated employees	Primary job Nature	Industry Group (TR)	Magnitude of TTP	Scale of TTP in person-years
32	Benefit evaluator examining eligibility for Govt. run benefits	3000	Financial services	Public Services	1-3 years	3000
33	Sales engineers selling hi-tech enterprise computer and server systems	100	Technical or Engineering	Communications & Networking	6 months	50
34	Customer service engineers troubleshooting and repairing complex semiconductor equipment	4000	Technical or Engineering	Semiconductors & Semiconductor Equipment	1-2 years	8000
35	Clinical staff and database administrators transitioning to new software for clinical trials data	1000	Technical or Engineering	Biotechnology & Medical Research	-	Unknown
36	Customer service helpdesk taking inbound calls for financial products	1000	Customer service helpdesk	Banking Services	1 year	1000
37	Healthcare professionals providing assisted living services for elders	200	Medical, Healthcare	Healthcare Providers & Services	3 months	50
38	Customer service engineers troubleshooting and repairing complex semiconductor equipment	5000	Technical or Engineering	Semiconductors & Semiconductor Equipment	1-2 years	10000
39	Customer service engineers troubleshooting and repairing complex semiconductor equipment	300	Technical or Engineering	Semiconductors & Semiconductor Equipment	1-2 years	600
40	Insurance agents selling insurance products	1000	Sales - Non-Technical	Investment Banking & Investment Services	-	unknown
42	Managers managing retail store chains	100	Managerial, Supervisory	Other Specialty Retailers	-	unknown

Project case ID	Case Title	Estimated employees	Primary job Nature	Industry Group (TR)	Magnitude of TTP	Scale of TTP in person-years
43	Plant maintenance engineers to troubleshooting production machine issues	500	Technical or Engineering	Machinery, Equipment & Components	-	unknown
44	Sales representatives upselling strategic service products	100	Sales - Non-Technical	Professional & Commercial Services	-	unknown
45	Reactor operators manufacturing chemical paints	1000	Technical or Engineering	Chemicals	1.5 - 2 years	2000
46	Customer service engineers troubleshooting and repairing complex semiconductor equipment	500	Technical or Engineering	Semiconductors & Semiconductor Equipment	6 months	250
47	Real estate agents booking mortgages and listings	10000	Sales - Non-Technical	Real Estate Operations	-	unknown
48	Truck assemblers assembling and fabricating automobiles	500	Assembly, Repair	Automobiles & Auto Parts	1 week	10
49	Maintenance engineers repairing and maintaining petroleum pipeline feeds	1000	Technical or Engineering	Oil & Gas Related Equipment and Services	1 year	1000
50	Machine operators fabricating mechanical parts for petroleum exploration equipment	2000	Production, Manufacturing	Oil & Gas Related Equipment and Services	1 month	166
52	Financial analysts assessing corporate insolvency cases	200	Management consulting	Professional & Commercial Services	-	unknown
53	Healthcare professionals providing residential care for severely disabled	200	Medical, Healthcare	Healthcare Providers & Services	9 months	150

Project case ID	Case Title	Estimated employees	Primary job Nature	Industry Group (TR)	Magnitude of TTP	Scale of TTP in person-years
54	Sales engineers selling construction products and equipment	200	Sales - Technical	Machinery, Equipment & Components	1.5 years	300
55	Customer service helpdesk taking inbound calls for internet phone service	1000	Customer service helpdesk	Telecommunications Services	3 months	250
56	Customer service helpdesk taking inbound calls for sales of financial products	10000	Sales - Non-Technical	Banking Services	-	Unknown
57	Customer service helpdesk taking inbound calls for banking services	5000	Customer service helpdesk	Investment Banking & Investment Services	1.5 month	7500
58	Design engineers developing complex semiconductor equipment	3000	Scientific or Development	Semiconductors & Semiconductor Equipment	3 years	9000
59	Customer service helpdesk taking inbound calls for upselling of financial products	100	Sales - Non-Technical	Investment Banking & Investment Services	3 months	75
60	Electrical engineers designing and repairing power plant equipment	500	Scientific or Development	Electrical Utilities & IPPs	2 years	1000
61	Sales engineers selling medical and surgical instruments	500	Sales - Technical	Healthcare Equipment & Supplies	Unknown	unknown
62	Business managers developing strategies for the unforeseen drop in gold prices	50	Strategic Management, Leadership	Metals & Mining	10-20 years event frequency	500
63	Underground miners preparing for unexpected underground fire during mining operations	1000	Production, Manufacturing	Metals & Mining	8-10 years event frequency	8000

5.5 WHAT IT MEANS TO YOU

Such a large-scale problem is not only impactful for an organization but also its employees in terms of their self-worth, confidence, and career progression. For instance, when the TTP is quite long in a job role, employees tend to feel disengaged or do not contribute much to the organization. They may well leave the organization even before reaching the target proficiency.

The TTP was so long in magnitude and far out in most of the jobs that it was worth doing something about it. As one project leader summarized:

> There is a universal problem all businesses have and if they work on their problem, they can make significant gains, which is just what you are saying that people simply are not getting up the speed as fast they can and it is very, very expensive when they are not. And, basically, it is the basic business case that we have started with... it is that every minute someone is not fully up to speed is costing you money and is worth doing something about it. It is probably the most significant issue. (Stephen, Project leader 53)

Researchers have appealed that it is worth doing something about such long TTP, though the impact of TTP and its scale has not been studied before (Fadde 2016; Hoffman, Andrews & Feltovich 2012).

I recommend a four-step approach to managers to take the learning from his chapter to your context:

CH5 / THE TRIGGERS

☞ **Establish clear and crisp measures of proficiency for each job role.** One must know whether the targeted employee group is at the desired proficiency. We typically measure proficiency in terms of numbers associated with the job. However, an enormous challenge is to align with all stakeholders to make sure that they are all clear about the definition and measurement of proficiency. Different job roles require different definitions, metrics, and hence measurement. Please refer to Chapter 2 for the measurement of proficiency.

☞ **Measure the TTP of the targeted group in terms of defined metrics.** The first cycle would typically take a long time. You can measure the TTP using a forward-looking approach, that is, you start measuring from today and mark the point in the future when an employee reaches that desired level. Or, you can use the backward-looking approach and measure proficiency using the analytics on historical performance or the data available. Refer to Chapter 4 for the definition and metrics of TTP.

☞ **Establish a baseline of historical average across all the employees serving a given job role.** The baseline is very important. We can base the baseline on individual employees or averaged across all employees in a job role or top employees in a job role, or it could be across the organization, depending on the goals of the employee development programs. You can then assign suitable goals based on the business needs to reduce this baseline in the next measurement cycle.

☞ **Educate your leaders and stakeholders about the TTP impact.** The key piece to driving shorter TTP is to educate your stakeholders about the TTP numbers in different job roles and explain how TTP manifests as an impact on business. Your HR team needs to know the target TTP for the job they are sourcing talent for. Hiring managers need to be clear about the current and target TTP values so that candidates with the right experience can be hired. The leaders need to know where their employees are on the proficiency curve, and what it means to stay ahead in the market and the risks associated with it.

CHAPTER 6
THE DRIVERS

THE BUSINESS DRIVERS TO REDUCE TTP

The need for accelerating the achievement of proficiency in sectors such as military, sports, utility, research, biotechnology, and information technology has been elucidated in the literature (see examples in Hoffman et al. 2014). Evidently, the TTP was very long in sectors such as military and sports. Hence, the need to accelerate proficiency was recognized as: '[In the US Air Force] it still ordinarily takes many years to achieve proficiency. Therefore, there would be great advantages if the USAF could establish regimens of training that could accelerate the achievement of that proficiency' (Hoffman, Andrews & Feltovich 2012, p. 1).

However, Ericsson & Charness (1994, p. 737), proponents of the 10-year deliberate practice rule, pointed out that there are no proven ways to develop expertise faster:

> Although these studies [on expertise] have revealed how beginners acquire complex cognitive structures and skills that circumvent the basic limits confronting them, researchers have not uncovered some simple strategies that would allow nonexperts to rapidly acquire expert performance.

Hoffman, Andrews & Feltovich (2012, p. 9) set the stage for looking into the methods for acceleration by stating that the 'empirical fact about expertise (i.e., that it takes a long time) sets the stage for an effort at demonstrating the acceleration of the achievement of proficiency.'

However, irrespective of the actual length, you would agree that the time to achieve a high level of proficiency to do any job consistently and reliably with a high degree of repeatability is generally very long. However, organizations cannot afford that much time (Fadde & Klein 2010). Market pressure, particularly in the last decade, has warranted accelerating the expertise cycle as a necessity (Clark & Mayer 2013). Several market forces collectively drive the need for shorter TTP in workplaces, such as time-to-market competitiveness (Lynn, Akgün & Keskin 2003); constant obsolescence of skills (Korotov 2007); increasing complexity of jobs and the skills required to perform them (Hoffman, Feltovich, et al. 2010); and attrition of senior or aging workforce, resulting in their constant replacement (Hoffman et al. 2014).

However, a richer understanding of how and why business dynamics dictate the need for accelerated proficiency and the benefits they are likely to accrue are apparently lacking. Hoffman, Andrews & Feltovich (2012, p. 9) suggested investigating the questions which had no direct answers in the literature:

> What might be the payoff if this problem were solved, say, by reducing the time to achieve journeyman level skill by some significant amount (e.g., from 4 years to 2)? (Hoffman, Andrews & Feltovich 2012, p. 9)

In the *TTP study,* I attempted to understand the business dynamics and challenges that drive the need for accelerated proficiency. I conducted a comprehensive analysis of the triggers, drivers, importance, and benefits of shorter TTP across 60 project cases. The findings shed light on how organizations were forced to start projects to reduce TTP. While it triggered the organizations to think about TTP in terms of its magnitude and scale, the real push came from the impact a long TTP caused on the business. The larger the magnitude and scale of the TTP, the larger is the business impact, and hence, the larger the push for organizations to start thinking about shortening TTP.

SPEED MATTERS

I noticed that this impact manifests significantly as one or more of these four business drivers: time-related pressures, speed-related competitiveness, skill-related deficiencies, and cost/financial implications. These four drivers, summarized and defined in Table 6-1, primarily drove organizations to do something to reduce the TTP of their workforce.

Table 6-1 Definition of business drivers

Drivers	Definition	Examples
Time-related pressures	The drivers in which operational metrics were consciously measured in the unit of time.	The time required to launch a product, The actual length of time-to-proficiency longer training duration
Speed-related competitiveness	The operational metrics in which speed was perceived as a measure of success.	Customer pressures to deliver fast; market urgencies to produce fast; business ramp-up speed; The speed of launch of new product, service or business; The need for rapid operational readiness; Rapid hiring sprints
Skill-related deficiencies	The needs that arise because of a lack of workforce skills or a lack of a qualified workforce.	Attrition and retirement; New hires replacing expert workforce; Performance issues due to a lack of skills and obsolete skills
Cost or financial implications	The factors and impacts which were measured in the unit of money.	The cost of training, the cost of someone not being proficient; Errors and mistakes; The cost of opportunity lost while someone was not proficient; Regulatory pressures that cost the company severely if not observed, such as safety

CH6 / THE DRIVERS

6.1 TIME-RELATED PRESSURES

Changing business landscapes and market dynamics bring different expectations on workforce competencies. A decade ago, the *Implications for 21st Century Work* report forecasted:

> One expected consequence of the technological advances is a continued growth in the demand for a high-skilled workforce capable of undertaking the basic R&D to develop new technologies, developing the applications and production processes that exploit the technological advances, and bringing the resulting products to the commercial marketplace. (Karoly 2007, p. 3)

The ability and readiness of the workforce to meet new business needs is a topic of constant concern to modern business managers (Salas et al. 2012). Thus, one of the critical business challenges is to bring the workforce up to speed to new job roles, new expectations, new standards, new products, and new business needs in as short a time as possible.

In the *TTP study*, 23 (38%) project cases showed 'time-related pressures' as the key driver. This represented those factors in which operational metrics were consciously measured in the unit of time. Examples included the time required to launch a product, the actual length of TTP, and the training duration:

> People simply are not getting up to the speed as fast they can and it is very, very expensive when they are not [coming up to the speed quickly]... the basic business case that we have started with is that every minute someone is not fully up to speed is costing you money and it is worth doing something about it. (Stephen, Project leader 53)

SPEED MATTERS

The only thing that counts within [this company] is time-to-market for the project. Every machine is delivered on the expected date to the customer. They never put up with even one day delay in shipping the machine... (Teresa, Project leader 58)

Case in point 6.1

> For instance, there was a customer helpdesk taking inbound calls at a large technical support center to remotely troubleshoot client computer and software issues. The support center experienced time-related pressures mainly because it was taking too long for the employees to reach the desired proficiency and the business needed rapid readiness to newer systems. In addition, there was a financial driver/cost-related implication here, which was due to the cost of training involved and, therefore, indirect.

Case in point 6.2

> In another instance, a sales organization's sales engineers selling construction products and equipment experienced mainly time-related pressures due to longer TTP and time value of proficiency. As cited by project leader: 'every minute someone isn't fully up to speed is costing you money and it's worth doing something about it.' The financial driver is implicit here due to the expectations associated with the job to

> start generating revenue as soon as possible. [quotes as stated by the project leader]

6.2 SPEED-RELATED COMPETITIVENESS

Global organizations have witnessed tremendous turmoil in their business environment. Several of them have experienced rapid growth between 2000 and 2016, which has made the environment extremely competitive, too (Deloitte 2017). The foremost organizational concern is increased competition. With globalization, most organizations now have access to the same markets, similar technologies, and similar capabilities (Kraiger, Passmore & Rebelo 2014; Kraiger 2014). The relative success of organizations may ultimately depend upon the time-to-market of the products, services, or solutions they develop or offer. Thus, competition and the rapid rate of technological change have created the need for a shorter time-to-market a critical business requirement for organizations.

The capabilities, competencies, and skills of the workforce are the most critical determinants of time-to-market and ultimately the competitive distinction among organizations (Wright & McMahan 2011). A company's competitiveness and its ability to stand out distinctly from its competitors in producing new products come from the capabilities, skills, and competencies possessed by its workforce (Huselid & Becker 2011; Wright & McMahan 2011). Thus, organizations worldwide are spending a significant amount of money on training and development interventions to develop their workforce because they believe 'a skilled workforce represents a competitive advantage' (Salas et al. 2012, p. 74). However, not just the capabilities but the efficiency with which companies do so [update worker's skills] can thus be critical in helping them maintain a competitive edge' (Koller 2005, p. 3).

There is a consensus among a large community of researchers that a team's TTP in supporting a new product, service, or technology does determine the "sweet spot" for the launch of the product or service (Langerak, Hultink & Griffin 2008). Shortening TTP of the workforce is likely to lead to a certain advantage in the time-to-market competitiveness for organizations (Fred 2002). In a recent survey, it was observed the importance of speed: 'Instead of mere efficiency, successful organisations must be designed for speed, agility, and adaptability to enable them to compete and win in today's global business environment' (Deloitte 2017, p. 20).

In the *TTP study*, 24 (38%) project cases showed 'speed-related competitiveness' as the driver that pushed organizations to reduce TTP. This driver included those operational metrics in which speed was perceived as a measure of success. Examples included customer pressures to deliver fast services; urgencies to produce faster in the market; the speed of business ramp-up to support new projects; the speed of launch of a new product, service, or business; and the need for rapid operational readiness and rapid hiring sprints:

> ... demand for this service was very high with investors, this online brokers' firm was hiring new service and sales personnel every single week. Almost every single week! In some cases, you might have 30 or 40 new employees per week or per month being hired in this continuous cycle of new employees to support the growth and of course to

support any turnover that occurs in the normal customer service and sales business. (Billy, Project leader 2)

... for them to go to their other clients and tell them [something like this that] "We lost this contract [with a client] because were not able to ramp-up people fast enough to get to the satisfaction scores that this company was requesting of us" is going to look really bad to the rest of the clients. (Mike, Project leader 36)

Case in point 6.3

A medical equipment company in the US was facing the challenge of rapid hiring of their sales engineers in order to support expansion and generate revenue targets.

They were required to develop proficient technical sales skills in their engineers in a shorter time.

The major driver was speed-related competitiveness as they had 'about 150 plus new salespeople coming into the organization every year.' The organization needed to get them ready in a shorter time to beat the competition. The real challenge, as expressed by the project leader, was, 'how do we really equip them to sell effectively and reduce the time it takes for quota?'

The time-related pressures were implicit, with the skill-related deficiencies inter-playing their role.

[quotes as stated by the project leader]

SPEED MATTERS

Case in point 6.4

A drug manufacturing company in the US, which was engaged in extensive data collection of clinical trials for developing a new drug, wanted to change the software used for gathering clinical trial information.

In order to bring the new software to use, it required the clinical staff and database administrators of the company to develop proficient data entry, management, and analytical skills.

They experienced the market urgency to use new products that required rapid readiness of employees. In the project leader's words, they are 'spending a lot of money implementing it, and they want to keep people using it right away.'

Skill-related deficiencies drove the need implicitly given the employees did not have any skills on the newer system and were required to quickly reach the speed to keep the operations running.

[quotes as stated by the project leader]

Case in point 6.5

A high-tech semiconductor equipment company in Singapore involved in the fast-paced technology business was faced with the challenge of keeping its customers' production running and keeping equipment uptime commitments.

> It required the company to develop proficient skills of its customer service engineers, who were involved in troubleshooting and repairing complex semiconductor equipment, in a shorter time.
>
> The case exhibited time-related pressures as well as speed-related competitiveness as drivers because of the customer expectations or pressures and the need to get their engineers ready with skills in a shorter time to be able to support their customers. The project leader stated, 'business need is typically the engineers should be proficient enough in around 3-6 months to be deployed in the field. That is the main target for now.' Longer training time and long TTP were the contributors to time-related pressures.
>
> Skill-related deficiencies were clearly evident in this case due to the fact that engineers were not able to perform the expected tasks proficiently. In the project leader's words, 'as per customer requirement, all engineers need to undergo formal training and get to be certified before they are allowed to maintain the tools on the customer site.'
>
> [quotes as stated by the project leader]

6.3 SKILL-RELATED DEFICIENCIES

In a survey conducted by Deloitte in 2017 with over 10,000 business leaders, they reported that skills were becoming obsolete at an accelerated rate and indicated that software engineers must redevelop their skills every 12–18 months (Deloitte 2017). They also speculated similar trends in other professions. New studies indicate that the half-life of job skills has gone down to 5 years, while the average tenure of an employee in a job is merely 4.5 years, indicating that every new job in a person's career potentially requires the mastery of altogether new skills (Gratton & Scott 2016). TTP, thus, is very important where knowledge and skills become obsolete very quickly.

Organizations increasingly realize the importance of bringing people up to desired speed faster. Also, employees are required to solve increasingly complex business problems characterized by multiple goals, many possible actions, several different and uncertain consequences, and dynamically changing environments (Fischer, Greiff & Funke 2011). Complexity is also evident in the ecosystem within which employees are required to operate in terms of processes, people, and systems (Andersson et al. 2014, 2014; Marks et al. 2012; Schmid et al. 2011). To cope up with such complexity, employees now need to learn much higher-ordered skills (Karoly 2007; Levy 2010). However, in some jobs, employees simply leave the job due to the frustration of not being able to handle such complex assignments, produce the desired results, and gain confidence quickly enough.

A *Workplace Learning Report* detailed that the 'cost of replacing an employee is 50% to 250% of their annual salary benefits' (LinkedIn 2017, p. 4). Therefore, it is wiser for organizations to make their new employees productive as fast as they can.

CH6/THE DRIVERS

In a case study, a large insurance company in the US was faced with the challenge of a very low retention rate of staff because the TTP was almost 18 weeks, which was rather long. However, when they reduced the TTP to 12 weeks, the retention rate went up by 50% (Pollock, Wick & Jefferson 2015, p. 285). The effect of an organization's inability to cope with the above market forces could be far-reaching. Fadde & Klein (2010, p. 5) indicated such an effect: 'The failure to get people up to speed can ripple through a team... These kinds of pressures put a premium on methods to build expertise at all levels of an organisation rapidly.' Thus, the speed of skill obsolescence and the pace of increasing complexity necessitate organizations to figure out methods and strategies to accelerate the TTP of their employees. The faster the workforce readiness, the higher is the organization's competitiveness in the market.

However, skill-related deficiencies or non-proficiency of employees could manifest as mistakes or errors and the impression carried by the customers. These factors also make a case to look at the concept of accelerating proficiency deeply. For example, in a study involving firefighting commanders in the US, we understood that fires do not happen frequently. Thus, the lack of events to gain experience and become proficient could endanger life and property when those events indeed occur, which require proficient people to handle them (Kuchenbrod 2016).

In the *TTP study*, more than half of the project cases, 32 (53%), showed 'skill-related deficiencies' as the key driver that pushed the need for a shorter TTP. The driver included those needs that arose because of the lack of skilled/qualified workforce. Examples included attrition and retirement, new hires replacing expert workforce, and performance issues due to a lack of skills and obsolete skills:

> People are reaching retirement age. So, they were going to begin losing the institutional knowledge of their senior personnel in short order. The [long] timeframe that it took to get the new engineers up to speed and learn the ins-and-outs of what the utility [company] and each department did - they were going to lose people sooner than get people to get up to speed. (Tony, Project leader 60)

Case in point 6.6

In one project case, military command in the US required proficiency in leadership skills to be developed among its young military leaders to deploy them in different operations at the earliest.

The command experienced skill-related deficiencies as the main driver of TTP because it required employees to exhibit better skills in a shorter time to run operations successfully. In the words of the project leader, the requirement was to 'profoundly accelerate the competency of young leaders to a new level of leadership ability.'

[quotes as stated by the project leader]

CH6 / THE DRIVERS

Case in point 6.7

> In one of the project cases, a high-tech manufacturing company pressed hard to keep production running but faced a very long TTP of its engineers.
>
> They needed to develop the proficient skills of their maintenance engineers in repair and service of production issues in a shorter time to avoid any impact on the production. They experienced skill-related deficiencies as a result of a long TTP. In the project leader's words, 'the person would either leave the company or possibly be terminated by the organization even before they had completed the training—which meant they had to refill the position and start the training process all over.'
>
> Time-related pressures were evident due to the urgency to resolve the issue quickly to avoid impact on production.
>
> [quotes as stated by the project leader]

Case in point 6.8

> In another case, the officials handling the technicians involved in troubleshooting and repairing complex navy electronics equipment in the US experienced skill-related deficiencies as the main driver in shortening TTP because the resolutions were not meeting the desired quality standards. The project leader expressed that 'their maintenance engineers did not perform as well as they should; at least the ones who just came out of

> school.' TTP was not an immediate goal but an expected outcome.
>
> [quotes as stated by the project leader]

6.4 COST OR FINANCIAL IMPLICATIONS

Organizations depend on training and learning interventions as the first line of defense to prepare employees for their initial operating proficiency (to start doing the job).

Some figures suggest that every year, organizations spend millions of dollars on training and learning programs to bring employees to the proficiency level to address their business needs. A *Training Industry Report* stated that the average annual training budget for large companies (those with over 10,000 employees) was $14.3 million, while the total training expenditures in the US alone were $70.6 billion (Training Magazine 2016, p. 29).

Several books showed case studies justifying the financial and business benefits of training (Bartel 2000; Kirkpatrick & Kirkpatrick 2009; Phillips 2012). Other studies showed the substantial financial or cost benefits of shorter training duration and faster readiness of the workforce (Jacobs 2014; Liu & Batt 2007; Sullivan, Brechin & Lacoste 1999) from the reduction of TTP (Borton 2007, p. 32; Pollock, Wick & Jefferson 2015, p. 285; Thompson 2017, p. 169).

On the same lines, a shorter TTP leads to substantial financial and operational benefits to the organization and a higher value to its customers, much beyond what one can achieve through shorter training (Fred 2002). 'If any time could be shaved off the "10000 clock," there would be potentially significant saving of money and time, an increase in overall organisational capability...' (Hoffman et al. 2014, p. 169).

There is also an opportunity cost or productivity loss while employees are away from their job undergoing training, no matter the training duration. Those times otherwise could have been used in producing revenue or handling critical jobs for the customers. In a case study conducted at one of the largest insurance companies in the US, it was observed that a TTP of 18 weeks for financial services advisors resulted in a revenue loss of hundreds of thousands of dollars. However, the revenue loss was observed to be subsequently reduced by 68% when the TTP was reduced to 12 weeks (Pollock, Wick & Jefferson 2015, p. 285). In another case study, that involved 14 new bankers, the net income increased by 13% (approx. $250,000) in the first 12 months of employment due to a 25% decrease in TTP (Thompson 2017).

The consequential costs associated with the non-proficiency of an employee cannot be ignored either. Non-proficient employees performing below the desired expectations may lead to errors or defects, customer dissatisfaction, financial losses for the business, and even life-threatening situations. Thus, we can say that bringing people up to proficiency faster leads to significant cost benefits.

SPEED MATTERS

In the *TTP study*, 20 (33%) of the project cases showed 'cost or financial implications' as the primary driver that drove the need for a shorter TTP. This driver included those factors and impacts which were measured in the unit of money. Examples included the cost of training, cost of an employee not being proficient, as indicated by errors and mistakes, cost of an opportunity lost while an employee was not proficient, and other regulatory pressures that costs a company severely if not observed, such as safety:

> The real costs of achieving proficient job performance in complex jobs come after training is done. These costs are substantial, but are rarely measured. We all know they exist—and they can be huge. These costs show up as: sub-par productivity, mistakes, dissatisfied customers, time spent getting help from others, manager's time reviewing and correcting work, attrition, due to employees feeling unprepared or overwhelmed by their jobs... If we can reduce the time it takes to become expert or at least proficient performers, we can save our organizations a lot of money, increase retention rates, reduce errors, and improve customer satisfaction. (McDonalds, Project leader 32)

Case in point 6.9

In a project case, a large biotechnology corporation in the US required its biotechnology scientists to strategize the business of brain implant technology for curing neurological diseases in as short a time as possible.

They were driven by implications related to cost or other financial factors whereby there was a risk of going out of business and running out of cash in about 7 months. Time-related pressures were implicit as well.

Case in point 6.10

Another project case involved a gold mining company in the US, engaged in mining and selling gold. They anticipated an inevitable decline in gold prices.

It was important for them to develop the strategic thinking skills of its managers to get prepared for a business situation its managers were never equipped to face.

They faced cost or financial implications as the driver to shorten the time to readiness of their business managers in developing strategies to tackle the unforeseen drop in gold prices. There was the risk of the cost of non-proficiency, such as the loss of revenue, which was likely to occur if employees were not prepared at enough speed to match the pace of business.

Time-related pressures were implicit here.

Case in point 6.11

In another project case, a mining company in the US engaged in underground mining operations required its miners to

> develop proficiency in handling unexpected and rare underground fire events during mining operations.
>
> The underground fire could cause losses to millions and in some cases render a mine completely destroyed or useless. In the words of the project leader, 'it (the underground mine fire) is an unusual event but it has huge costs.' In such a case, it was driven by cost or financial implications.
>
> [quotes as stated by the project leader]

6.5　INTERPLAY OF DRIVERS

Even if the general thought is that cost drives all decisions in a company, what I found was quite contrary to that. In reality, the skill-related deficiencies drove the programs on accelerated proficiency, followed by time-related or speed-related drivers, across all (100%) the project cases. The prevalence analysis (counting the code presence), as shown in Table 6-2, suggests that skill-related drivers were the main trigger that forced organizations to implement initiatives/projects to accelerate proficiency. However, the intent of saving costs or other financial gains was not seen to be the main trigger for organizations to institute initiatives/projects to reduce TTP. In addition, factors such as time-to-market, the requirement to being competitive, and market leadership mattered more than the money that could be saved.

The skill-related drivers were more prevalent in management, manufacturing, and highly technical jobs, which faced high competition, required a high level of skills from people, and faced faster obsolescence of skills. The drivers were also prevalent in jobs driven by regulatory pressures, such as oil & gas and medical research, in which skill deficiencies were stated as damaging to the business. Time- and speed-related drivers were seen as the next most prevalent drivers, predominantly in technical, engineering, and science jobs due to time-to-market and pressure to remain competitive. The cost-related drivers were more prevalent in technical sales jobs due to the direct impact on revenue in such jobs.

Table 6-2 Prevalence of business drivers across project classification parameters

	Prevalence of business driver present in each value of					
	COMPL EXITY	SKILLS	JOBS	BUSINESS SECTOR	ECONOMIC SECTOR	Overall Prevalence
Time-related pressures	100%	67%	64%	65%	80%	75%
Speed-related competitiveness	100%	87%	86%	60%	70%	80%
Skill-related deficiencies	100%	87%	79%	85%	100%	90%
Cost/financial implications	100%	67%	57%	55%	70%	70%

Organizations now realize that the faster their employees learn the skills required to do the job up to the set performance standards, the faster will they be able to handle new customer needs, meet new market needs, perform to new expectations, and deliver new technologies, or adopt new changes (Attri & Wu 2015; Attri 2014). It is not an overstatement to say that TTP is becoming one of the most important business metrics in fast-paced technology organizations.

Interestingly, none of the business drivers appeared in isolation; rather, there was an interconnection among the drivers, with one impacting the other. In practice, all or several of the business drivers may drive the need for a shorter TTP of the workforce. This interconnection and chain of impact are explained through some project case examples below.

Case in point 6.12

> In a project case, a large aircraft engine manufacturer in the US was faced with an unacceptably long TTP of its computer numerical control (CNC) machinists, who were involved in manufacturing highly sophisticated engine parts.
>
> They were required to develop their proficiency in precision manufacturing skills in a shorter time.
>
> Skill-related deficiencies were seen as 'a severe skill shortage' of this kind of specific job skill. The shortage led the organization to hire people at a rapid pace to sustain the business. 'Massive recruitment efforts yielded few potential employees.' The need to bring new employees up to speed was driven by speed-related competitiveness like customer expectations and time-to-market. '[T]he longer that it takes somebody to learn, the more difficult it is to complete our process and ship to the customer on time.'

> The skill-related drivers were amplified by the need for the precision involved in the job and the need to prepare employees to a proficiency level of error-free work. 'The sooner people are fully competent to perform job, the new employee becomes safer and more productive.'
>
> Though not the primary drivers, the usual cost-related drivers of the organization came up in this project case due to the impact of non-proficiency resulting in the loss of production and opportunity cost during the waiting period. 'In addition, the company wanted to reduce costs (including recruitment costs).'
>
> [quotes as stated by the project leader]

Case in point 6.12

> Another project case involved an oil & gas company which conducted exploratory operations in the US. They were faced with the rapid retirement of their aged and experienced board operators.
>
> The company was required to develop the technical and decision-making skills of younger, newly hired operators to proficiency before the current experts were gone.
>
> Amidst those situations, the company faced the challenge of speed-related competitiveness due to the urgency of moving to a new control system for exploration operations without the loss of productivity and efficiency. In the project leader's

words, 'this ability to accelerate... even more necessary now because of the rapid pace of change... they realized they have to train all of the crew over.'

The company also experienced skill-related deficiencies mainly because the older system was no longer in use, making existing skills outdated, and the expert workforce was retiring, which created the need to develop younger, newer employees faster. 'Expected retirement of a large population of its experienced workforce... a lot of mature workers were scheduled to retire within a couple of years... they were dealing with or continued to deal with a pretty rapid rate of attrition among the operators, and losing their less experienced operators, needing to bring newer people up to the speed really quickly... a bunch of new, young, fairly unskilled engineers and operation staff coming into the organization and not having the knowledge and experience of the more mature workers... seeing significant losses due to retirements and workforce is getting younger very fast... Sites likely will lose substantial expert knowledge at a time when it is of the greatest need. This will ratchet up pressure to more quickly develop expertise in newer operators.'

Financial or business drivers were indirectly related to the regulations requiring employees to exhibit proficiency in error-free work. 'Very high-tech operational settings where there are regulatory changes that are occurring almost monthly where they now have to do things differently and change the way they work... Bringing new operators up to speed quickly to maintain safe and efficient operations... making sure they are maintaining operations within those regulatory requirements.'

CH6 / THE DRIVERS

[quotes as stated by the project leader]

Case in point 6.12

Another project case noticed a large IT infrastructure and services company in the US, which was faced with the challenge of hiring sales engineers responsible for selling their high-tech enterprise communication products.

The group exhibited a longer TTP before they could support revenue targets. The company needed to develop proficient technical sales skills in their engineers in a shorter time. The organization experienced all four types of drivers due to rapid hiring and the need to get them ready in a shorter time.

Financial drivers were indirect and arose from the expectation associated with the job role to start producing revenue as soon as possible. The financial implications were evident as the business wanted their engineers to 'start contributing to the bottom line.' The business set the time-related pressures as the organization experienced that the 'total time to proficiency would be one year.'

Speed-related competitiveness drove that required their product readiness goals 'to be completed and ready for launch in four months in 18 time zones and 13 global sites.' This required that 'these associates must get up to speed on [Company C]'s myriad products, technical solutions, and methodologies within a short time.'

> Some level of skill-related deficiencies as drivers also surfaced as it involved young, inexperienced learners. Thus, 'understanding the next generations' learning preferences is a key to creating classroom environments that engage the user and accelerate learning.'
>
> [quotes as stated by the project leader]

Case in point 6.12

> One of the project cases involved a major chemical manufacturing company in the US who was faced with a high turnover of chemical reactor operators and a very long training cycle of new operators.
>
> The company needed to develop the proficiency of their operators in a shorter time.
>
> They experienced time-related pressures mainly because it was taking too long for the employees to come up to the desired performance specs, which impacted the quality of output. 'It was a lengthy and time-consuming process to get a new chemical reactor operator trained.'
>
> Cost or financial implications showed up: 'Then there is the time away from their work, and then there is the time in this session and the opportunity costs associated with this.'

CH6 / THE DRIVERS

> Skill-related deficiencies drove the need for a shorter TTP due to faster turnover, which required preparing the new employees in a shorter time.
>
> [quotes as stated by the project leader]

Case in point 6.12

> One of the project cases involved a major chemical manufacturing company in the US, faced with a high turnover of chemical reactor operators and a very long training cycle of new operators.
>
> An information technology company in the US with 65 software development centers worldwide and 5000 software developers offshored 1800 of them to low-cost countries, replacing the existing expert workforce.
>
> While formal training was too long, coaching using the leaving experts was not feasible either. They needed to develop the skills of offshored employees to the desired proficiency in a shorter timeframe, before the existing experts were gone.
>
> In this case, speed-related competitiveness showed up as the driver because the hiring of the new engineers took place rapidly and they were to be developed to the desired level of proficiency in a shorter timeframe: 'We recruited people rapidly into those development centers... 1,800 in 15 months.' The replacement of the existing workforce caused serious skill-related deficiencies: 'We were replacing vastly

> experienced people across Europe and North America.' But formal training created time-related pressures as 'the formal structured training programs just took too long, just were taking too much time over too long.'
>
> The long training period also implicitly led to cost and financial implications: 'To reduce these training programs from five days to three days. And if we do that, there will be huge cost savings.'
>
> [quotes as stated by the project leader]

It must be noted that the drivers need to be assessed in the overall organizational system and not in isolation. Shortening TTP is not a simple training problem. It is one of the complex business problems of today's time, which requires a multipronged approach. Thus, it is important that project leaders view the driving factors in context and then develop or put their systems, processes, and strategies in play in order to reduce TTP successfully.

I must mention here that a business or financial goal alone may not push for a shorter TTP. Several non-financial factors, such as the impact of non-proficiency in critical professions, are important drivers (e.g., firefighters need to be proficient all the time no matter an event occurs or not).

6.6 WHAT IT MEANS TO YOU

☛ **The TTP problem is too big to ignore:** It must be recognized that the TTP business problem is too big for organizations to ignore, and organizations must address this business challenge because of the impact it has on the workforce, business metrics, profitability, and market competitiveness.

☛ **Focus first on the skill deficiencies and how they need to be addressed at an accelerated rate.** The skill-deficiency-related business drivers are the most foundational. That means, even if everything has a dollar value, the capabilities, and speed with which you develop employees is the most fundamental driver to think about while attempting to shorten TTP.

☛ **Be aware of the automatic chain reaction.** Once you close the skills gaps at a faster rate or prepare the workforce at a higher speed, the chain reaction is a better time and speed advantage, better time-to-market performance, and overall better cost-efficiency.

SPEED MATTERS

☞ **Identify the driver that is really driving the need.** There are times when leaders would associate the length of training or overall TTP directly with the potential cost-saving or the financial gains they can get by reducing it. While this is an undebatable relationship, I observed that the projects which start with the goal of saving cost for employee development may not end up in overall better competitiveness. However, when projects are initiated to gain competitive advantages or skill efficiencies, cost savings and financial gains are invariably achieved.

CHAPTER 7
THE BENEFITS

THE BUSINESS BENEFITS OF REDUCING TTP

Before we talk about the benefits that can be achieved from a shortened TTP, a legitimate question that arises is, 'Can TTP be really shortened?'

Several researchers have argued against the possibility of shortening TTP. Universally, it is thought that it takes 10 years or 10,000 hours for an employee to become an expert. But here, our goal is not to make every employee a world-class expert. Some experts event went on to say, 'nature takes its own course.' In that club are several organizational leaders too who continued to downplay the possibility of shortening TTP.

However, I believe that we need to break this mindset. Several practitioners have already established that it indeed is possible to reduce TTP up to 30% (Rosenbaum & Williams 2004). My research on TTP suggested that, if executed right, the reduction in TTP could be as large as 80%, as seen in 60 project cases. In this chapter, I first discuss the extent of TTP reduction before getting on to the benefits accrued from a shorter TTP.

7.1 MAGNITUDE OF REDUCTION IN TTP

In the *TTP study*, I observed two indicators that suggested attaining a shorter TTP—direct and indirect.

7.1.1 Direct indicators

Direct indicators of the reduction in the TTP of employees included reduction in the time to readiness of a business operation and reduction in training duration at the training course level. Out of the total number of project cases considered, 54 (90%) reported results with direct indicators.

Some observations based on Table 7-1 are:

- Out of the 60 project cases, 24 (41%) were about shortening the TTP of employees in a job role, while 13 (25%) addressed the TTP problem at the group, business, or organizational level to get ready for new businesses, processes, or operations, expressed in terms of time to readiness.

- Out of the 60 project cases, 7 (12%) reported training duration reduction as the means to shorten TTP because proficiency was being developed primarily in the training settings. This showed that only a relatively small number of programs were geared toward shortening TTP with training, thus affirming an earlier postulation that TTP is more than just reducing the duration of the training program.

7.1.2 Indirect indicators

Only 6 (10%) of the project cases, as shown in Table 7-1, did not report any direct results because the corresponding consultants or project leaders did not have any access to the clients or results. However, the project leaders had a positive feeling of the end results being good in those cases.

In such cases, project leaders reported the results using indirect indicators such as improvements in performance compared to that of experienced staff, percentage of population crossing the desired thresholds, and the visible evidence of the improved rate of learning. The indirect results indicated positive trends toward acceleration. This observation suggested that the strategies reported in each project case worked in a majority of their contexts toward shortening TTP.

Table 7-1 Indicators of TTP reduction

Indicator type	No of projects	Sub-indicator	When used	Reported as the only indicator	Reported with more than one indicator
Direct indicators	54 projects (90%)	Time to proficiency	If the time to proficiency of the people in a job role is reduced compared to a baseline	24 (41%)	32 (55%)
		Time to readiness	If the time to the readiness of a given operation (process, product, system, equipment, business unit, group-wise certification, etc.) is reduced compared to the expected time	13 (25%)	15 (25%)
		Training program duration	If the duration of the training program (where it is the primary vehicle to develop proficiency) is reduced compared to the duration before	7 (12%)	17 (28%)
Indirect indicators	6 projects (10%)	Comparative performance	If new people are performing comparable to experienced staff, means time-to-proficiency of new people is relatively shorter than previous staff	1 (2%)	6 (10%)

	Proficient population	If % of proficient people increased at the end of the project, means time-to-proficiency of the group is shortened	1 (2%)	1 (2%)
	Rate of learning	If time to learning representative tasks is reduced compared to average indications before	3 (5%)	16 (36%)

Also, 20 (33%) project cases reported indirect results alongside the direct results, thus legitimating the use of indirect results as a sign of acceleration.

7.1.3   Before and after comparison

The results of each project case were reported mostly in comparison to a baseline number established for that indicator before the new practices/strategies (as shared by the project leaders) were implemented. I made the following observations from Table 7-2, by comparing the data before and after implementing new practices/strategies:

- When compared with the baselines established at the beginning of the project cases (the baseline was specific to each project case), the new practices/strategies shared by the project leaders in the interviews reduced the TTP of employees by 20% in some cases and by as much as 83% in other cases, depending on the context. This vast variation was due to the diversity in the contexts included in the *TTP study*.

- When compared with the baseline estimates established at the beginning of the project cases (the baseline was specific to each project case), the new practices/strategies shared by the project leaders reduced the time to readiness of a business or operation by 50% in some cases and by as much as 90% in other cases, depending on the context. This significant variation was also because of the diversity in the contexts included in the *TTP study*.

- When compared with the baseline durations of training programs at the beginning of the project cases (the baseline was specific to each project case), the new practices/strategies shared by project leaders reduced the duration of the training programs by 20% in some cases and as much as 80% in other cases, depending on the context. This significant variation was due to the nature of the training program and also the diversity in the contexts included in the *TTP study*. Out of the 60 project cases, 28% realized the reduction achieved in the training duration as a side benefit besides the major benefit of a reduced TTP.

- To reach the performance comparable to that of experienced peers already serving a given job role, the new performers took 34% less time to reach that performance compared with the new performers who came to the same job before implementing the new practices/strategies shared by the project leaders.

- Compared to 35%, performers in a given job role being deemed proficient in performing the job role at the beginning of the project cases, within eight weeks of implementation of new practices/strategies, the number of proficient performers increased to 55%.

Table 7-2 Direct and indirect indicators of TTP reduction across all project cases

Project case ID	Project case title	Direct indicators			Indirect indicators
		Time to Proficiency reduction	Time to Readiness reduction	Time to Training Reduction	
1	Customer service engineers troubleshooting and repairing complex semiconductor equipment	67% (53 weeks to 18 weeks)	-	45% (from 13 weeks to 7 weeks)	-
2	Customer service helpdesk taking inbound calls for sales of investment products	33% (from 12 weeks to 8 weeks)	-	INCREASED (from 4 weeks to 12 weeks)	Productivity- 34% faster (achieved the same productivity and quality scores in 8 weeks as the 12 weeks old graduates)
4	Software engineers developing large scale information applications (books)	-	The readiness of offshore centers Reduced by several months	-	-
5	Cybersecurity analysts analyzing and identifying cyber-threats on client enterprise networks	50% (180 days to 90 days)	-	-	Producing in 30 days equivalent to previously trained people's

#	Role	Col A	Col B	Col C	Col D
6	Insurance agents selling insurance products	83% (18 months to 3 months)	-	-	Strong performance equivalent to tenure staff
7	Customer service engineers troubleshooting and repairing complex semiconductor equipment	over 50% (from several months to 5 weeks)	-	-	-
8	Console operators monitoring and controlling the processes at petrochemical plants	-	(Simulated) - from several years to a few days for 10% rare events	-	-
9	Service engineers troubleshooting and repairing telecommunication network equipment	-	-	13 hours per week (5 hours a week)	Reduce training development from 240 hours to 166 hours
10	Console operators monitoring and controlling the processes at petrochemical plants	-	(Simulated) - from several years to a few days for 10% rare events	-	-
11	Pharmaceutical biochemists manufacturing sophisticated cancer drugs	50% (from 6 months to 15 weeks)	-	-	-
12	Managers managing retail donut baking stores	50% (4 weeks to 2 weeks)	-	50% (4 weeks to 2 weeks)	Consistent and better skill ratings than before

#	Role				
13	Claim processing executives examining and processing health insurance claims	80% (5 months to 1 month)	-	-	33% (from 15 weeks to 10 weeks -check)??	-
14	Sales representative selling pharmaceutical products	25% (From 24 weeks to 18 weeks)	-	-	-	-
15	Insurance agents selling insurance products	-	Certification: Over 50% (from X days to 90 days)	-	-	-
16	Console operators monitoring and controlling the processes at petrochemical plants	-	-	-	-	Most successful transition compared to peers (as cited by client)
17	Customer service helpdesk taking inbound calls for hotel and travel-related services	-	-	-	25% (from 4 weeks to 3 weeks)	Strong performance equivalent to tenure staff, much shorter time to readiness (able to handle live calls out of training)
18	Managers managing supermarket chains	80% (14 months to 14 weeks)	-	-	50% (13 weeks to 5-7 weeks)	-
19	Energy Corporation top executives transferring knowledge to successors	50% (as compared to time taken by veterans)	-	-	-	Improvement in Proficiency scores
20	Hospital medical doctors and nursing staff providing pediatrics care services	-	Ramp-up: 66% (Expected 12 months to 4 months)	-	-	-

21	Customer helpdesk taking inbound calls to remotely troubleshoot client computer and software issues	22% (9 weeks to 7 weeks)	-	60% (5 weeks to 2 weeks)	Higher level performance in 4 weeks compared to previous graduates, 10 points higher for the graduate of 3 weeks training than graduates of 5 weeks training
22	Customer service engineers troubleshooting and repairing complex semiconductor equipment	Target 75% (from 2-3 years to 6 months) - work in progress	-	-	-
23	The school administrator and teachers instituting school improvement programs	-	Certification: over 50% (from X years to 4 months)	-	-
24	Warehouse professionals adopting SAP for supply chain and logistics transactions	-	Accelerated ramp-up of 12 sites by several months	-	-
25	Console operators monitoring and controlling the processes at petrochemical plants	-	-	-	Accelerated knowledge acquisition for new hires
26	Young military officers on the leadership pathway	-	-	-	time with improved effectiveness (Young leader ready to lead

				sooner than before)
27	Military officers setting up a new command center to prevent cyberterrorism	-	Ramp-up 50% (from 1 year to 6 months)	-
28	Biotechnology scientists strategizing business of brain implant technology for curing neurological diseases	-	(simulated) - 2 years' worth of change in 2 days for anticipated rare events	-
29	Machinists fabricating aircraft engine mechanical parts	40% (151 days to 92 days)	-	At a better rate than average time to competence
30	Sales engineers selling hi-tech enterprise communication products	50% (1 year to 6 months)	-	Productivity - 10% increase in efficiency than past graduates, much shorter time to readiness (becoming productive sales representatives at a faster speed) Time-to-proficiency - Shortened compared to veterans Performance

				Indicators - immediately start generating revenue (earning during 120 days of hiring)
31	Electronics technicians to troubleshoot and repair of complex Navy electronics equipment	-	-	
32	Benefit evaluators examining eligibility for Govt. run benefits	over 50% (from 1-3 years to a few months)	-	42% (7 weeks to 4 weeks)
				Employee up to speed in a shorter time with improved effectiveness (able to handle cases right away)
33	Sales engineers selling hi-tech enterprise computer and server systems	50% (26 weeks to 12 weeks for new hires and 6 weeks for experienced sellers)	-	Productivity - 70% higher sales by new hires over 3 quarters Productivity - 2X likely to achieve average quota than experienced sellers
34	Customer service engineers troubleshooting and repairing complex semiconductor equipment	Target 50% (1-2 years to 6 -12 months) - work in progress	-	Employee up to speed in a shorter time with improved

#	Role	Metric 1	Metric 2	Metric 3
35	Clinical staff and database administrators transitioning to new software for clinical trials data	-	-	Much shorter time to readiness (on a new system)
36	Customer service helpdesk taking inbound calls for financial products	66% (1 year to 4 months)	-	50% (from X to Y)
37	Healthcare professionals providing assisted living services for elders	77% (90 days to 20 days)	-	-
38	Customer service engineers troubleshooting and repairing complex semiconductor equipment	-	Certification: Target 50% (1-2 years to less than 1 year) - work in progress	Much shorter time to readiness
39	Customer service engineers troubleshooting and repairing complex semiconductor equipment	Over 50% (from 1-2 years to 6 months)	-	Much shorter time to readiness
40	Insurance agents selling insurance products	-	-	80% (5 days to 1 day)	Employee up to speed in a shorter time with improved effectiveness
42	Managers managing retail store chains	-	-	87% (8 weeks to 1-week instructor-led)	Much shorter time to readiness (doing most essential tasks in XX weeks)

43	Plant maintenance engineers to troubleshooting production machine issues	-	-	66% (18 weeks of instructor-led to 6 weeks on-the-job training)	Reduced time of learning
44	Sales representatives upselling strategic service products		Significant shorter time to sales quota		
45	Reactor operators manufacturing chemical paints	50% (18-24 months to 9-12 months)	-	-	
46	Customer service engineers troubleshooting and repairing complex semiconductor equipment	-	Certification: 80% (6 months to 6 weeks) for 80% population	66% (6 weeks to 2 weeks)	
47	Real estate agents booking mortgages and listings				Reduced time of sales performance (results interrupted due to acquisition)
48	Truck assemblers assembling and fabricating automobiles	90% (from 5 days to 0.5 days)	-	-	Productivity - Improved by 66% (3 defects to 1 defect per week)
49	Maintenance engineers repairing and maintaining petroleum pipeline feeds	Target 75% (1 year to 3 months)	-	-	
50	Machine operators fabricating mechanical parts for petroleum exploration equipment	50% (4 weeks to 2 weeks) for 95% of cases	-	-	
52	Financial analysts assessing corporate insolvency cases				Excelled in simulated performance,

	Job	Time to proficiency reduction	Other outcomes
53	Healthcare professionals providing residential care for severely disabled	77% (9 months to 2 months)	-
54	Sales engineers selling construction products and equipment	33% (from 18 months to 12 months)	-
55	Customer service helpdesk taking inbound calls for internet phone service	over 30% (from 12 weeks to 8 weeks)	-
56	Customer service helpdesk taking inbound calls for sales of financial products	-	30% (from 51 days to 36 days)
57	Customer service helpdesk taking inbound calls for banking services	66% (6 weeks to 2 weeks) - post-training	-
58	Design engineers developing complex semiconductor equipment	Target 66% (from 3 years to 1 year) - work in progress	-
59	Customer service helpdesk taking inbound calls for upselling of financial products	50% (3 months to 1.5 months)	-
60	Electrical engineers designing and repairing power plant equipment	(Expected) 33% to 50% reduction (from 2 years to 1 year)	-
61	Sales engineers selling medical and surgical instruments	-	Significant shorter time to quota

Additional column (New hires up to speed on basic decision-making / readiness):
- 56: Population to Proficiency - Increased from 33% to 55% (or 68%) in 10 weeks
- 57: 50% (12 weeks to 6 weeks)
- 58: Much shorter time to readiness
- 59: Much shorter time to readiness (faster on the floor)

| 62 | Business managers developing strategies for an unforeseen drop in gold prices | - | (Simulated) - From 10-20 years to 3 days for anticipated rare events |
| 63 | Underground miners preparing for unexpected underground fire during mining operations | - | (Simulated) - From 8-10 years to 2 days for anticipated rare events |

This page is kept blank intentionally.

CH7/THE BENEFITS

7.1.4 Examples from the semiconductor industry

There were 7 project cases from the semiconductor equipment manufacturing companies that involved troubleshooting and repairing complex semiconductor equipment by customer service engineers. All of these cases fell under the technology equipment sector and were located in different countries. There was a reduction in the TTP in the range of 50% to 80%, depending upon the nature of the project case. In some cases, the TTP was reduced to as little as 5 weeks, as shown in Table 7-3.

The point here is that it is possible to significantly reduce TTP depending upon the context, the nature of the job role, and other factors if the right strategies are implemented.

Table 7-3 TTP reduction in hi-tech project cases

Case Title	Time to Proficiency	Time to Training
Customer service engineers troubleshooting and repairing complex semiconductor equipment	Reduced 67% (53 weeks to 18 weeks)	Cut by 45% (from 13 weeks to 7 weeks)
Customer service engineers troubleshooting and repairing complex semiconductor equipment	Reduced over 50% (from several months to 5 weeks)	-
Customer service engineers troubleshooting and repairing complex semiconductor equipment	Target to reduce by 75% (from 2-3 years to 6 months) – work in progress	-
Customer service engineers troubleshooting and repairing complex semiconductor equipment	Target to reduce by 50% (1-2 years to 6 -12 months) – work in progress	-
Customer service engineers troubleshooting and repairing complex semiconductor equipment	Target to reduce by 50% (1-2 years to less than 1 year) – work in progress	-

Customer service engineers troubleshooting and repairing complex semiconductor equipment	Significant reduction (from original 1-2 years)	-
Customer service engineers troubleshooting and repairing complex semiconductor equipment	Reduced 80% (6 months to 6 weeks) for 80% of the population	Cut by 66% (6 weeks to 2 weeks)

7.1.5 Examples from sales-related jobs

Sales-related jobs, technical or non-technical, in various industries, showed a reduction in TTP was of the order of 25% to 50% depending upon the nature of the project case. In some cases, the TTP was reduced down to as little as 6 weeks, as shown in Table 7-4.

Table 7-4 TTP reduction in sales-related project cases

Case Title	Time to Proficiency	Time to Training
Sales representative selling pharmaceutical products	Reduced by 25% (From 24 weeks to 18 weeks)	-
Sales engineers selling hi-tech enterprise communication products	Reduced 50% (1 year to 6 months)	-
Sales engineers selling hi-tech enterprise computer and server systems	Reduced to 12 weeks for new hires and 6 weeks for experienced sellers	-
Sales engineers selling construction products and equipment	Reduced by 33% (from 18 months to 12 months)	-
Sales engineers selling medical and surgical instruments	Significant shorter time to quota	-

7.1.6 Examples from plant maintenance roles

In another example on the same lines, plant maintenance roles in various industries showed a reduction in TTP in the range of 25% to 75%, depending on the project case. In some cases, the TTP was reduced down to as little as 3 months, as shown in Table 7-5. A reduction of 42–67% was observed in the training duration. In some cases, the training was made as short as 4 weeks.

Table 7-5 TTP reduction in plant maintenance-related project cases

Case Title	Time to Proficiency	Time to Training
Electronics technicians to troubleshoot and repair of complex navy electronics equipment	-	Cut by 42% (7 weeks to 4 weeks)
Plant maintenance engineers to troubleshooting production machine issues	-	Cut by 66% (18 weeks of instructor-led training to 6 weeks OJT)
Maintenance engineers repairing and maintaining petroleum pipeline feeds	Reduce by 75% (1 year to 3 months) Reduced by 25% (from 18 months to 13.5 months)	-
Electrical engineers designing and repairing power plant equipment	(Expected) to reduce by 33% to 50% (from 2 years) – work in progress	-

7.2 BENEFITS OF A SHORTER TTP

Some of the previous research studies have shown case studies, indicating the financial and business benefits of training (Bartel 2000; Kirkpatrick & Kirkpatrick 2009; Phillips 2012). While previous studies have made speculative statements on the possible need and potential benefits of shortening TTP, in the *TTP study*, I have quantified the TTP values and presented the numbers. In addition, I have gathered qualitative indications of the actual business benefits accrued in the 60 project cases. I identified four business benefits that most organizations accrued out of a shorter TTP: business gains, improvement in operational metrics, improvement in productivity, and cost savings, which are defined in Table 7-6. I also observed that "cost savings" were invariably realized in every project case.

Table 7-6 Definition and metrics of business benefits

Benefit	Definition and metrics
Business gains	Increased market share, Shorter sales cycle, increased profit or revenue, Competitiveness, The readiness of staff, Improved sales, Higher customer satisfaction
Improvement in operational metrics	An increase in staff retention, Need for fewer staff, High training capacity Shorter courses, Improvement in skill scores
Improvement in productivity	An improvement in processing rate, Reduction in errors, Improved output, Availability of staff, Efficiency and saving of time
Cost savings	Shorter time-to-proficiency, Shorter training duration Less travel required, Cost savings aggregated on a larger population

7.2.1 Business gains

A shorter TTP of the employees could give some advantage in time-to-market (Fred 2002). Researchers have supported that a team's TTP could determine the "sweet spot" for the launch of the product or service (Langerak, Hultink & Griffin 2008).

In this *TTP study*, 'business gains' represented gains such as increased market share, shorter sales cycle, increased profit or revenue, competitiveness, the readiness of staff, improved sales, and higher customer satisfaction realized because of shorter TTP values. For example, in a project case involving sales representatives upselling strategic service products in the industrial and commercial services sector in the US, the organization '*shortened the sales cycle substantially and increased market share*' by shortening the TTP of its employees.

Some project leaders cited benefits such as:

- $1.8M additional net profit per seller
- Clients citing phenomenal results
- Onboarding of 400 new staff in a shorter time
- 5X increase in stock, 3X increase in the market cap, and no debt
- Improved sales and internal efficiencies
- High customer satisfaction

7.2.2 Improvement in operational metrics

'Improvement in operational metrics' represented an increase in staff retention, need for lesser number of staff, high training capacity with shorter courses, and improved skill scores of the staff. For example, in a project case involving healthcare professionals providing residential care for the severely disabled at a leading healthcare provider offering assisted living, the project leader cited that *'employee retention improved from 55% to 95%'* when the TTP was reduced by 77%, that is, from 90 days to 20 days.

Some project leaders cited benefits such as:

- 40% fewer staff to execute the program
- Manager-to-employee ratio reduced by 50% (from 1:20 to 1:40)
- Retention increased by 50% and cost reduced by 70%
- Engineers' on-the-job availability increased
- Training load reduced by 75%
- Retention improved in one case from 10% to 25.5% in 4 years; in another case, it improved from 50% to 95%, while in another case it increased by more than 50% and in some cases even improved to 90%
- Scores and statistics improved year on year

7.2.3 Improvement in productivity

The cost incurred by an organization due to lack of proficiency of employees (such as low productivity, substandard work, errors, defects, and lack of compliance) could be way too large to ignore.

CH7 / THE BENEFITS

That was where 'improvement in productivity' represented an improvement in the processing rate, reduction in errors, improved output, availability of staff, efficiency, and saving of time.

For example, in a project case involving a customer helpdesk group taking inbound calls to remotely troubleshoot client computer and software issues, a large software & IT services company realized higher customer satisfaction. This was the result of reducing the TTP by 22% (from 9 weeks to 7 weeks), which also included a reduction in the training duration by 60% (from 5 weeks to 2 weeks). The project leader also noticed a higher level of performance in 4 weeks compared with the previous graduates; in fact, 10 points higher for graduates who had undergone 3 weeks of training when compared with those who had undergone 5 weeks of training.

In a project case involving technicians in charge of troubleshooting and repairing complex electronics equipment belonging to the US Navy, I found that the productivity improved from 45% to 95% in terms of the number of faults troubleshot. The increase occurred as a result of a reduction in TTP, which included the reduction in training duration by 42%, that is, from 7 weeks to 4 weeks.

Some project leaders cited benefits such as:

- 53% drop in misdirected calls
- Improvement in quality by 66% (3 defects to 1 defect per week)
- 10% increase in efficiency compared to past graduates
- 26% higher quota attainment over 6 quarters
- A saving of 45,500 hours of 1250 people per year

- 25% increase in claim processing and a 60% reduction in errors
- 2X more likely to achieve average quota than experienced sellers
- 2X increase in the troubleshooting rate (from 45% to 90%)
- Improvement in productivity by 300%
- Decrease in the preparation time of facilitators
- Improvement in productivity by 25% (from 120 to 150 per day)
- Reduced need to take people away from the job
- A saving of 4.9 hours on an average for 62% workforce
- Increase in the troubleshooting performance (from 45% to 100%)

As an example, Table 7-7 shows the reduction in TTP and training duration and the productivity improvement accrued from it in sales-related project cases.

Table 7-7 TTP reduction and productivity improvement in sales-related project cases

Case Title	Time to Proficiency	Time to Training	Business Benefits
Sales engineers selling hi-tech enterprise communication products	Reduced 50% (1 year to 6 months)	-	10% increase in efficiency than past graduates immediately start generating revenue (earning during 120 days of hiring)

CH7/THE BENEFITS

Sales engineers selling hi-tech enterprise computer and server systems	Reduced to 12 weeks for new hires and 6 weeks for experienced sellers	-	Productivity - 2X likely to achieve average quota than experienced sellers

7.2.4 Cost savings

Several previous studies have shown substantial financial or cost benefits of shorter training duration and faster readiness of the workforce (Jacobs 2014; Liu & Batt 2007; Sullivan, Brechin & Lacoste 1999). Some studies have shown financial gains from the reduction of TTP (Borton 2007, p. 32; Pollock, Wick & Jefferson 2015, p. 285; Thompson 2017, p. 169). There is also an opportunity cost or productivity loss because of long training that could have been otherwise used to earn additional hundreds of thousands of dollars of revenue. From a case study conducted in one of the largest banks in the US, it was observed that the opportunity cost could be reduced by 68% by simply reducing the TTP of financial services advisors from 18 weeks to 12 weeks (Pollock, Wick & Jefferson 2015, p. 285). Similarly, from another case study, it was observed that, a decrease of 25% of TTP of new bankers led to an increase in the revenue by 13% (approx. $250,000) in the first 12 months of employment (Thompson 2017).

In the *TTP study*, 'cost savings' represents the cost savings aggregated on a larger population on account of a shorter TTP, shorter training duration, and reduced need for travel. For example, in a project case involving a customer service helpdesk group of a large US bank taking inbound calls for the sales of financial products in the banking and investment services sector, the bank *'saved $5.68M in 2 years'* by shortening TTP, which included shortening training by 30%, that is, from 51 days to 36 days.

Some project leaders cited benefits such as:

- Cost avoidance of $145K in 1 year
- Saved millions of dollars corresponding to 600 people
- Reduced cost by 24%
- Saved travel expenses by 40%

As an example, Table 7-8 shows the reduction in TTP and training duration and the cost-saving accrued from it.

Table 7-8 TTP reduction and cost savings in hi-tech project cases

Case Title	Time to Proficiency	Time to Training	Business Benefits
Customer service engineers troubleshooting and repairing complex semiconductor equipment	Reduced 67% (53 weeks to 18 weeks)	Cut by 45% (from 13 weeks to 7 weeks)	Cost-saving - Saved travel expenses by 40%
Customer service engineers troubleshooting and repairing complex semiconductor equipment	Reduced 80% (6 months to 6 weeks) for 80% of the population	Cut by 66% (6 weeks to 2 weeks)	$8-10M cost savings Reduced training load by 75% High customer satisfaction

7.2.5 Interplay of benefits

I noted that all four benefits were uniform across all the project cases, with no specific strong prevalence of one of them. Table 7-9 shows this as prevalence scores summarized across various project

CH7/THE BENEFITS

classification parameters. In fact, each project realized more than one type of business benefit.

Table 7-9 Prevalence of various business benefits across project classification parameters

	COMPLEXITY	SKILLS	JOBS	BUSINESS SECTOR	ECONOMIC SECTOR	Overall prevalence
BUSINESS GAINS	80%	40%	21%	40%	60%	48%
COST SAVINGS	80%	40%	36%	30%	50%	47%
IMPROVEMENT IN OPERATIONAL METRICS	80%	33%	36%	30%	50%	45%
IMPROVEMENT IN PRODUCTIVITY	80%	53%	36%	35%	50%	51%

Case in point 7.1

> A high-tech semiconductor equipment company in Singapore involved in the fast-paced technology business was faced with the challenge of keeping its customers' production running and keeping equipment uptime commitments.
>
> It required the company to develop proficient skills of its customer service engineers, who were involved in troubleshooting and repairing complex semiconductor equipment, in a shorter time.
>
> The case exhibited several benefits of reducing TTP:
>
> Customer satisfaction: 'Another side benefit of this whole thing is that your customer satisfaction goes up. Because the people that are working on the [equipment] actually know how to work on the things that actually happen on the tool, the

> customer will have a higher degree of confidence in the individual's ability.'
>
> Operational metrics: 'So, overall, that benefit is probably because we have reduced our training load by about 75%. So, that is the direct impact that we have seen.'
>
> Cost savings: 'We have also done cost avoidance savings that are probably around 8–10 million dollars, I believe that.'
>
> [quotes as stated by the project leader]

While it is reasonable to assume that the reduction in TTP is always driven by the financial or cost-saving interests of an organization, a contrasting fact was revealed. I found that reducing costs and financial implications are not usually the primary drivers that drive organizations to institute initiatives/projects to reduce TTP. The thought process is driven by other market forces such as competition, time-to-market, and skill shortage. However, financial gains are invariably attained in every such initiative/project. Table 7-10 summarizes the business benefits across the project cases analyzed in the *TTP study*.

Table 7-10 Business benefits across project cases

Project case ID	Case title	Business gains (Business, productivity, operational metrics)
1	Customer service engineers troubleshooting and repairing complex semiconductor equipment	Cost-saving - Saved travel expenses by 40%
4	Software engineers developing large scale information applications (books)	Productivity- Saved 45500 hours of 1250 people per year Productivity -

CH7/THE BENEFITS

Project case ID	Case title	Business gains (Business, productivity, operational metrics)
		saved 4.9 hours per month on an average for 62% productivity of the workforce - Reduced need to take people away from the job
6	Insurance agents selling insurance products	Operation Metrics - Retention improved from 10% to 25.5% (4 years) Operation Metrics - Retention rates increased by more than 50% (1st year)
9	Service engineers troubleshooting and repairing telecommunication network equipment	Business gains - The client cited phenomenal results
11	Pharmaceutical biochemists manufacturing sophisticated cancer drugs	Productivity-- Supervisor more productive
13	Claim processing executives examining and processing health insurance claims	Productivity - 25% increase in claim processing and 60% reduction in errors. Productivity - Reduction in errors and spills (payment errors are expected to drop by 60%)
14	Sales representative selling pharmaceutical products	Cost-saving - Millions of dollars for 600 people
16	Console operators monitoring and controlling the processes at petrochemical plants	Business gains - The client cited phenomenal results
18	Managers managing supermarket chains	Cost-saving - Tremendous savings with OJT
20	Hospital medical doctors and nursing staff providing pediatrics care services	Business gains - Onboarding of 400 new staff in a shorter time
21	Customer helpdesk taking inbound calls to remotely troubleshoot client computer and software issues	Business gains - High customer satisfaction
24	Warehouse professionals adopting SAP for supply chain and logistics transactions	Business gains -12 site ready with software deployments
28	Biotechnology scientists strategizing business of brain implant technology for curing neurological diseases	Business gains - stock 5X, market cap 3X and 0 debt
29	Machinists fabricating aircraft engine mechanical parts	Cost-saving - cost avoidance of $145K in 1 year
30	Sales engineers selling hi-tech enterprise communication products	Business gains - Needed 40% fewer staff to execute the program Cost-saving - Reduced cost by 24%
31	Electronics technicians to troubleshoot and repair of complex Navy electronics equipment	Productivity - Troubleshooting performance increased from 45% to 100%
33	Sales engineers selling hi-tech enterprise computer and server systems	Business gains - $1.8M additional net profit per seller Productivity - 26% higher quota attainment over 6 quarters

Project case ID	Case title	Business gains (Business, productivity, operational metrics)
37	Healthcare professionals providing assisted living services for elders	Business gains - improved sales and internal efficiencies
43	Plant maintenance engineers to troubleshooting production machine issues	Operation Metrics - Increased engineer's availability on-the-job
44	Sales representatives upselling strategic service products	Business gains - Shortened sales cycle substantially and increased market share
45	Reactor operators manufacturing chemical paints	Productivity - Reduction in errors and spills
46	Customer service engineers troubleshooting and repairing complex semiconductor equipment	Cost-Saving - 8-10 Million dollars Operation Metrics - Reduced training load by 75% Business gains - High customer satisfaction
53	Healthcare professionals providing residential care for severely disabled	Operation Metrics - Retention improved from 55% to 95%
54	Sales engineers selling construction products and equipment	Operation Metrics - Retention improved in 1st year
55	Customer service helpdesk taking inbound calls for internet phone service	Operation Metrics - Retention improved in 1st year
56	Customer service helpdesk taking inbound calls for sales of financial products	Productivity - 53% drop in misdirected calls Cost-saving - $682K in 1 year and 5.68M in 2 years with a shorter course
57	Customer service helpdesk taking inbound calls for banking services	Operation Metrics - Cut Manager-to-employee ratio by 50% (1:20 to1:40) 20% reduction in new hire induction training cycle (this is not the job training) Productivity - improved 25% from 120 to 150 per day
59	Customer service helpdesk taking inbound calls for upselling of financial products	Operation Metrics - Retention improved to 90%

7.3 WHAT IT MEANS TO YOU

Be clear about the end goal. In the business context, several strategies are put into play to address different aspects of the business challenges. The business benefits cannot be isolated or attributed to one kind of strategy or others. Thus, the overall

CH7/THE BENEFITS

business benefits one derived at the end could be aggregated effect of other strategies, including the ones specifically employed to shorten.

☛ **Business benefits are not directly proportional to the magnitude of TTP improvement.** The business benefits are contextual and, therefore, subject to several contextual factors, systems, strategies, and the nature of jobs. While TTP reduction invariably will lead to some business benefits, there is no direct relationship between the quantum of TTP reduction and the business benefits. For example, while a small reduction in TTP may show up drastic business benefits, a large reduction may not necessarily mean huge business benefits. The benefits need to be explained in the context of the goals of the TTP project.

☛ **Developing a business case.** Any non-monetary business gain derived from a shorter TTP usually leads to some kind of monetary benefits downstream. For instance, the improvement in productivity would lead to cost savings or other business gains at the end. Therefore, work out an overall business proposal by considering how non-monetary benefits lead to dollar value downstream when quantifying ROI for a project initiative meant to invest in resources to shorten TTP.

CHAPTER 8
THE SYSTEM

THE CLOSED-LOOP OF TTP

In Chapter 2, I laid the foundation of why organizational leaders need to focus on the proficiency aspect of workforce performance. In Chapter 3, I appealed that TTP is one of the most overlooked, but the most powerful of the metrics organizations can have. In Chapter 4, I built a business case of the magnitude and scale of TTP in various settings and concluded that they are so large to ignore. In Chapter 5, I explained how the magnitude and scale of TTP manifested in the form of business drivers that pushed organizational leaders to think of solving the TTP problem. In Chapter 6, I described the range and nature of business benefits one can accrue from a shorter TTP. This last chapter will focus on the inter-relationship among these elements and explain a closed-loop model to guide practitioners.

8.1 THE CLOSED-LOOP OF TTP

I would like to emphasize that the triggers, drivers, and benefits of TTP are not three separate manifestations. They are, in fact, interlinked with each other as a closed-loop system. Figure 8.1 shows the conceptual interactions, which are explained below.

Triggers—magnitude and scale of TTP: How long is TTP in a given job role? That is the trigger point in organizations. The magnitude of the problem of TTP in a given job role and its scale multiplied by the number of employees serving the same role acts as the trigger. This trigger manifests its impact on the business. With so many things to handle, the business managers may not react to problems that do not seem to carry a big impact.

CH8 / THE SYSTEM

Business drivers to TTP: We see the impact in the form of four business drivers: time-related pressures, speed-related competitiveness, skill-related deficiencies, and cost/financial implications. The size of the problem manifests itself in the form of one of these business drivers. This usually makes the leaders start thinking that a long TTP is a problem worth solving. The larger the scale, the more significant the impact seen on these drivers.

Inputs—project efforts to reduce TTP: These drivers then push organizations to see the need for a shorter TTP in relationship to their business metrics. Once the impact is recognized on any aspect of the business, project efforts are initiated by defining the proficiency and establishing the measures. Part of this process is to baseline current TTP based on historical data or other estimations. We establish the new targets for TTP based on the business needs driving the initiative/project or other organizational goals.

Accelerated proficiency appears to be a system in which the various elements must work effectively in coordination to shorten TTP. At various business levels, in the *TTP study*, I found that 24 strategies and 6 business practices lead to the successful reduction in TTP. There are complex interactions among these practices and strategies as a closed-loop system. Like any other system, there are several decisions and trade-offs involved. It is not mandatory to implement each of the 24 strategies in a given context for a given business challenge. We can use and leverage several existing systems, resources, methods, and information sources or as a proxy to implement the six practices at a high level.

Outputs—reduced TTP: The new target for TTP becomes the reference for monitoring any improvement in TTP in the project. The project leaders have to come out with ways to put systems, processes, or strategies in play to reduce TTP successfully.

The actual strategies found in the *TTP study* are out of the scope of this book. But, eventually, such efforts are likely to reduce TTP in a given job role.

Feedback loop: The resultant TTP is measured or monitored against the target TTP. If the resultant TTP has still not reached the goal, its magnitude and scale could be large enough to manifest in the form of one or more of the business drivers. That pushes the project leaders to investigate the factors that were not known earlier and now coming on the way to accelerate proficiency. Or, we can now incorporate the new accelerators not identified earlier to drive the correction. We can then continue monitoring the TTP until we achieve the desired TTP.

Based on that, we make the necessary corrections or adjustments in strategies. Eventually, with appropriate correction and adjustment, the desired TTP is achieved. The outcome may depend on the degree of the orchestration of all the practices/processes. Usually, it requires a closed-loop system approach to monitor and correct the performance.

Outcomes—business benefits of TTP: As a result of shortening TTP, the organizations typically enjoyed four business benefits out: business gains, improved productivity, improved operational metrics, and cost savings.

CH8/THE SYSTEM

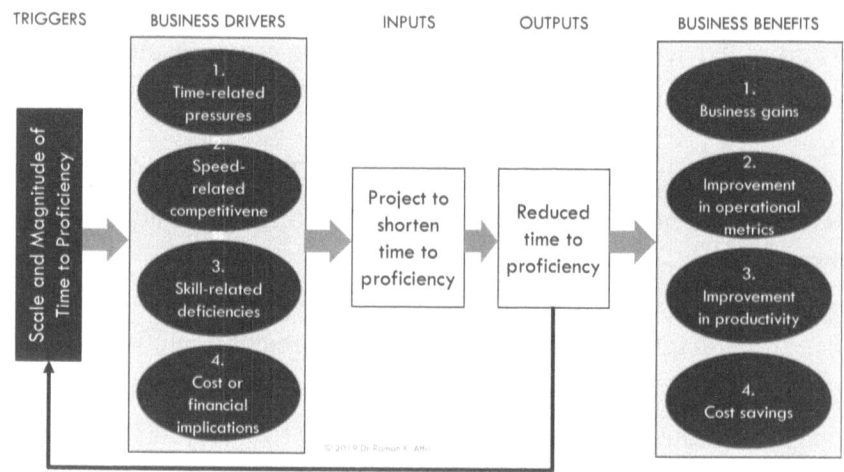

Figure 8.1 Closed-loop conceptual model of TTP.

8.2 WHAT IT MEANS TO YOU

☞ **Complexly interrelated:** There is a highly dependent, often non-linear, and non-proportionate relationship among the triggers, drivers, and benefits of TTP. They are complexly interrelated and depend on each other. They impact or get impacted by other business conditions, measurements, and metrics.

SPEED MATTERS

☞ **Chain reaction:** There is undoubtedly a chain reaction, though it is not always easy to quantify how severely or lightly the magnitude and scale of TTP contribute toward making a given business driver irresistible. Similarly, it may not be a direct equation to link the business drivers with the resultant business benefits.

☞ **A closed-loop system:** Accelerating TTP is a process that acts as a system in which various elements work effectively with each other to shorten the TTP. In turn, the quantum of TTP drives the changes and optimizations like a closed-loop system.

☞ **Trade-offs:** Like any other system, there are several decisions and trade-offs involved, and it is not necessary to implement every strategy in a given context for a given business challenge. You can use or leverage several existing systems, resources, methods, and information sources or as a proxy to implement the six practices at a high level.

PUBLICATIONS

1. Attri, RK 2020, *Accelerated Proficiency for Accelerated Times: A Review of Key Concepts and Methods to Speed up Performance,* Speed to Proficiency Research, Singapore.
2. Attri, RK 2019, *Models of Skill Acquisition and Expertise Development: A Quick Reference of Summaries*, Speed To Proficiency Research, Singapore.
3. Attri, RK 2019, *Speed to Proficiency in Organizations: A Research Report on Model, Practices and Strategies to Shorten Time to Proficiency*, Speed To Proficiency Research, Singapore, viewed 26 Jun 2019 <https://www.amazon.com/gp/product/B07NYS81HQ/>.
4. Attri, RK 2019, *Designing Training to Shorten Time to Proficiency: Online, Classroom and On-the-job Learning Strategies from Research*, Speed To Proficiency Research, Singapore, viewed 26 Jun 2019 <https://www.amazon.com/gp/product/9811406324>.
5. Attri, RK 2018, *Accelerate your leadership development in training domain: Proven success strategies for new training & learning managers*, Speed To Proficiency Research: S2Pro©, Singapore, available at <https://www.amazon.com/ /dp/9811400660/>.
6. Attri, RK 2018, "Modelling accelerated proficiency in organisations: practices and strategies to shorten time-to-proficiency of the workforce," PhD thesis, Southern Cross University, Lismore, Australia.
7. Attri, RK 2014, "Rethinking professional skill development in competitive corporate world: accelerating time-to-expertise of employees at workplace," in J Latzo (ed.), *Proceedings of Conference on Education and Human Development in Asia*, Hiroshima, 2-4 March, PRESDA Foundation, Kitanagova, pp. 1–11, http://dx.doi.org/10.13140/RG.2.1.5125.7043.

8. Attri, RK & Wu, WS 2018, "Model of accelerated proficiency in the workplace: six core concepts to shorten time-to-proficiency of employees," *Asia Pacific Journal of Advanced Business and Social Studies*, vol. 4, no. 1, http://dx.doi.org/10.25275/apjabssv4i1bus1.
9. Attri, RK & Wu, WS 2017, "Model of accelerated proficiency in the workplace: six core concepts to shorten time-to-proficiency of employees," *First Australia and New Zealand Conference on Advanced Research (ANZCAR)*, Melbourne, Asia Pacific Institute of Advanced Research, Melbourne, 17-18 June, pp. 1-10, viewed 24 July 2017, <http://apiar.org.au/wp-content/uploads/2017/07/1_ANZCAR_2017_BRR713_Bus-1-10.pdf>.
10. Attri, RK & Wu, WS 2016, "Classroom-based instructional strategies to accelerate proficiency of employees in complex job skills," paper presented to the Asian American Conference for Education, Singapore, 15-16 January, viewed 24 June 2017, <https://www.researchgate.net/publication/303803099>.
11. Attri, RK & Wu, WS 2016, "E-learning strategies at workplace that support speed to proficiency in complex skills," in M Rozhan and N Zainuddin (eds.), *Proceedings of the 11th International Conference on E-Learning: ICEl2016*, Kuala Lampur, 2-3 June, Academic Conference and Publishing, Reading, pp. 176–184, viewed 24 June 2017, <https://www.researchgate.net/publication/303802961>.
12. Attri, RK & Wu, WS 2015, E-Learning Strategies to Accelerate Time-to-Proficiency in Acquiring Complex Skills: Preliminary Findings. Paper presented at *E-learning Forum Asia Conference*, Jun 2015. Singapore: SIM University, available at <https://www.researchgate.net/publication/282647943>.
13. Attri, RK & Wu, W 2015, 'Conceptual model of workplace training and learning strategies to shorten time-to-proficiency in complex skills: preliminary findings', paper presented to the *9th International Conference on Researching in Work and Learning (RWL)*, Singapore, 9-11 December, viewed 24 June 2017, <https://www.researchgate.net/publication/286623558>.

REFERENCES

Accenture 2013, *Top-Five Focus Areas for Improving Sales Effectiveness Initiatives*, viewed 24 June 2017, <https://www.accenture.com/t20150523T052741__w__/us-en/_acnmedia/Accenture/Conversion-Assets/DotCom/Documents/Global/PDF/Strategy_4/Accenture-Top-Five-Improvements-Sales-Effectiveness.pdf>.

Ackerman, PL 1988, 'Determinants of individual differences during skill acquisition: cognitive abilities and information processing', *Journal of Experimental Psychology General*, vol. 117, no. 3, pp. 288–318, http://dx.doi.org/10.1037/0096-3445.117.3.288.

Alexander, PA 2003a, 'Can we get there from here?', *Educational Researcher*, vol. 32, no. 8, pp. 3–4, http://dx.doi.org/10.3102/0013189X032008003.

―――― 2003b, 'The development of expertise: the journey from acclimation to proficiency', *Educational Researcher*, vol. 32, no. 8, pp. 10–14, http://dx.doi.org/10.3102/0013189X032008010.

Alorica 2017, 'Think quick: increase speed to proficiency,' viewed 24 June 2018, <https://www.alorica.com/wp-content/uploads/2017/09/ebook_SpeedtoProficiency.pdf>.

Andersson, AW, Jansson, A, Sandblad, B & Tschirner, S 2014, Recognizing complexity: visualization for skilled professionals in complex work situations, in A Ebert, G van der Veer, G Domik, N Gershon & I Scheler (eds.), *Building Bridges: HCI, Visualization, and Non-formal Modeling*, Lecture notes in computer science, vol 8345, Springer, Berlin Heidelberg, Germany, pp. 47–66, http://dx.doi.org/10.1007/978-3-642-54894-9_5.

REFERENCES

Andrews, DH & Fitzgerald, P 2010, 'Accelerating learning of competence and increasing long-term learning retention', paper presented to the ITEC Conference, London, 18-20 May, viewed 24 June 2017, <http://www.dtic.mil/cgi-bin/GetTRDoc?AD=ADA522088>.

Angelo, RL, Ryu, RK, Pedowitz, RA, Beach, W, Burns, J, Dodds, J, Field, L, Getelman, M, Hobgood, R, McIntyre, L & others 2015, 'A proficiency-based progression training curriculum coupled with a model simulator results in the acquisition of a superior arthroscopic bankart skill set', *Arthroscopy: The Journal of Arthroscopic & Related Surgery*, vol. 31, no. 10, pp. 1854–1871, viewed 24 June 2017, <https://www.ucc.ie/en/media/academic/assertforhealth/assertdocs/1.1-s2.0-S0749806315005836-main.pdf>.

Attri, RK 2018, 'Modelling accelerated proficiency in organisations: practices and strategies to shorten time-to-proficiency of the workforce', PhD thesis, Southern Cross University, Lismore, Australia.

Attri, RK 2014, 'Rethinking professional skill development in competitive corporate world: accelerating time-to-expertise of employees at workplace', in J Latzo (ed.), *Proceedings of Conference on Education and Human Development in Asia*, Hiroshima, PRESDA Foundation, Kitanagova, pp. 1–11, http://dx.doi.org/10.13140/RG.2.1.5125.7043.

Attri, RK & Wu, W 2015, 'Conceptual model of workplace training and learning strategies to shorten time-to-proficiency in complex skills: preliminary findings', paper presented to the 9th International Conference on Researching in Work and Learning (RWL), Singapore, 9-11 December, viewed 24 June 2017, <http://www.rwl2015.com/papers/Paper100.pdf>.

Bachlechner, D, Kohlegger, M, Maier, R & Waldhart, G 2010, 'Taking pressure off knowledge workers with the help of situational applications-improving time-to-proficiency in knowledge work settings', in A Fred & J Filipe (eds.), *Proceedings of the International Conference on Knowledge Management and Information Sharing (KMIS-2010)*, Valencia, 25-28 October, SCITEPRESS Science and Technology, Setúbal, Portugal, pp. 378–381, http://dx.doi.org/10.5220/0003118203780381.

Baker, T 2016, *The end of the job description: Shifting from a job-focus to a performance-focus*, Palgrave MacMillan, London, http://dx.doi.org/10.1007/978-1-137-58146-4.

_____ 2017, *Performance Management for Agile Organisations*, Springer, Cham, http://dx.doi.org/10.1007/978-3-319-40153-9.

Bartel, AP 2000, 'Measuring the employer's return on investments in training: evidence from the literature', *Industrial Relations: A Journal of Economy and Society*, vol. 39, no. 3, pp. 502–524, viewed 24 June 2017, <http://sis.ashesi.edu.gh/courseware/cms/file.php/57/aaLIBRARY/Training_Development/Bartel_-_employer_s_ROI_from_training_devpt.pdf>.

Bedi, A 2003, 'Student profiling: the Dreyfus model revisited', *Education for Primary Care*, vol. 14, no. 3, pp. 360–363, viewed 24 June 2017, <https://www.researchgate.net/publication/293527610>.

Benner, P 1984, *From novice to expert: excellence and power in clinical nursing practice*, Addison-Wesley, Palo Alto, http://dx.doi.org/10.1097/00000446-198412000-00025.

―――― 2001, *From novice to expert: excellence and power in clinical nursing practice*, Commemorative edn, Prentice Hall, London, http://dx.doi.org/10.1097/00000446-198412000-00025.

―――― 2004, 'Using the Dreyfus model of skill acquisition to describe and interpret skill acquisition and clinical judgment in nursing practice and education', *Bulletin of Science, Technology and Society*, vol. 24, no. 3, pp. 188–199, http://dx.doi.org/10.1177/0270467604265061.

Bersin, J 2013, 'The end of a job as we know it,' blog post, 30 January, viewed 24 June 2017, <http://blog.bersin.com/the-end-of-a-job-as-we-know-it/>.

Beta, G & Lidaka, A 2015, 'The aspect of proficiency in the theoretical overview of pedagogical practice of nurses', *Procedia-Social and Behavioral Sciences*, vol. 174, no. 2015, pp. 1957–1965, http://dx.doi.org/10.1016/j.sbspro.2015.01.861.

Binder, C 2017, 'What it really means to be accomplishment based', *Performance Improvement*, vol. 56, no. 4, pp. 20–25, http://dx.doi.org/10.1002/pfi.21702.

Bologa, R & Lupu, AR 2007, 'Accelerating the sharing of knowledge in order to speed up the process of enlarging software development teams - a practical example', in C Long, V Mladenov & Z Bojkovic (eds.), *Proceedings of the 6th WSEAS International Conference on Artificial Intelligence, Knowledge Engineering and Data Bases*, Corfu Island, Greece, 16-19 February, World Scientific and Engineering Academy and Society, pp. 90–95, viewed 24 June 2017, <http://www.wseas.us/e-library/conferences/2007corfu/papers/540-225.pdf>.

REFERENCES

Borman, WC & Motowidlo, SJ 1993, Expanding the criterion domain to include elements of contextual performance, in E Schmitt & W Borman (eds.), *Personnel Selection in Organisations*, Jossey-Bass, San Francisco, pp. 71–98.

_____(eds.) 1997, *Organisational citizenship behavior and contextual performance: a special issue of human performance*, Kindle edn, Psychology Press, London, http://dx.doi.org/10.4324/9781315799254.

Borton, G 2007, 'Managing productivity: measuring the business impact of employee proficiency and the employee job life cycle', *Management Services*, no. 7, pp. 28–33, viewed 24 June 2017, <http://www.ims-productivity.com/user/custom/journal/2007/autumn/IMSaut07pg28-33.pdf>.

Bower, M, Dalgarno, B, Kennedy, GE, Lee, MJ & Kenney, J 2015, 'Design and implementation factors in blended synchronous learning environments: outcomes from a cross-case analysis', *Computers & Education*, vol. 86, no. 8, pp. 1–17, http://dx.doi.org/10.1016/j.compedu.2015.03.006.

Boyatzis, R 1998, *Transforming qualitative information: thematic analysis and code development*, Sage, Thousand Oaks.

Bransford, JD, Brown, AL, Cocking, RR, Donovan, MS & Pellegrino, JW (eds.) 2004, *How people learn brain, mind, experience, and school*, Expanded edn, National Academy Press, Washington, D.C., http://dx.doi.org/10.17226/6160.

Braun, V & Clarke, V 2006, 'Using thematic analysis in psychology', *Qualitative Research in Psychology*, vol. 3, no. 2, pp. 77–101, http://dx.doi.org/10.1191/1478088706qp063oa.

_____ 2013, *Successful qualitative research: a practical guide for beginners*, Sage, Thousand Oaks, viewed 24 June 2017, <http://eprints.uwe.ac.uk/21156/3/SQR%2520Chap%25201%2520Research%2520Repository.pdf>.

Bruck, B 2007, 'Speed to proficiency: strategically using training to drive profitability,'', viewed 24 June 2017, <http://www.q2learning.com/docs/WP-S2P.pdf>.

_____ 2015, *Speed to proficiency: creating a sustainable competitive advantage*, CreateSpace, USA, viewed 24 June 2017, <http://www.readings.com.au/products/20647385/speed-to-proficiency-creating-a-sustainable-competitive-advantage>.

Campbell, JP 1990, Modeling the performance prediction problem in industrial and organisational psychology, in M Dunnette & L Hough (eds.), *Handbook of industrial and organisational psychology, Vol. 1*, Consulting Psychologists Press, Palo Alto, pp. 687–732.

―――― 1999, The definition and measurement of performance in the new age, in D Ilgen & E Pulakos (eds.), *The changing nature of performance: Implications for staffing, motivation, and development*, Jossey-Bass, San Francisco, pp. 399–429.

Campbell, JP, McCloy, RA, Oppler, SH & Sager, CE 1993, A theory of performance, in N Schmitt & W Borman (eds.), *Personnel selection in organisations*, Jossey-Bass, San Francisco, pp. 35–70.

Campbell, JP, McHenry, JJ & Wise, LL 1990, 'Modeling job performance in a population of jobs', *Personnel Psychology*, vol. 43, no. 2, pp. 313–575, http://dx.doi.org/10.1111/j.1744-6570.1990.tb01561.x.

Campbell, JP & Wiernik, BM 2015, 'The modeling and assessment of work performance', *Annual Review of Organisational Psychology and Organisational Behavior*, vol. 2, no. 1, pp. 47–74, http://dx.doi.org/10.1146/annurev-orgpsych-032414-111427.

Carpenter, MA, Monaco, SJ, O'Mara, FE & Teachout, MS 1989, *Time to Job Proficiency: A Preliminary Investigation of the Effects of Aptitude and Experience on Productive Capacity*, Report No. AFHRK-TP-88-17, Air Force Systems Command, Brooks Air Force Base, San Antonio, viewed 24 June 2017, <https://www.researchgate.net/publication/235105070>.

Charness, N & Tuffiash, M 2008, 'The role of expertise research and human factors in capturing, explaining, and producing superior performance', *Human Factors*, vol. 50, no. 3, pp. 427–32, http://dx.doi.org/10.1518/001872008X312206.

Chase, WG & Simon, HA 1973, 'Perception in chess', *Cognitive Psychology*, vol. 4, no. 1, pp. 55–81, http://dx.doi.org/10.1016/0010-0285(73)90004-2.

Chevalier, R 2003, 'Updating the behavior engineering model', *Performance Improvement*, vol. 42, no. 5, pp. 8–14, http://dx.doi.org/10.1002/pfi.4930420504.

―――― 2004, 'The link between learning and performance', *Performance Improvement*, vol. 43, no. 4, pp. 40–44, http://dx.doi.org/10.1002/pfi.4140430410.

REFERENCES

Chi, MT 2006, Two approaches to the study of experts' characteristics, in R Hoffman, N Charness & P Feltovich (eds.), *The Cambridge Handbook of Expertise and Expert Performance*, Cambridge University Press, New York, pp. 21–30, http://dx.doi.org/10.1017/CBO9780511816796.002.

Chi, MT, Glaser, R & Farr, M (eds.) 1988, *The nature of expertise*, Lawrence Erlbaum, Hillsdale, http://dx.doi.org/10.4324/9781315799681.

Chi, MT, Glaser, R & Rees, E 1981, *Expertise in Problem Solving*, Technical Report No. 5, University of Pittsburgh, Pittsburgh, viewed 24 June 2017, <http://www.dtic.mil/cgi-bin/GetTRDoc?AD=ADA100138>.

Chi, MT 1982, Expertise in problem solving, in R Sternberg (ed.), *Advances in psychology of human intelligence, Vol.1*, Erlbaum, Hillsdale, pp. 7-75, viewed 24 June 2017, <http://www.dtic.mil/cgi-bin/GetTRDoc?AD=ADA100138>.

Clark, RC 2008, *Building expertise: cognitive methods for training and performance improvement*, 3rd ed., Pfeiffer, San Francisco, http://dx.doi.org/10.1002/pfi.4140390213.

⎯⎯⎯⎯ 2013, 'Accelerating expertise with scenario-based e-learning', *The Watercooler Newsletter*, viewed 24 June 2017, <http://www.watercoolernewsletter.com/accelerating-expertise-with-scenario-based-elearning//#.Um0wNXD-ok>.

⎯⎯⎯⎯ & Mayer, RE 2013, *Scenario-based e-learning: evidence-based guidelines for online workforce learning*, Pfeiffer, San Francisco.

Clavarelli, A, Platte, WL & Powers, JJ 2009, 'Teaching and assessing complex skills in simulation with application to rifle marksmanship training', *Interservice Industry Training, Simulation and Education Conference (I/ITSEC)*, Orlando, 30 November - 2 December, National Training and Simulation Association (NTSA), Arlington, viewed 24 June 2017, <http://www.dtic.mil/cgi-bin/GetTRDoc?AD=ADA535072>.

Crichton, M & Flin, R 2004, 'Identifying and training non-technical skills of nuclear emergency response teams', *Annals of Nuclear Energy*, vol. 31, no. 12, pp. 1317–1330, http://dx.doi.org/doi:10.1016/j.anucene.2004.03.011.

Cross, J 2013, 'How to shorten time-to-proficiency', blog post, 23 February, viewed 24 Jun 2017, <http://www.internettime.com/2013/02/how-to-shorten-time-to-proficiency/>.

Dall'Alba, G & Sandberg, J 2006, 'Unveiling professional development: a critical review of stage models', *Review of Educational Research*, vol. 76, no. 3, pp. 383–412, http://dx.doi.org/10.3102/00346543076003383.

Day, J 2002, 'What is an expert?', *Radiography*, vol. 8, no. 2, pp. 63–70, viewed <http://www.blumehaiti.org/uploads/2/8/3/8/2838360/fallcelloday.pdf>.

Dean, PJ 2016, 'Tom Gilbert: engineering performance with or without training', *Performance Improvement*, vol. 55, no. 2, pp. 30–38, http://dx.doi.org/10.1002/pfi.21556.

Deloitte 2017, *Rewriting the rules for the digital age: 2017 Deloitte Global Human Capital Trends*, Deloitte University Press, UK, viewed 24 June 2017, <https://www2.deloitte.com/us/en/pages/human-capital/articles/introduction-human-capital-trends.html>.

DiBello, L & Missildine, W 2011, 'Future of immersive instructional design for the global knowledge economy: a case study of an IBM project management training in virtual worlds', *International Journal of Web Based Learning and Teaching Technologies*, vol. 6, no. 3, pp. 14–34, http://dx.doi.org/10.4018/jwltt,2011070102.

Dixon, V 2015, 'Time to proficiency: orientation and onboarding', viewed 24 June 2018, <https://talentculture.com/time-to-proficiency-orientation-and-onboarding/>.

Dörfler, V, Baracskai, Z & Velencei, J 2009, 'Knowledge levels: 3-D model of the levels of expertise', paper presented to The 68th Annual Meeting of the Academy of Management, Chicago, 7-11 August, viewed 24 June 2017, <http://www.viktordorfler.com/webdav/papers/KnowledgeLevels.pdf>.

Dreyfus, HL & Dreyfus, SE 1986, *Mind over machine: the power of human intuition and expertise in the era of the computer*, The Free Press, New York, http://dx.doi.org/10.1109/mex.1987.4307079.

———— 2004, 'The ethical implications of the five-stage skill-acquisition model', *Bulletin of Science, Technology and Society*, vol. 24, no. 3, pp. 251–264, http://dx.doi.org/10.1177/0270467604265023.

———— 2005, 'Peripheral vision: expertise in real world contexts', *Organisation Studies*, vol. 26, no. 5, pp. 779–792, http://dx.doi.org/10.1177/0170840605053102.

———— 2009, The relationship of theory and practice in the acquisition of skill, in P Benner, C Tanner & C Chesla (eds.), *Expertise in nursing practice: Caring, clinical judgment, and ethics*, Springer, New York, pp. 1–23,

REFERENCES

viewed 24 June 2017,
<http://lghttp.48653.nexcesscdn.net/80223CF/springer-static/media/samplechapters/9780826125446/9780826125446_chapter.pdf>
.

Dreyfus, SE 2004, 'The five-stage model of adult skill acquisition', *Bulletin of Science, Technology & Society*, vol. 24, no. 3, pp. 177–181, http://dx.doi.org/10.1177/0270467604264992.

Deutscher, C, Gürtler, O, Prinz, J & Weimar, D 2017, 'The payoff to consistency in performance', *Economic Inquiry*, vol. 55, no. 2, pp. 1091–1103, http://dx.doi.org/10.1111/ecin.12415.

Duguay, SM & Korbut, K a 2002, 'Designing a training program which delivers results quickly!', *Industrial and Commercial Training*, vol. 34, no. 6, pp. 223–228, http://dx.doi.org/10.1108/00197850210442458.

Dumas, A & Hanchane, S 2010, 'How does job-training increase firm performance? the case of morocco', *International Journal of Manpower*, vol. 31, no. 5, pp. 585–602, http://dx.doi.org/10.1108/01437721011066371.

Enos, MD, Kehrhahn, MT & Bell, A 2003, 'Informal learning and the transfer of learning: how managers develop proficiency', *Human Resource Development Quarterly*, vol. 14, no. 4, pp. 369–387, http://dx.doi.org/10.1002/hrdq.1074.

Eraut, M 1994, *Developing professional knowledge and competence*, Routledge, London, http://dx.doi.org/10.4324/9780203486016.

Ericsson, KA 2000, 'Expertise in interpreting: an expert-performance perspective', *Interpreting*, vol. 5, no. 2, pp. 187–220, http://dx.doi.org/10.1075/intp.5.2.08eri.

———— 2002, Attaining excellence through deliberate practice: insights from the study of expert performance, in M Ferrari (ed.), *The Pursuit of Excellence Through Education*, Lawrence Erlbaum, Mahwah, pp. 21–55, http://dx.doi.org/10.1002/9780470690048.ch1.

———— 2003, Development of elite performance and deliberate practice: an update from the perspective of the expert performance approach, in J Starkes & K Ericsson (eds.), *Expert Performance in Sports: Advances in Research on Sport Expertise*, Human Kinetics, Champaign, pp. 53–83, viewed 24 June 2017,
<http://drjj5hc4fteph.cloudfront.net/Articles/2003%20Starkes%20and%20Ericsson%20Chapt%203.pdf>.

_____ 2004, 'Deliberate practice and the acquisition and maintenance of expert performance in medicine and related domains', *Academic Medicine*, vol. 79, no. 10, pp. 70–81, http://dx.doi.org/10.1097/00001888-200410001-00022.

_____ 2006, The influence of experience and deliberate practice on the development of superior expert performance, in K Ericsson, N Charness, P Feltovich & R Hoffman (eds.), *The Cambridge Handbook of Expertise and Expert Performance*, Cambridge University Press, New York, pp. 683–704, http://dx.doi.org/10.1017/CBO9780511816796.038.

_____ 2007, 'Deliberate practice and the modifiability of body and mind: toward a science of the structure and acquisition of expert and elite performance', *International Journal of Sport Psychology*, vol. 38, no. 1, pp. 4–34, viewed 24 June 2017, <http://drjj5hc4fteph.cloudfront.net/Articles/2007 IJSP - Ericsson - Deliberate Practice target art.pdf>.

_____ 2008, 'Deliberate practice and acquisition of expert performance: a general overview', *Academic Emergency Medicine*, vol. 15, no. 11, pp. 988–94, http://dx.doi.org/10.1111/j.1553-2712.2008.00227.x.

_____ 2009a, 'Discovering deliberate practice activities that overcome plateaus and limits on improvement of performance', in A Willamon, S Pretty & R Buck (eds.), *International Symposium on Performance Science*, Auckland, 15-18 December, European Association of Conservatoires (AEC), Utrecht, The Netherlands, pp. 11–21, viewed 24 June 2017, <http://www.performancescience.org/ISPS2009/Proceedings/Rows/003Ericsson.pdf>.

_____ 2009b, Enhancing the development of professional performance: implications from the study of deliberate practice, in K Ericsson (ed.), *Development of professional expertise: Toward measurement of expert performance and design of optimal learning environments*, Cambridge University Press, New York, pp. 405–431, http://dx.doi.org/10.1017/cbo9780511609817.022.

_____ 2014, 'Why expert performance is special and cannot be extrapolated from studies of performance in the general population: a response to criticisms', *Intelligence*, vol. 45, no. 4, pp. 81–103, http://dx.doi.org/10.1016/j.intell.2013.12.001.

Ericsson, KA & Charness, N 1994, 'Expert performance: its structure and acquisition', *American Psychologist*, vol. 49, no. 8, pp. 725–747, http://dx.doi.org/10.1037/0003-066X.49.8.725.

REFERENCES

Ericsson, KA, Krampe, RTR, Tesch-romer, C, Ashworth, C, Carey, G, Grassia, J, Hastie, R, Heizmann, S, Kellogg, R, Levin, R, Lewis, C, Oliver, W, Poison, P, Rehder, R, Schlesinger, K, Schneider, V & Tesch-Römer, C 1993, 'The role of deliberate practice in the acquisition of expert performance', *Psychological Review*, vol. 100, no. 3, pp. 363–406, http://dx.doi.org/10.1037/0033-295X.100.3.363.

Ericsson, KA, Prietula, MJ & Cokely, ET 2007, 'The making of an expert', *Harvard Business Review*, vol. 85, nos. 7-8, pp. 114–121, 193, viewed 24 June 2017, <https://www.researchgate.net/publication/6196703>.

Ericsson, KA & Towne, TJ 2010, 'Expertise', *Wiley Interdisciplinary Reviews: Cognitive Science*, vol. 1, no. 3, pp. 404–416, http://dx.doi.org/10.1002/wcs.47.

Ericsson, KA & Ward, P 2007, 'Capturing the naturally occurring superior performance of experts in the laboratory: toward a science of expert and exceptional performance', *Current Directions in Psychological Science*, vol. 16, no. 6, pp. 346–350, http://dx.doi.org/10.1111/j.1467-8721.2007.00533.x.

Fadde, PJ 2007, 'Instructional design for advanced learners: training recognition skills to hasten expertise', *Educational Technology Research and Development*, vol. 57, no. 3, pp. 359–376, http://dx.doi.org/10.1007/s11423-007-9046-5.

―――― 2009a, Training complex psychomotor performance skills: a part-task approach, in K Silber & W Foshay (eds.), *Handbook of Training and Improving Workplace Performance, Volume I: Instructional Design and Training Delivery*, Pfeiffer, San Francisco, pp. 468–507, http://dx.doi.org/10.1002/9780470587089.ch14.

―――― 2009b, 'Training of expertise and expert performance', *Technology, Instructional, Cognition and Learning*, vol. 7, no. 2, pp. 77–81, viewed 24 June 2017, <http://web.coehs.siu.edu/Units/CI/Faculty/PFadde/Research/xbtintro.pdf>.

―――― 2009c, 'Expertise-based training: getting more learners over the bar in less time', *Technology, Instructional, Cognition and Learning*, vol. 7, no. 2, pp. 171–197, viewed 24 June 2017, <http://web.coehs.siu.edu/units/ci/faculty/pfadde/Research/xbttraining.pdf>.

―――― 2012, 'What's wrong with this picture? video-annotation with expert-model feedback as a method of accelerating novices' situation awareness', *The Interservice Industry Training, Simulation and Education Conference*

(I/ITSEC), London, 3-6 December, National Training and Simulation Association (NTSA), Arlington, viewed 24 June 2017, <http://www.peterfadde.com/Research/iitsec12.pdf>.

_____ 2013, 'Accelerating the acquisition of intuitive decision-making through expertise-based training (XBT)', paper presented to the The Interservice Industry Training, Simulation and Education Conference (I/ITSEC), Orlando, 2-5 December, National Training and Simulation Association (NTSA), Arlington, viewed 24 June 2017, <http://peterfadde.com/Research/iitsec13.pdf>.

_____ 2016, 'Instructional design for accelerated macrocognitive expertise in the baseball workplace', *Frontiers in Psychology*, vol. 7, no. 292, pp. 1–16, http://dx.doi.org/10.3389/fpsyg.2016.00292.

Fadde, PJ & Klein, G 2010, 'Deliberate performance: accelerating expertise in natural settings', *Performance Improvement*, vol. 49, no. 9, pp. 5–14, http://dx.doi.org/10.1002/pfi.

_____ 2012, 'Accelerating expertise using action learning activities', *Cognitive Technology*, vol. 17, no. 1, pp. 11–18, viewed 24 June 2017, <http://peterfadde.com/Research/cognitivetechnology12.pdf>.

Faneuff, RS, and Stone, BM, Curry, GL & Hageman, DC 1990, *Extending the Time to Proficiency Model for Simultaneous Application to Multiple Jobs*, Report No. AFHRL-TP-90-42, Air Force Systems Command Brooks Air Force Base, San Antonio, viewed 24 June 2017, <http://www.dtic.mil/docs/citations/ADA224759>.

Farrington-Darby, T & Wilson, JR 2006, 'The nature of expertise: a review', *Applied Ergonomics*, vol. 37, no. 1, pp. 17–32, http://dx.doi.org/10.1016/j.apergo.2005.09.001.

Fischer, A, Greiff, S & Funke, J 2011, 'The process of solving complex problems keywords', *The Journal of Problem Solving*, vol. 4, no. 1, pp. 19–42, http://dx.doi.org/10.7771/1932-6246.1118.

Fitt, PM & Posner, M 1967, *Learning and skilled performance in human performance*, Brock-Cole, Belmont.

Fred, CL 2002, *Breakaway: Deliver value to your customers—Fast!*, Jossey-Bass, San Francisco, viewed 24 June 2017, <http://www.wiley.com/WileyCDA/WileyTitle/productCd-0787961647.html>.

REFERENCES

Gander, SL 2006, 'Beyond mere competency: measuring proficiency with outcome proficiency indicator scales', *Performance Improvement*, vol. 45, no. 4, pp. 38–44, http://dx.doi.org/10.1002/pfi.2006.4930450409.

Ge, X & Hardré, PL 2010, 'Self-processes and learning environment as influences in the development of expertise in instructional design', *Learning Environments Research*, vol. 13, no. 1, pp. 23–41, http://dx.doi.org/10.1007/s10984-009-9064-9.

Gilbert, TF 2013, *Human Competence: Engineering Worthy Performance*, Tribute edn, Pfeiffer, San Francisco.

Glaser, R & Chi, MTH 1988, Overview, in M Chi, R Glaser & M Farr (eds.), *The nature of expertise*, Lawrence Erlbaum, Mahwah, pp. xv–xxviii.

Gordon, TJ 1994, The Delphi method, in J Glenn & T Gordon (eds.), *Futures research methodology - Version 3.0*, The Millennium Project, Washington, D.C., viewed 24 June 2017, <http://millennium-project.org/FRMv3_0/04-Delphi.pdf>.

Government Publishing Office 2013, *Pilot Certification and Qualification Requirements for Air Carrier*, No. 78, Government Publishing Office, USA.

Gratton, L 2016, 'Rethinking the manager's role', *MIT Sloan Management Review*, vol. 58, no. 1, p. 8, viewed 24 June 2017, <http://sloanreview.mit.edu/article/technology-and-the-end-of-management/>.

Grenier, RS & Kehrhahn, M 2008, 'Toward an integrated model of expertise redevelopment and its implications for hrd', *Human Resource Development Review*, vol. 7, no. 2, pp. 198–217, http://dx.doi.org/10.1177/1534484308316653.

Griffin, MA, Neal, A & Parker, SK 2007, 'A new model of work role performance: positive behavior in uncertain and interdependent contexts', *Academy of Management Journal*, vol. 50, no. 2, pp. 327–347, http://dx.doi.org/10.5465/amj.2007.24634438.

De Groot, A 1965, *Thought and choice in chess (translated from the Dutch original, 1946)*, Reprinted edn, G Baylor (ed.), Ishi Press, New York.

De Groot, A 1966, Perception and memory versus thought: some old ideas and recent findings, in B Kleinmuntz (ed.), *Problem solving*, John Wiley, New York, pp. 19–50.

Guskey, T 2009, 'Mastery learning,'", viewed 24 June 2017, <http://www.education.com/reference/article/mastery-learning/>.

Hayes, JR 1989, *The complete problem solver*, 2nd edn, Erlbaum, Hillsdale.

Hintze, NR 2008, 'First responder problem solving and decision making in today's asymmetrical environment', Naval Postgraduate School, Monterey, viewed 24 June 2017, <http://www.dtic.mil/cgi-bin/GetTRDoc?AD=ADA479926>.

Hoffman, RR 1998, How can expertise be defined? implications of research from cognitive psychology, in R Williams, W Faulkner & J Fleck (eds.), *Exploring expertise*, Palgrave Macmillan, Edinburgh, Scotland, pp. 81–100, http://dx.doi.org/10.1007/978-1-349-13693-3_4.

―――― 2012, *Expertise out of context*, Psychology Press, New York.

Hoffman, RR & Andrews, DH 2012, 'Cognition and cognitive technology for research on accelerated learning and developing expertise', *Cognitive Technology*, vol. 17, no. 1, pp. 5–6, viewed 24 June 2017, <http://cmapsinternal.ihmc.us/rid=1LM7CN14D-1335H6-1B3K/CogTech%20for%20Accelerated%20Learning-2013.pdf>.

Hoffman, RR, Andrews, DH & Feltovich, PJ 2012, 'What is 'accelerated learning'?', *Cognitive Technology*, vol. 17, no. 1, pp. 7–10.

Hoffman, RR, Andrews, DH, Fiore, SM, Goldberg, S, Andre, T, Freeman, J, Fletcher, JD & Klein, G 2010, 'Accelerated learning: prospects, issues and applications', *Proceedings of the Human Factors and Ergonomics Society 54th Annual Meeting*, San Francisco, 27 September - 1 October, Sage, Thousand Oaks, pp. 399–402, http://dx.doi.org/10.1177/154193121005400427.

Hoffman, RR, Feltovich, PJ, Fiore, SM & Klein, G 2010, *Accelerated Proficiency and Facilitated Retention: Recommendations Based on an Integration of Research and Findings from a Working Meeting*, Report No. AFRL-RH-AZ-TR-2011-0001, Air Force Research Laboratory, Mesa, http://dx.doi.org/10.21236/ada536308.

Hoffman, RR, Feltovich, PJ, Fiore, S, Klein, G & Moon, B 2008, *Program on Technology Innovation: Accelerating the Achievement of Mission-Critical Expertise: A Research Roadmap*, Report No. 1016710, Electric Power Research Institute (EPRI), Palo Alto, viewed 24 June 2017, <http://perigeantechnologies.com/publications/AcceleratingAchievementofExpertise.pdf>.

REFERENCES

Hoffman, RR, Feltovich, PJ, Fiore, SM, Klein, G & Ziebell, D 2009, 'Accelerated learning (?)', *IEEE Intelligent Systems*, vol. 24, no. 2, pp. 18–22, http://dx.doi.org/10.1109/MIS.2009.21.

Hoffman, RR, Ward, P, Feltovich, PJ, DiBello, L, Fiore, SM & Andrews, DH 2014, *Accelerated Expertise: Training for high proficiency in a complex world*, Expertise: Research and Applications Series, Psychology Press, New York, http://dx.doi.org/10.4324/9780203797327.

Houger, VP 2006, 'Trends of employee performance collaborative effort between managers and employees', *Performance Improvement*, vol. 45, no. 5, pp. 26–31, http://dx.doi.org/10.1002/pfi.2006.4930450508.

Hughes, C 2004, 'The supervisor's influence on workplace learning', *Studies in Continuing Education*, vol. 26, no. 2, pp. 275–287, http://dx.doi.org/10.1080/158037042000225254.

Huselid, MA & Becker, BE 2011, 'Bridging micro and macro domains: workforce differentiation and strategic human resource management', *Journal of Management*, vol. 37, no. 2, pp. 421–428, http://dx.doi.org/10.1177/0149206310373400.

Imel, S 2002, 'Accelerated learning in adult education and training and development', *Trends and Issue Alerts No. 33*, pp. 1–2, viewed 24 June 2017, <http://www.calpro-online.org/ERIC/docs/tia00101.pdf>.

Jacobs, RL 1997, "A taxonomy of employee development: toward an organizational culture of expertise," *Proceedings of the Academy of Human Resource Development*, Academy of Human Resource Development, Baton Rouge, pp. 278–283.

_____ 2001. Managing employee competence and human intelligence in global organisations. In F. Richter (ed.), *Maximizing Human Intelligence in Asia Business: The Sixth Generation Project*. Prentice-Hall, New York, pp. 44-54.

_____ 2003, *Structured on-the-job training: Unleashing employee expertise in the workplace*, 2nd edn, Berrett-Koehler, San Francisco.

_____ 2014, Structured on-the-job training, in R Poell, T Rocco & G Roth (eds.), *The Routledge Companion to Human Resource Development*, Routledge, Oxon, pp. 272–284.

Jacobs, RL & Bu-Rahmah, MJ 2012, 'Developing employee expertise through structured on-the-job training (S-OJT): an introduction to this training approach and the KNPC experience', *Industrial and Commercial Training*, vol. 44, no. 2, pp. 75–84, http://dx.doi.org/10.1108/00197851211202902.

Jacobs, R & Washington, C 2003, 'Employee development and organisational performance: a review of literature and directions for future research', *Human Resource Development International*, vol. 6, no. 3, pp. 343–354, http://dx.doi.org/10.1080/13678860110096211.

Jenkins, JT, Currie, A, Sala, S & Kennedy, RH 2016, 'A multi-modal approach to training in laparoscopic colorectal surgery accelerates proficiency gain', *Surgical Endoscopy*, vol. 30, no. 7, pp. 3007–3013, http://dx.doi.org/10.1007/s00464-015-4591-1.

Jung, E, Kim, M & Reigeluth, CM 2016, 'Learning in action: how competent professionals learn', *Performance Improvement Quarterly*, vol. 28, no. 4, pp. 55–69, http://dx.doi.org/10.1002/piq.21209.

Kanfer, R & Kantrowitz, TM 2002, Ability and non-ability predictors of job performance, in S. Sonnentag (ed.), *Psychological management of individual performance*, John Wiley, San Francisco, pp. 27–50, http://dx.doi.org/10.1002/0470013419.ch2.

Kang, S "Pil" 2017, 'What do hpt consultants do for performance analysis?', *TechTrends*, vol. 61, no. 1, pp. 32–45, http://dx.doi.org/10.1007/s11528-016-0129-1.

Karoly, LA 2007, *Forces Shaping the Future Us Workforce and Workplace: Implications for 21st Century Work*, Report No. CT-273, Rand Corporation, Santa Monica, viewed 24 June 2017, <http://www.rand.org/content/dam/rand/pubs/testimonies/2007/RAND_CT 273.pdf>.

Kaufman, SB & Kaufman, JC 2007, 'Ten years to expertise, many more to greatness: an investigation of modern writers', *The Journal of Creative Behavior*, vol. 41, no. 2, pp. 114–124, http://dx.doi.org/10.1002/j.2162-6057.2007.tb01284.x.

Khan, K & Ramachandran, S 2012, 'Conceptual framework for performance assessment: competency, competence and performance in the context of assessments in healthcare-deciphering the terminology', *Medical Teacher*, vol. 34, no. 11, pp. 920–928, http://dx.doi.org/10.3109/0142159X.2012.722707.

Khan, RAG, Khan, FA & Khan, MA 2011, 'Impact of training and development on organisational performance', *Global Journal of Management and*

REFERENCES

Business Research, vol. 11, no. 7, pp. 63–67, viewed 24 June 2017, <https://globaljournals.org/GJMBR_Volume11/8-Impact-of-Training-and-Development-on-Organisational-Performance.pdf>.

Kim, MK 2012, 'Theoretically grounded guidelines for assessing learning progress: cognitive changes in ill-structured complex problem-solving contexts', *Educational Technology Research and Development*, vol. 60, no. 4, pp. 601–622, http://dx.doi.org/10.1007/s11423-012-9247-4.

―――― 2015, 'Models of learning progress in solving complex problems: expertise development in teaching and learning', *Contemporary Educational Psychology*, vol. 42, no. 3, pp. 1–16, http://dx.doi.org/10.1016/j.cedpsych.2015.03.005.

Kirkman, MA 2013, 'Deliberate practice, domain-specific expertise, and implications for surgical education in current climes', *Journal of Surgical Education*, vol. 70, no. 3, pp. 309–317, http://dx.doi.org/10.1016/j.jsurg.2012.11.011.

Kirkpatrick, DL & Kirkpatrick, JD 2009, *Transferring Learning to Behavior: Using the Four Levels to Improve Performance*, Berrett-Koehler, Oakland.

Klein, GA & Baxter, HC 2009, Cognitive transformation theory: contrasting cognitive and behavioral learning, in D Schmorrow, J Cohn & D Nicholson (eds.), *The PSI handbook of virtual environment for training and education: Developments for the military and beyond, Volume 1, Education: Learning, requirements and metrics*, Praeger Security International, Santa Barbara, pp. 50–65, viewed 24 June 2017, <https://pdfs.semanticscholar.org/99f0/b9bdbce6432c3232fdeffeae0fddea7bcebd.pdf>.

Klein, GA & Borders, J 2016, 'The shadowbox approach to cognitive skills training an empirical evaluation', *Journal of Cognitive Engineering and Decision Making*, vol. 10, no. 3, pp. 268–280, http://dx.doi.org/10.1177/1555343416636515.

Koopmans, L, Bernaards, CM, Hildebrandt, VH, Schaufeli, WB, de Vet Henrica, C & van der Beek, AJ 2011, 'Conceptual frameworks of individual work performance: a systematic review', *Journal of Occupational and Environmental Medicine*, vol. 53, no. 8, pp. 856–866, http://dx.doi.org/10.1097/JOM.0b013e318226a763.

Korotov, K 2007, Accelerated development of organisational talent, in V Vaiman & C Vance (eds.), *Smart Talent Management: Building Knowledge*

Assets for Competitive Advantage, Dward Elgar, Cheltenham, pp. 139–157, http://dx.doi.org/10.4337/9781848442986.00015.

Kraiger, K 2014, 'Looking back and looking forward: trends in training and development research', *Human Resource Development Quarterly*, vol. 25, no. 4, pp. 401–408, http://dx.doi.org/10.1002/hrdq.21203.

Kraiger, K, Passmore, J & Rebelo, N 2014, The psychology of training, development, and performance improvement, in K Kraiger, J Passmore, N Santos & S Malvezzi (eds.), *The Wiley Blackwell Handbook of the Psychology of Training, Development, and Performance Improvement*, John Wiley, San Francisco, pp. 535–544, http://dx.doi.org/10.1002/9781118736982.ch1.

Kuchenbrod, R 2016, 'Accelerating expertise to facilitate decision making in high-risk professions using the DACUM system', PhD thesis, Eastern Illinois University, Charleston, viewed 24 June 2017, <http://thekeep.eiu.edu/cgi/viewcontent.cgi?article=3462&context=theses>.

Lajoie, SP 2003, 'Transitions and trajectories for studies of expertise', *Educational Researcher*, vol. 32, no. 8, pp. 21–25, http://dx.doi.org/10.3102/0013189X032008021.

Langan-Fox, J, Armstrong, K, Balvin, N & Anglim, J 2002, 'Process in skill acquisition: motivation, interruptions, memory, affective states, and metacognition', *Australian Psychologist*, vol. 37, no. 2, pp. 104–117, http://dx.doi.org/10.1080/00050060210001706746.

Langerak, F, Hultink, EJ & Griffin, A 2008, 'Exploring mediating and moderating influences on the links among cycle time, proficiency in entry timing, and new product profitability', *Journal of Product Innovation Management*, vol. 25, no. 4, pp. 370–385, http://dx.doi.org/10.1111/j.1540-5885.2008.00307.x.

Lee, PWY 2011, 'Structured proficiency based progression phacoemulsification training curriculum using virtual reality simulator technology', Masters thesis, Royal College of Surgeons in Ireland, Dublin, Ireland, viewed 24 June 2017, <http://epubs.rcsi.ie/cgi/viewcontent.cgi?article=1007&context=mchresthes es>.

Levy, F 2010, *How Technology Changes Demands for Human Skills*, Working Paper No. 45, OECD Publishing, Paris, France, http://dx.doi.org/10.1787/5kmhds6czqzq-en.

REFERENCES

Li, X, Wang, J & Ferguson, MK 2014, 'Competence versus mastery: the time course for developing proficiency in video-assisted thoracoscopic lobectomy', *The Journal of Thoracic and Cardiovascular Surgery*, vol. 147, no. 4, pp. 1150–4, http://dx.doi.org/10.1016/j.jtcvs.2013.11.036.

Lincoln, YS & Guba, EG 1985, *Naturalistic inquiry*, Sage, Newbury Park.

LinkedIn 2017, *2017 Workplace Learning Report: How Modern L&D Professionals Are Tackling Top Challenges*, LinkedIn Solutions, Sunnyvale, viewed 24 June 2017, <http://www.linkedin.com>.

Liu, X & Batt, R 2007, 'The economic pay-offs to informal training: evidence from routine service work', *Industrial and Labor Relations Review*, vol. 61, no. 1, pp. 75–89, http://dx.doi.org/10.1177/001979390706100104.

Lynn, GS, Skov, RB & Abel, KD 1999, 'Practices that support team learning and their impact on speed to market and new product success', *Journal of Product Innovation Management*, vol. 16, no. 5, pp. 439–454, http://dx.doi.org/10.1111/1540-5885.1650439.

Macmillan, PJ 2015, 'Thinking like an expert lawyer: measuring specialist legal expertise through think-aloud problem solving and verbal protocol analysis', PhD thesis, Bond University, Robina, Australia, viewed 24 June 2017, <http://epublications.bond.edu.au/cgi/viewcontent.cgi?article=1167&context=theses>.

Marker, A, Villachica, SW, Stepich, D, Allen, D & Stanton, L 2014, 'An updated framework for human performance improvement in the workplace: the spiral hpi framework', *Performance Improvement*, vol. 53, no. 1, pp. 10–23, http://dx.doi.org/10.1002/pfi.21389.

Marks, A, Richards, J, Hagemann, V, Kluge, A & Ritzmann, S 2012, 'Flexibility under complexity: work contexts, task profiles and team processes of high responsibility teams', *Employee Relations*, vol. 34, no. 3, pp. 322–338, http://dx.doi.org/10.1108/01425451211217734.

Mason, J 2002, *Qualitative researching*, 2nd edn, Sage, Thousand Oaks.

Merriam, SB & Tisdell, EJ 2016, *Qualitative research: a guide to design and implementation*, 4th edn, Jossey-Bass, San Francisco.

Miles, MB & Huberman, AM 1994, *Qualitative Data Analysis: An Expanded Sourcebook*, 2nd edn, Sage, Thousand Oaks.

Miles, MB, Huberman, AM & Saldana, J 2014, *Qualitative Data Analysis: A Methods Sourcebook*, 3rd edn, Sage, Thousand Oaks.

Millington, R 2018, 10.10: Measuring time-to-full productivity, in *How to Calculate the ROI of online Communities*, FeverBee Ltd, London, viewed 24 October 2018, <https://www.feverbee.com/roi/measuring-time-to-full-productivity/>.

Moon, YK, Kim, EJ & You, Y-M 2013, 'Study on expertise development process based on Arête, *International Journal of Information and Education Technology*, vol. 3, no. 2, pp. 226–230, http://dx.doi.org/10.7763/IJIET.2013.V3.269.

Motowidlo, SJ, Borman, WC & Schmit, MJ 1997, 'A theory of individual differences in task and contextual performance', *Human Performance*, vol. 10, no. 2, pp. 71–83, http://dx.doi.org/10.1207/s15327043hup1002_1.

Motowidlo, SJ & Van Scotter, JR 1994, 'Evidence that task performance should be distinguished from contextual performance', *Journal of Applied Psychology*, vol. 79, no. 4, pp. 475-480, http://dx.doi.org/10.1037//0021-9010.79.4.475.

Nagel, D 2011, 'Beyond seat time: advancing proficiency-based learning', *The Journal: Transforming Education*, viewed 24 June 2017, <https://thejournal.com/articles/2011/08/10/beyond-seat-time-advancing-proficiency-based-learning.aspx>.

Patchan, MM, Schunn, CD, Sieg, W & McLaughlin, D 2015, 'The effect of blended instruction on accelerated learning', *Technology, Pedagogy and Education*, vol. 25, no. 3, pp. 1–18, http://dx.doi.org/10.1080/1475939X.2015.1013977.

Peña, A 2010, 'The Dreyfus model of clinical problem-solving skills acquisition: a critical perspective', *Medical Education Online*, vol. 15, no. 1, art. 4856, pp. 1-11, http://dx.doi.org/10.3402/meo.v15i0.4846.

Pershing, JA (ed.) 2006, *Handbook of human performance technology: principles, practices, and potential*, 3rd edn, Pfeiffer, San Francisco.

Phillips, JJ 2012, *Return on investment in training and performance improvement programs*, Routledge, New York.

Pinder, CC & Schroeder, KG 1987, 'Time to proficiency following job transfers', *Academy of Management Journal*, vol. 30, no. 2, pp. 336–353, http://dx.doi.org/10.2307/256278.

REFERENCES

Pollock, RV, Wick, CW & Jefferson, A 2015, *The six disciplines of breakthrough learning: how to turn training and development into business results*, 3rd edn, John Wiley, San Francisco.

Quartey, SH 2012, 'Effect of employee training on the perceived organisational performance: a case study of the print-media industry in ghana', *Human Resource Management (HRM)*, vol. 4, no. 15, viewed 24 June 2017, <https://www.academia.edu/6817560/>.

Radler, D & Bocianu, I 2017, 'Accelerated teaching and learning: roles and challenges for learners and tutors', *The International Scientific Conference eLearning and Software for Education*, Bucharest, 27-28 April, ProQuest, Ann Arbor, pp. 601–608, http://dx.doi.org/10.12753/2066-026X-17-170.

Ramsburg, L 2010, 'An initial investigation of the applicability of the Dreyfus skill acquisition model to the professional development of nurse educators', PhD thesis, Marshall University Graduate College, Huntington, viewed 24 June 2017, <http://mds.marshall.edu/cgi/viewcontent.cgi?article=1371&context=etd>.

Rosenbaum, S 2018, *Up to Speed: Secrets of Reducing Time to Proficiency*, BookBaby, US.

Rosenbaum, S 2014, How we bring employees up to speed in record time using leaning path methodology, in R Pollock, C Wick & A Jefferson (eds.), *The field guide to the 6Ds*, Wiley & Sons, San Francisco, CA, pp. 345–351.

Rosenbaum, S & Pollock, R 2015, 'Creating a conducive talent development and learning culture', paper presented to the ATD International Conference and Exposition, Orlando, FL, 17-23 May.

Rosenbaum, S & Williams, J 2004, *Learning paths: increase profits by reducing the time it takes employees to get up to speed*, Jossey-Bass, San Francisco, viewed 24 June 2017, <http://www.wiley.com/WileyCDA/WileyTitle/productCd-0787975346.html>.

Rosenthal, ME, Castellvi, AO, Goova, MT, Hollett, LA, Dale, J & Scott, DJ 2009, 'Pretraining on southwestern stations dcreases training time and cost for proficiency-based fundamentals of laparoscopic surgery training', *Journal of the American College of Surgeons*, vol. 209, no. 5, pp. 626–631, http://dx.doi.org/10.1016/j.jamcollsurg.2009.07.013.

Roth, R 2009, 'Acquiring and maintaining expert ability', [Unpublished Manuscript], viewed 24 June 2017,

<http://www.r2research.com/Research_files/ExpertAbility_Roth_2009.pdf>

Saks, A, Haccoun, R & Belcourt, M 2010, *Managing performance through training and development*, 5th ed., Nelson Education, Canada, viewed 24 June 2017, <https://www.amazon.com/Managing-Performance-Through-Training-Development/dp/0176507337>.

Schmid, U, Ragni, M, Gonzalez, C & Funke, J 2011, 'The challenge of complexity for cognitive systems', *Cognitive Systems Research*, vol. 12, no. 3-4, pp. 211–218, http://dx.doi.org/10.1016/j.cogsys.2010.12.007.

Schraagen, JM 1993, 'How experts solve a novel problem in experimental design', *Cognitive Science*, vol. 17, no. 2, pp. 285–309, http://dx.doi.org/10.1207/s15516709cog1702_4.

Schreiber, BT, Bennett Jr, W, Colegrove, CM, Portrey, AM, Greschke, DA & Bell, HH 2009, Evaluating pilot performance, in K Ericsson (ed.), *Development of professional expertise*, Cambridge University Press, New York, pp. 247–270, http://dx.doi.org/10.1017/cbo9780511609817.014.

Scobey, BW 2006, 'The journey to expertise: pathways to expert knowledge traveled by Texas juvenile probation officers', PhD thesis, Texas State University, San Marcos, viewed 24 June 2017, <https://digital.library.txstate.edu/bitstream/handle/10877/4267/fulltext.pdf?sequence=1>.

Shanteau, J 2015, 'Why task domains (still) matter for understanding expertise', *Journal of Applied Research in Memory and Cognition*, vol. 4, no. 3, pp. 169–175, http://dx.doi.org/10.1016/j.jarmac.2015.07.0032211-3681.

Shuell, TJ 1986, 'Individual differences: changing conceptions in research and practice', *American Journal of Education*, vol. 94, no. 3, pp. 356–377, http://dx.doi.org/10.1086/443854.

Simonton, DK 1997, 'Creative productivity: a predictive and explanatory model of career trajectories and landmarks.', *Psychological Review*, vol. 104, no. 1, pp. 66-89, viewed 24 June 2017, <https://pdfs.semanticscholar.org/abb5/02a8b01b50790a44cf5438f01f9f5ac9bf42.pdf>.

Soderstrom, NC & Bjork, RA 2015, 'Learning versus performance: an integrative review', *Perspectives on Psychological Science*, vol. 10, no. 2, pp. 176–199, http://dx.doi.org/10.1177/1745691615569000.

REFERENCES

Sonnentag, S & Frese, M 2002, Performance concepts and performance theory, in S Sonnentag (ed.), *Psychological management of individual performance*, John Wiley, New York, pp. 3–25, http://dx.doi.org/10.1002/0470013419.ch1.

Spiro, RJ, Collins, BP, Thota, JJ & Feltovich, PJ 2003, 'Cognitive flexibility theory: hypermedia for complex learning, adaptive knowledge application, and experience acceleration', *Educational Technology*, vol. 43, no. 5, pp. 5–10, viewed 24 June 2017, <https://eric.ed.gov/?id=EJ675158>.

Spiro, RJ & Jehng, J-C 1990, Cognitive flexibility and hypertext: theory and technology for the nonlinear and multidimensional traversal of complex subject matter, in D Nix & R Spiro (eds.), *Cognition, education, and multimedia: Exploring ideas in high technology*, Erlbaum, Hilldale, pp. 163–205.

Stake, RE 2006, *Multiple case study analysis*, The Guilford Press, New York, viewed 24 June 2017, <http://www.guilford.com/books/Multiple-Case-Study-Analysis/Robert-Stake/9781593852481>.

Sternberg, RJ 1999, 'Intelligence as developing expertise.', *Contemporary Educational Psychology*, vol. 24, no. 4, pp. 359–375, http://dx.doi.org/10.1006/ceps.1998.0998.

Stolovitch, HD 2000, 'Human performance technology: research and theory to practice', *Performance Improvement*, vol. 39, no. 4, pp. 7–16, http://dx.doi.org/10.1002/pfi.4140390407.

Stolovitch, HD & Keeps, EJ 1999, What is performance technology?, in H Stolovitch & E Keeps (eds.), *Handbook of human performance technology. Improving individual and organisational performance worldwide.*, Jossey-Bass/Pfeiffer, San Francisco, pp. 3–23.

Sudnickas, T 2016, 'Different levels of performance evaluation-individual versus organisational', *Viesoji Politika Ir Administravimas*, vol. 15, no. 2, http://dx.doi.org/10.13165/VPA-16-15-2-01.

Sullivan, ME, Yates, KA, Inaba, K, Lam, L & Clark, RE 2014, 'The use of cognitive task analysis to reveal the instructional limitations of experts in the teaching of procedural skills', *Academic Medicine*, vol. 89, no. 5, pp. 811–816, http://dx.doi.org/10.1097/ACM.0000000000000224.

Swanson, RA & Holton, EF 2001, *Foundations of human resource development*, Berrett-Koehler, Oakland, viewed 24 June 2017,

<https://www.bkconnection.com/static/Foundations_of_Human_Resource_Development_EXCERPT.pdf>.

Teodorescu, T 2006, 'Competence versus competency: what is the difference?', *Performance Improvement*, vol. 45, no. 10, pp. 27–30, http://dx.doi.org/10.1002/pfi.027.

Thompson, KS 2017, Training's impact on time-to-proficiency for new bankers in a financial services organisation, in S Frasard & P Frederick (eds.), *Training Initiatives and Strategies for the Modern Workforce*, IGI Global, Hershey, pp. 169–185, http://dx.doi.org/10.4018/978-1-5225-1808-2.ch009.

Thomson Reuters 2012, *Thomson Reuters Business Classification (TRBC)*, Thomson Reuter, New York, viewed 24 June 2017, <http://financial.thomsonreuters.com/en/products/data-analytics/market-data/indices/trbc-indices.html>.

Van Tiem, D, Moseley, JL & Dessinger, JC 2012, *Fundamentals of performance improvement: optimizing results through people, process, and organisations*, 3rd edn, Pfeiffer, San Francisco.

Training Magazine 2016, '2016 training industry report', *Training Magazine*, vol. 53, no. 6, pp. 28–41, viewed 24 June 2017, <https://trainingmag.com/sites/default/files/images/Training_Industry_Report_2016.pdf>.

Trekles, AM & Sims, R 2013, 'Designing instruction for speed: qualitative insights into instructional design for accelerated online graduate coursework', *Online Journal of Distance Learning Administration*, vol. 16, no. 3, viewed 24 June 2017, <http://www.westga.edu/~distance/ojdla/winter164/trekles_sims164.html>.

Turner, JR & Müller, R 2003, 'On the nature of the project as a temporary organisation', *International Journal of Project Management*, vol. 21, no. 1, pp. 1–8, http://dx.doi.org/10.1016/s0263-7863(02)00020-0.

Viswesvaran, C 1993, *Modeling Job Performance: Is There a General Factor?*, University of Iowa, Iowa, viewed 24 June 2017, <http://www.dtic.mil/dtic/tr/fulltext/u2/a294282.pdf>.

Viswesvaran, C & Ones, DS 2000, 'Perspectives on models of job performance', *International Journal of Selection and Assessment*, vol. 8, no. 4, pp. 216–226, viewed 24 June 2017, <https://www.researchgate.net/profile/Deniz_Ones/publication/229645528>.

REFERENCES

Vohra, V 2014, 'Using the multiple case study design to decipher contextual leadership behaviors in Indian organisations', *Electronic Journal of Business Research Methods*, vol. 12, no. 1, pp. 54–65, viewed 24 June 2017, <http://www.ejbrm.com/issue/download.html?idArticle=334>.

Wallace, GW 2006, Modeling mastery performance and systematically deriving the enablers for performance improvement, in J Pershing (ed.), *Handbook of human performance technology: Principles, practices, and potential*, Pfeiffer, San Francisco, viewed 24 June 2017, <http://widyo.staff.gunadarma.ac.id/Downloads/files/20372/HANDBOOK+OF+HPT_THIRD+EDITION.pdf#page=284>.

Ward, P, Hodges, NJ, Starkes, JL & Williams, AM 2007, 'The road to excellence: deliberate practice and the development of expertise', *High Ability Studies*, vol. 18, no. 2, pp. 119–153, http://dx.doi.org/10.1080/13598130701709715.

Van de Wiel, MWJ & Van den Bossche, P 2013, 'Deliberate practice in medicine: the motivation to engage in work-related learning and its contribution to expertise', *Vocations and Learning*, vol. 6, no. 1, pp. 135–158, http://dx.doi.org/10.1007/s12186-012-9085-x.

Wilcox, V, Trus, T, Salas, N, Martinez, J & Dunkin, BJ 2014, 'A proficiency-based skills training curriculum for the sages surgical training for endoscopic proficiency (step) program', *Journal of Surgical Education*, vol. 71, no. 3, pp. 282–288, http://dx.doi.org/10.1016/j.jsurg.2013.10.004.

Wray, A & Wallace, M 2011, 'Accelerating the development of expertise: a step-change in social science research capacity building', *British Journal of Educational Studies*, vol. 59, no. 3, pp. 241–264, http://dx.doi.org/10.1080/00071005.2011.599790.

Wright, PM & McMahan, GC 2011, 'Exploring human capital: putting 'human' back into strategic human resource management', *Human Resource Management Journal*, vol. 21, no. 2, pp. 93–104, http://dx.doi.org/10.1111/j.1748-8583.2010.00165.x.

Yin, RK 2014, *Case study research: design and methods*, 5th edn, Sage, Thousand Oaks.

INDEX

10 years 86, 112, 123-124, 129-130, 132, 134, 138, 152, 191, 207
10,000 hours 86, 123, 191
10-year rule 123

A
ability 42-43, 51, 54, 62, 68, 72, 77-78, 80, 83, 93, 162, 164, 171, 181, 219
academic 14, 49, 77, 95, 99, 116
accelerate 3-7, 11-14, 32, 34, 59, 67, 79, 87, 93, 95, 98-103, 105, 107-113, 115, 117, 119-120, 124, 128, 159-160, 168, 170-171, 177, 181, 183, 186, 193-194, 200, 226-227, 229
accelerate the TTP 11-12, 170
accelerated expertise 12
accelerated learning 108-109, 120
accelerated proficiency 3, 6-7, 11-13, 32, 34, 59, 87, 93, 95, 99-103, 107-111, 115, 119-120, 160, 177, 226
accelerating expertise 108, 112
accelerating learning 108, 119
accelerating training 108
accelerating TTP 101, 112, 229

acceleration of proficiency 5, 102, 107
acceptable level of performance 96
accomplishment 38-40, 73
achieve 4, 12, 45-47, 60-61, 63, 66, 69, 71, 74, 80, 82, 84, 87, 89, 93, 95-96, 99, 101-102, 105-106, 109-110, 114-115, 118, 123-124, 159-160, 174-175, 187, 191, 195, 197, 203, 215-216, 227
achievement of proficiency 159
acquire 3-4, 45, 47-49, 51-52, 55-58, 68, 79, 83-84, 86, 96, 99-100, 102, 117-119, 123, 127-128, 130, 159, 201, 205
aerospace 20, 26, 140, 149
analysis 21, 25-27, 29-33, 40, 47, 53, 60, 71, 74, 76, 106-107, 116, 125-126, 131-132, 135, 139-140, 142, 147, 160, 177
analysts 25, 27, 128, 147, 151, 197, 205
analytical 7, 25, 30-31, 53-55, 123, 125, 129-130, 147, 167, 197, 219
analytics 120, 154
assignments 169

INDEX

attain 51, 57, 61, 69-70, 80, 84, 97, 106, 109, 111, 114, 118, 123, 130, 191, 214, 219-220
attitude 78-80
attrition 94, 160-161, 170, 175, 181
automatic 56, 186
automaticity 47-48, 84
automobile 19-20, 27, 135, 138, 151, 205
aviators 94
avionics 94

B

baseline 105, 120, 147, 154-155, 193-195, 226
baseline TTP 105, 120, 147
beginner 48, 54, 159
behavior 38-44, 50, 64-65, 68, 73-74, 76-78, 80, 107, 114, 117-118
behavioral performance 38, 65
benchmark 74, 120
benefits 5, 7-8, 13, 26, 34, 150, 160, 169, 173-174, 189, 191, 202, 210-219, 221-222, 225, 227-229
best practices 34
biochemistry 128
biochemists 25, 148, 198, 220
biotechnology 20, 26, 128, 136, 140, 149-150, 159, 175, 201, 220
bounded project case 18, 29-30
business 3-8, 11-14, 18-19, 21-23, 26-34, 37, 39, 41, 44-46, 57, 65-75, 77-78, 80, 82, 87-89, 93, 95-98, 101-106, 108-111, 114-118, 125-127, 130, 132-135, 137-138, 140, 144-146, 149, 152-153, 155, 160-169, 173-176, 178-179, 181-182, 185-186, 191-193, 195, 201, 207, 210-212, 215, 217-222, 225-229
business benefits 5, 8, 13, 34, 173, 210-211, 215, 217-219, 221-222, 225, 227, 229
business drivers 5, 34, 161, 178-179, 181, 186, 225-227, 229
business gains 8, 211-212, 218-222, 227
business metrics 29, 66-68, 71, 78, 80, 97, 179, 186, 226
business practices 34, 226
business results 72-73, 75, 108, 114

C

capability 62, 83, 85, 162, 164-165, 174, 186
capacity 211, 213
capital 97-98
career 63, 95, 99-100, 153, 169
categorization 60, 135
categorized 18, 125-126, 131
certification 59, 146, 193, 199-200, 204-205
certified 124, 146, 168
chain reaction 186, 229
challenge 3, 6, 11-12, 14, 29, 31, 46, 51, 59, 65, 77, 87, 93, 101, 117, 154, 160, 162, 166-167, 170, 180, 182, 186, 218, 221, 226, 229
characteristics 7, 31, 37, 46, 52-53, 57, 60-61, 65, 70, 75, 77, 81-82, 99, 103, 107
characterize 43-44, 46, 50, 57, 69, 84-85, 95, 102, 125, 169
chemical 19-20, 27, 72, 134-135, 138, 151, 183-184, 204, 221
chemist 72-73, 115
classification 19, 22, 62, 126, 133-135, 178, 218
classified 19, 22, 137
classroom 6, 129, 183

clinical 26, 49, 53, 55, 150, 167, 203
closed-loop system 8, 225-227, 229
coach 85, 109
coaching 15, 27, 184
cognitive 42, 64, 85-86, 102, 159
colleagues 12, 94, 96
command 26, 86, 149, 171, 201
commanders 170
communicate 42, 144
communication 14-15, 20, 25-26, 39, 94, 124, 134, 136, 141, 143, 147, 149-150, 182, 201, 209, 215, 220
community 165
company 3, 67, 90, 95, 116, 125, 142, 145-146, 161, 163-168, 170-177, 180-184, 208, 214, 218
comparable 29, 193, 195
comparative 33, 125, 142, 193
compared 30-31, 33, 86, 102, 111, 120, 144, 193-195, 199-200, 202, 214
comparing 29, 54, 76, 85, 123, 194
comparison 31, 73-76, 194
compelling 95, 126, 145
compete 165
competence 7, 55, 59, 61-63, 66, 77, 79-82, 87, 93, 95-96, 98-99, 104, 113, 201
competency 44, 77-78, 81, 96-97, 117, 162, 164, 171
competent 48, 54, 63, 81, 84, 113, 180
competition 3, 87, 93, 164, 166, 178, 219
competitive 5, 37, 98, 164-165, 177-178, 187
competitiveness 7, 40, 160-161, 164-166, 168, 170, 178-180, 182, 184, 186-187, 211-212, 226
competitors 3, 164
complete 31, 43, 49, 76, 96, 115, 179
completely 4, 61, 68, 177
completeness 18, 29
complex 3-4, 20, 25-27, 49, 55, 64, 76, 78, 93, 127, 129-132, 139-143, 145-147, 149-152, 159, 168-169, 172, 175, 185, 197-198, 200, 202-206, 208-210, 214, 217-221, 226
complex tasks 49, 55
complexity 7, 18, 21-22, 30-31, 117-118, 125, 129-131, 160, 169-170
compliance 213
components 20, 27, 52, 85, 136, 140, 150-151
composition 77, 137
comprehensive 6, 12-13, 106, 125, 160
compressing 113
computer 15, 26-27, 74, 111, 143, 149-150, 163, 179, 200, 203, 209, 214, 216, 220
conceived 95
concentration 85
concept 3, 5-7, 12, 32-34, 41, 47, 50-51, 54, 56, 58-60, 64, 66, 79, 86, 95, 97, 99, 101-102, 106, 108, 110, 170
conceptual 32, 37, 225, 228
conceptualized 12, 109
concern 57, 70, 81, 102, 162, 164
conditions 78, 102, 228
conducted 4-6, 11, 29, 31, 33, 44-45, 65, 95, 125, 160, 168, 174, 180, 216
confidence 71, 73, 153, 169, 219
confirmed 86
confronting 159
confuse 108, 119
connections 109

INDEX

conscious 100, 161-162
consensus 32, 165
consequence 37, 117, 162, 169
consequential 174
consistency 69-70, 82
consistent 29, 45, 69-70, 80, 107-108, 124, 198
consistent results 124
consistently 41, 45, 69-70, 72, 80, 82, 88, 90, 109, 112, 118, 159
console 25-27, 128, 148-149, 198-200, 220
consolidation 51
constant 31, 51, 84-85, 160, 162
constituent 70
constrained 33
constraining 77
construct 7, 12, 59, 64, 77, 80-82, 84, 108, 116
construction 27, 143, 151, 163, 206, 209, 221
consultant 14, 16, 192
consulting 15, 20, 27, 129, 140, 151
consumer 19, 25-27, 133, 135, 138
consuming 183
contended 51, 59, 67, 87, 102
content 107-109, 115
context 3, 11, 14, 31, 34, 41-42, 48-49, 52-55, 93-94, 109, 124-126, 131, 137, 153, 185, 193-195, 208, 221-222, 226, 229
contextual 7, 13, 18-19, 30-31, 37, 53-56, 65, 222
contextual variables 18-19, 30-31
continuous 50, 52, 114, 165
continuum 47-48, 59-61, 82
contract 146, 166
contradictory 39
contrary 69, 77, 177
contrast 79
contribute 38, 96, 109, 117, 153, 229

contribution 39, 95, 109
contributors 168
control 86, 105, 179-180
controlled performance 71, 76
controlling 25-27, 108, 148-149, 198-200, 220
conversation 27, 108
convert 68
convey 50, 80, 82, 89, 112, 115, 144
convince 13
coordination 226
corporate 27, 151, 205
corporation 26, 148, 175, 199
correct 43, 50, 66, 85, 227
correlation 131
corresponding 50, 192, 217
cost 3, 7-8, 73, 94, 161, 163, 169, 173-178, 180, 183-187, 211, 213, 216-222, 226-227
cost or financial implications 7, 161, 173, 175-177, 183
cost savings 8, 185, 187, 211, 216-219, 222, 227
costing 153, 162-163
course 68, 146, 165, 191-192, 211, 213, 221
covers 33-34
create 11, 64, 102
created 59, 77, 79, 164, 181, 185
creating 5, 32, 103, 183
credibility 11, 33
crew 181
criteria 14, 47, 73, 75, 104
critical 3, 7, 11, 18, 20, 24, 40, 46, 56, 85, 87, 93, 98, 105, 107, 114, 119, 131-132, 138, 162, 164-165, 174, 185
criticized 62, 124
cross-case analysis 29, 31
cultural 116
current 4, 15-16, 64, 75, 85, 146, 155, 180, 226

curriculum 81, 114
curve 100, 102, 108, 155
customer 3, 5, 20, 25-27, 65, 67-68, 71-76, 78, 97, 112, 116, 129, 138-139, 141-142, 145-152, 161, 163, 165-168, 170, 174-175, 178-179, 197-200, 203-206, 208-209, 211-212, 214, 216-221
cybersecurity 25, 128, 134, 147, 197
cyberterrorism 26, 149, 201
cycle 102, 112, 133, 154-155, 160, 165, 183-184, 211-212, 221
cyclical 19, 25-27, 133, 135, 138

D
data 13, 21, 26, 29-30, 32-33, 74, 76, 105, 120, 125-126, 129-130, 132-133, 140, 150, 154, 167, 194, 203, 226
data analysis 30, 32-33, 74
database 14, 26, 40, 128, 150, 167, 203
decision 39, 43, 52-55, 177, 180, 205, 226, 229
decision making 46
defense 20, 26, 140, 149, 173
deficiencies 7, 161, 166-168, 170-172, 177-179, 181, 183-184, 186, 226
deficiency related 186
defined 18, 38, 40-42, 44-45, 47, 49-50, 58, 60, 65-68, 70-71, 73, 76, 80, 83, 86, 89, 93-94, 97, 99, 119, 154, 161, 211
definition 41, 45, 55, 57, 63, 78, 82, 89, 95, 103-107, 119, 154, 161, 211
definition of proficiency 89, 103-106, 119
deliberate 55, 83-87, 100, 123-124, 159

deliberate practice 83, 85-87, 123-124, 159
deliberately 84
deliberation 43
deliverables 67, 69, 82, 88
Delphi method 32
demonstrate 40-41, 77
demonstrating 39, 49, 68, 73, 78, 89, 120, 159
describe 7, 32, 37, 44-45, 56, 62, 65, 69, 74, 81, 84, 95, 102, 107, 119, 126, 225
description 29, 38, 53, 56-57
design 21, 25-27, 54, 58, 115-116, 118, 128, 131-132, 140-141, 145, 152, 206
designer 16, 81, 115
designing 6, 27, 144, 152, 206, 210
desired proficiency 37, 45, 70, 76, 87, 95, 100, 102, 114, 127-128, 154, 163, 184
determinant 31, 40, 42, 46, 58, 164
determine 41, 68, 70, 76, 79-80, 131, 165, 212
develop 46, 49, 51, 54, 58-60, 78, 83, 86-89, 94, 97, 102, 109, 137, 159, 162, 164, 166-168, 172, 176-177, 179-186, 193, 218
developed 5, 11, 20, 25-28, 32, 37, 45-51, 53-55, 57-60, 65, 69, 81, 84, 86-88, 93, 98, 107, 111-112, 114, 116, 128-129, 140-141, 145, 147-149, 152, 155, 162, 164, 167, 171, 176, 184, 187, 192, 197-198, 206-207, 219, 222
developing employees 87, 93
development of expertise 86, 112
differentiate 13, 44-45, 59, 68-69, 78-79, 81, 83, 108, 110, 119
direct indicators 191-193, 197

INDEX

distinction 47, 62, 80, 107-108, 112, 164
distinctly 164
distinguished 61
distinguishing 48, 59-60, 64
distribution 11, 15, 17-19, 22
distribution profile 15, 17-19, 22
doctoral 6, 11
doctorate 15-16
doctors 26, 148, 200, 220
documentation 33
domain related 85
Dreyfus and Dreyfus model 43, 48-49, 52, 56-58
drivers 5, 7-8, 34, 157, 160-161, 168, 177-183, 185-186, 219, 225-229
duration 107, 110-111, 123, 133, 137, 143, 161-162, 173-174, 192-193, 195, 210-211, 214-217

E

earning 202, 215
economic 7, 18-19, 22, 31, 126, 133-134, 137-138, 178, 218
ecosystem 119, 127, 169
educate 3, 155
education 15-17, 20, 25-26, 53, 59, 129, 140, 149
effectively 61, 64, 78, 96, 166, 226, 229
effectiveness 98, 201-204
efficiency 70, 165, 180, 186-187, 201, 211-212, 214-215, 220
efficient 61, 70, 181
efficiently 115
effort 39, 67, 84-85, 89, 100-102, 106, 112, 159, 179, 226-227
effortlessly 56
electrical 15, 20, 27, 141, 143-144, 152, 206, 210

electronic 15, 20, 26, 128, 141, 143, 149, 172, 202, 210, 214, 220
elements 29, 43, 52, 54-55, 83, 89, 225-226, 229
emergency 52
emphasize 13, 44-46, 56, 69, 77, 118, 225
empirical 50, 102, 159
employed 221
employee 3-7, 11-12, 27, 37, 40-42, 45-48, 51-52, 54, 58-59, 61, 65-70, 75, 77, 79-80, 86-89, 93-95, 97-98, 100-114, 116-117, 119-120, 123-124, 126-128, 130-132, 144-147, 153-155, 163, 165, 167, 169-171, 173-176, 178-181, 183-184, 186-187, 191-192, 194, 202-204, 212-213, 221, 225
employee development 5, 11, 45, 98, 107, 155, 187
employers 93
employment 174, 216
encourage 6, 34, 89
endanger 170
endeavor 45, 106, 119
energy 15, 19, 25-27, 128, 133-135, 138, 148, 199
enforcement 105
engaged 33, 86, 167, 176
engagement 44, 84
engine 26, 149, 179, 201, 220
engineer 25-28, 109, 126-128, 131, 142-152, 163, 166, 168, 171-172, 181-182, 184, 197-198, 200-201, 203-206, 208-210, 213, 215-221
engineering 20, 25-27, 86, 128-129, 138-141, 145, 147-151, 178
enterprise 25-26, 93, 102, 143, 147, 149-150, 182, 197, 201, 203, 209, 215-216, 220

environment 31, 50, 74, 94, 164-165, 169, 183
equipment 19-20, 25-28, 126, 128, 134-136, 139-152, 163, 166-168, 172, 193, 197-198, 200, 202-206, 208-210, 214, 217-221
error 115, 161, 170, 174-175, 180, 211, 213-215, 220-221
essential 37, 41, 204
established 34, 41, 48, 65, 67, 82, 89, 94, 118, 120, 124, 191, 194-195
estate 19-20, 27, 127, 135, 139, 151, 205
estimate 123-124, 195
estimation 73, 226
evaluated 70, 114
evaluation 51
evaluator 26, 150, 202
evidence 14, 18, 50, 73-74, 76, 193
exceptions 53, 129-130, 132, 134-136
exchanges 29
execute 213, 220
execution 21, 26, 132, 140-141
executive 25-26, 74, 127, 145, 148, 199, 220
exemplary 120
expectation 37, 66-67, 71-72, 97, 105, 162-163, 168, 174, 178-179, 182
expected 48, 65, 70, 75, 82, 88, 93, 124, 162-163, 168, 173, 181, 193, 200, 206, 210, 220
expenditures 173
expense 94, 217, 219
expensive 153, 162
experience 4, 15-17, 27, 33, 41, 43, 46-47, 49, 52, 54-59, 61-62, 70, 83, 85, 95, 103-104, 109, 117, 131, 155, 170, 181

experienced 33, 47, 60-64, 68, 73, 75-76, 93, 95, 99, 131, 143, 163-164, 167, 171-172, 180-183, 185, 193, 195, 203, 209, 215-216
expert 3, 14, 32, 34, 46-48, 50, 52-53, 55-64, 83-88, 97, 100, 123-124, 159, 161, 171, 175, 180-181, 184, 191
expert performance 83-87, 123-124, 159
expertise 12, 44, 46-48, 50-51, 56-57, 59-60, 62, 79, 83-87, 99, 102-103, 108, 112, 123-124, 159-160, 170, 181
expert-level performance 84
exploratory 13, 180
exposure 61, 84, 132
extremes 59

F
failure 57, 114, 170
fast 3-5, 11, 34, 70, 97, 99, 102, 106-107, 109-112, 119, 153, 159, 161-162, 165-167, 169-170, 173-174, 178-179, 181, 184, 186, 197, 202, 206, 216, 218
fast-paced world 11
feed-forward 32
field 62, 116, 123, 168
figure 15, 17-18, 22, 40, 98, 100-101, 125, 144, 170, 173, 225, 228
firefighters 114, 185
five stages 48, 53, 57
flexibility 102
focus group 32, 34
formal 46, 104, 112, 114, 168, 184-185
formal training 104, 112, 168, 184-185
formalized 81

INDEX

foundation 225
foundational 5, 7, 13, 50, 103, 107, 186
framework 30, 33, 51, 62, 73, 86
full productivity 7, 93, 96
function 39, 41, 44, 48, 60-63, 65, 68, 77, 85-87, 131
functional 4
functioning 111
fundamental 51, 59, 186

G

generalizability 11, 29, 32-34
generalizable 34
global 3, 14, 164-165, 182
globalization 164
globally 144
government 19, 26, 124, 133, 135, 140, 150, 202
grade 146
gradual 49, 85
gradually 47, 49, 52, 86
graduate 106, 197, 200-201, 214-215
grand 19-21, 141
graphical 15, 17-18, 22
grasp 6, 48, 55
grasping 54
ground 7, 40, 87
grounded 47
group 7, 18-19, 23, 30, 32, 34, 49, 108-109, 126, 135-138, 145, 147, 154, 182, 192-194, 214, 216
grouped 31, 71
grow 50, 145
growth 100, 162, 164-165
guarantee 109
guidance 64
guide 78, 225
gurus 93

H

hallmark 45, 69, 76, 80
hand 60, 62, 87, 113, 127
handle 46, 48, 55, 68, 128-130, 132, 134, 169-170, 178, 199, 202, 225
handling 27, 54, 132, 172, 174, 177
happen 37, 86, 97, 115, 117, 128-130, 132, 134, 170, 218
hasten 99
hazardous 38
healthcare 19-20, 25-28, 49, 53, 129, 133-136, 139, 148, 150-152, 203, 205, 213, 220-221
heavily 46, 70
helpdesk 20-21, 25-27, 129, 132, 138-139, 141, 145, 147-152, 163, 197, 199-200, 203, 206, 214, 216, 220-221
hierarchy 30
high 21, 25-28, 34, 44, 46-48, 51, 55, 59-60, 67, 70, 73, 84, 87, 96, 99, 103, 123-124, 129-130, 134, 146, 159, 162, 165, 167, 172, 178, 181-184, 211-213, 217-218, 220-221, 226, 229
high proficiency 47-48, 59-60, 123
higher 15, 29, 41, 47-48, 50, 52-53, 55, 58, 61, 75, 99, 102, 130-131, 169-170, 174, 186, 200, 203, 211-212, 214, 219-220
highest 63, 123, 134
highlighted 42
hire 96, 143, 161, 170, 179, 201, 203, 205, 209, 216, 221
hiring 103, 155, 161, 165-166, 182, 184, 202, 215
historical 105, 120, 154, 226
holding 15
holistic 43, 53
home 43
horizontal 101
hospital 26, 148, 200, 220
HRD 16, 79-80

human 3, 15, 39, 62-63, 65, 73, 82, 109
human competence 62-63, 82
human performance technology 73
hundreds 144, 174, 216
hypothetical 102

I
idea 47, 50, 70, 102, 106, 110
ideals 61
identified 6, 12, 30, 39, 52, 66, 69, 71, 85, 97, 103, 105, 120, 211, 227
identify 31, 43, 54, 78, 93, 120, 187
identifying 25, 58, 94, 105, 107, 147, 197
immediately 74, 114, 116, 202, 215
immersed 43
impact 57, 95, 114, 125-126, 144, 153, 155, 160-161, 172, 175, 178-180, 185-186, 219, 225-226, 228
impact of TTP 153
impacted 183, 228
impactful 153
impacting 179
impediment 13
imperative 45, 83
implant 26, 149, 175, 201, 220
implement 177, 226, 229
implementation 196
implemented 29, 194, 208
implication 7, 56, 58, 63-64, 95, 161-163, 173, 175-178, 182-183, 185, 219, 226
implicit 48, 163, 166, 176
implied 38, 70, 82, 102
importance 7, 42, 57, 93, 106, 116, 160, 165, 169
important 4, 12, 14, 32, 39, 43, 46, 52, 55, 59, 66, 70, 72, 79, 85, 93, 97, 107, 111, 116, 125, 131, 154, 169, 176, 179, 185

impression 170
improve 54-55, 85, 115, 118, 175
improved 33, 84, 193, 201-205, 211-214, 220-221, 227
improvement 8, 26, 39, 75, 97, 103, 106, 113-114, 149, 193, 199-200, 211, 213-215, 218, 222, 227
inability 170
inbound 25-27, 145, 147-152, 163, 197, 199-200, 203, 206, 214, 216, 220-221
incidentally 14
inclination 69
included 31, 33, 39, 57, 84, 162, 165, 170, 175, 191, 194-195, 214, 217
increase 5, 49-50, 54, 102, 109, 174-175, 201, 211-216, 220
increased 49, 53, 93, 164, 174, 194, 196-197, 206, 211-213, 220-221
increasing 62, 88, 111, 160, 170
increasingly 43, 169
incrementally 84
increments 49
independent 57
independently 65, 67-68, 72, 80, 88, 94, 98
in-depth 33
indicate 42, 100, 169
indicated 42, 47, 66, 80-81, 84, 87, 110, 125, 168, 170, 175, 193
indicating 46, 145, 169, 210
indication 54, 60, 90, 194, 211
indicator 39, 47, 49, 59, 67, 71, 74-75, 117, 191-194, 197, 202
indirect 163, 182, 191-194, 197
indirect indicators 192-193, 197
individual 38-40, 42-45, 47, 52, 57-58, 60, 62-63, 65, 67-68, 72, 77, 80, 82-86, 90, 94-96, 98-

265

INDEX

99, 102, 106, 108-110, 119-120, 123, 125, 131, 154, 219
individualized 85
inducements 95
induction 221
industrial 19, 26-27, 133, 135, 140, 143, 212
industry 3-4, 7, 14-15, 18-19, 23, 30-33, 96, 114, 116, 126-127, 133-138, 144, 147, 173, 208-210
inefficiencies 31
inevitable 176
inexperienced 183
inferences 33, 108, 131
influence 4, 57, 77-78
informal 46, 104
information 15-16, 25, 32, 94, 115, 147, 159, 167, 184, 197, 219, 226, 229
informed 13
infrastructure 97, 182
inherently 4
initial 110-111, 127, 173
initiate 61, 100
initiated 187, 226
initiative 4-5, 13, 67, 177, 219, 222, 226
initiator 48
innovation 21, 25-27, 131-132, 140-141
input 31-32, 49, 59, 72-73, 226
insight 31, 73, 133-134
insignificant 113
insolvency 27, 151, 205
instance 42, 70, 73, 88, 96, 105, 110, 112, 115-116, 153, 163, 222
institute 7, 101, 177, 219
institution 146
institutional 171
instruction 54, 61-62
instructional 16, 58, 115-116, 118
instructor 204, 210
instruments 28, 152, 206, 209
insurance 19-20, 25, 27, 127, 135-136, 139, 147-148, 150, 170, 174, 198-199, 204, 220
intensive 11, 123
intent 74, 108, 110, 120, 177
inter 166, 225
interaction 50, 114, 225-226
interactive 98
interacts 50
interchange 119
interconnection 179
interest 44, 51, 219
interested 116
interesting 98
interestingly 179
interlinked 225
internet 15, 27, 151, 206, 221
interpersonal 38
interplay 44, 177, 217
interpretations 81
interrelated 228
interrupted 205
intervals 76, 101
intervention 80, 98, 107, 110, 112-114, 116-118, 164, 173
interviews 14, 29, 32-33, 59, 194
intrigued 4, 123
intuition 46, 56-57
intuition based 53
intuitive 48, 55
intuitively 53
invariably 74, 187, 211, 219, 222
invest 13, 45, 222
investigate 6, 227
investigated 70
investigating 160
investment 19-20, 25-27, 67, 74, 95, 106, 135-136, 139, 147, 150, 152, 197, 217
investors 165
invited 32

isolated 39, 45, 78, 81, 221
isolated skills 78, 81
isolation 179, 185
issue 26-27, 29, 51, 84, 106, 144, 149-150, 153, 161, 163, 171-172, 200, 204, 210, 214, 220-221
iterated 65, 117
iterative 32

J

job performance 38, 40-42, 44, 64, 79, 109, 175
job role 4, 11, 18, 31, 45, 47, 65-68, 70-72, 75, 77-78, 82-83, 87-88, 94, 96, 101, 104-107, 109, 111, 114, 120, 125-126, 128, 130-131, 143-144, 146, 153-155, 162, 182, 192-193, 195, 208, 225, 227
job-role proficiency 7, 81-82, 88, 107
jobs 14, 18, 30, 37, 49, 57, 67, 70, 73, 93, 101-102, 105, 114, 126-132, 137, 153, 160, 169, 174-175, 177-178, 209, 222
job specific 38, 42, 79
journey 46, 51, 64, 69, 108, 112
journeyman 48, 61, 63-64, 68, 87-88, 93, 95, 99-100, 160
judged 55
judgements 61
judgment 46, 49, 61, 81
jumping 127
junior 100
justifying 173

K

know 6, 12, 14, 37, 41, 53, 79, 89, 94, 104, 106-107, 134, 154-155, 175, 218
knowledge 3, 26, 41, 44, 47-52, 55-57, 59-60, 62, 67-68, 77-80, 83-84, 96, 98, 109, 118-119, 148, 169, 171, 181, 199-200
knowledge acquisition 118

L

labor 93
laboratory 86
labored 43
large 4, 6, 25, 33, 60, 83, 125-127, 130, 144-147, 153, 163, 165, 170, 173, 175, 179, 181-182, 191, 197, 213-214, 216, 219, 222, 225, 227
largely 51
larger 11, 33, 64, 77, 144, 160, 211, 216, 226
launch 3, 161-162, 165, 182, 212
launching 3
lead 73, 89, 105, 109, 119, 165, 174, 201, 222, 226
leader 3-8, 13-15, 29, 32, 37, 45, 65-81, 87-88, 93, 96, 103-113, 115-119, 127, 145-146, 153, 155, 162-164, 166-168, 171-173, 175, 177, 180, 182-185, 187, 191-195, 201, 212-214, 217, 219, 225-227
leadership 4, 16, 20, 26, 28, 32, 127, 129, 138-140, 148-149, 152, 171, 177, 201
leading 6, 12, 14, 65, 71, 73, 75, 82, 85-86, 93, 96-97, 114, 213
learn 3, 53, 57, 97, 108-109, 115-116, 127, 169, 171, 178-179
learned 54
learner 43, 47, 52-53, 55, 58, 85, 104, 115, 183
learning 5-6, 13-15, 31, 44-46, 49, 58, 65, 77, 82-83, 89, 93, 97-98, 103, 107-110, 112-113, 115-120, 153, 169, 173, 183, 193-194, 204
learning intervention 112, 118, 173

INDEX

learning progress 49
length 94-95, 123, 126, 159, 161-162, 187
lengthy 183
level 11, 13, 18, 29, 31, 34, 37, 41-42, 45-52, 56, 58-67, 69-72, 74-79, 82, 84, 86-89, 93-101, 109-110, 112-113, 115, 120, 123-124, 137, 154, 159-160, 170-171, 173, 178, 180, 183-184, 192, 200, 214, 226, 229
leverage 131, 226, 229
literature 44, 46, 49-51, 60, 64, 68-69, 81, 83, 88, 99, 102, 124, 159-160
long 3-4, 12, 54, 70, 76, 86-87, 94, 96, 98-99, 104, 106, 112, 117, 123, 126-129, 132-133, 136-137, 139, 144-146, 148, 153-154, 159-160, 163, 168, 170-172, 179, 183-185, 216, 225-226
long TTP 12, 126, 153, 160, 168, 172, 179, 226
longer 8, 112-113, 123, 127, 161, 163, 168, 179, 181-182
longest 136

M

machine 27, 75, 113, 128, 144, 150-151, 163, 204-205, 210, 221
machinery 20, 27, 136, 140, 150-151
machining 21, 26-28, 132, 138-140
machinists 26, 128, 149, 179, 201, 220
magazine 14, 33, 173
magnitude 7, 125-126, 129-133, 135-136, 142-147, 153, 160, 191, 222, 225, 227, 229
maintain 77, 97, 165, 168, 181
maintained 39, 46, 50, 84, 113
maintaining 27, 39, 45, 82, 144, 151, 181, 205, 210
maintenance 27, 70, 128, 143-144, 150-151, 172, 204-205, 210, 221
major 4, 32, 40, 58, 63, 126, 130, 166, 183-184, 195
majority 29, 33, 87, 111, 193
management 13, 15, 20, 26-28, 39, 71, 127, 129, 138-140, 148-149, 151-152, 167, 177
manager 3, 16, 25-28, 37, 41, 69, 95-96, 103, 105-108, 112-113, 119, 127, 129-130, 132, 134, 148, 150, 152-153, 155, 162, 175-176, 198-199, 204, 207, 213, 220, 225
managerial 20, 25-27, 127, 129, 131, 138, 148, 150
managing 25-27, 148, 150, 198-199, 204, 220
mandatory 114, 226
manufacturer 72-73, 145, 179
manufacturing 15, 20, 25-28, 129, 138-140, 142, 148-149, 151-152, 167, 172, 177, 179, 183-184, 198, 204, 208, 220-221
mapped 131
mapping 131
maps 32-33
market 4, 11, 102, 155, 159-165, 167, 170, 177-179, 186, 211-212, 219-221
marketing 71
marketplace 162
master 15-16, 48, 61-63, 67, 85, 98
mastered 76
mastery 41, 47, 51-52, 60-61, 70, 85, 98-99, 109, 115, 169
materials 19, 27-28, 133, 138
matrix 30-33, 76
matrix analysis 30, 33
maxims 53, 55

maximum 102, 126
mean 3, 15, 44, 50, 60, 62, 68, 73, 81, 84, 88, 95-97, 101, 104-108, 115, 119-120, 153, 155, 186, 192-194, 221-222, 228
meaning 4-5, 13, 34, 58, 104, 109
meaningful 31
measurable 49, 63-64, 66, 71-73, 75, 105
measure 31, 40-42, 50, 57-59, 64, 71, 73-75, 77-79, 90, 96, 103-107, 119-120, 123, 127, 154, 161, 165, 226
measure of performance 41-42
measured 40-42, 45, 49, 67-68, 71-75, 77, 82, 86, 89-90, 94, 96, 104, 107, 115, 119-120, 161-162, 175, 227
measurement 5, 34, 37, 44, 49, 70-73, 77, 86, 94, 103, 119-120, 123-124, 126, 154-155, 228
measures of proficiency 58, 154
measuring 7, 39-40, 77, 103, 125, 154
mechanical 26-27, 149, 151, 201, 205, 220
mechanism 7, 14, 47, 51, 53, 59, 84-86, 114, 118
medical 19-21, 25-28, 48, 126, 129, 132, 134-136, 139-140, 148-152, 166, 178, 200, 206, 209, 220
medium 14-15, 21, 25-28, 129-131
meeting 45, 65, 67, 69, 71-72, 76, 89, 98, 172
member 61, 116
memory 84
mental 50, 94
mention 14, 185
mentioned 5, 34, 69, 105
merged 31, 102
metals 20, 28, 136, 138, 152

method 6, 12-13, 18, 31-33, 51, 58, 63, 72, 74, 94, 110-111, 159, 170, 226, 229
methodology 110, 116, 182
metric 4-5, 7-8, 11-13, 29, 37, 39, 49, 66-68, 70-72, 76, 78, 80, 90-91, 93-94, 96-97, 103-107, 116, 125, 154, 161-162, 165, 179, 186, 211, 213, 218-221, 225-228
military 15, 19-20, 26, 86, 94, 114, 127, 133, 135, 140, 149, 159, 171, 201
mindset 191
mineral 19, 28, 135, 138
modalities 116
model 6, 8, 31-34, 39, 43-44, 48-49, 51-53, 56-58, 60, 62-64, 84-85, 94, 100, 106, 115, 118, 225, 228
modeling 94, 123
modelling 6, 11
monitor 95, 105, 227
monitored 85, 103, 227
motivate 60, 83
motivations 44
multidimensional 40

N
naïve 48, 61
need 3, 5, 12-14, 18, 37, 41, 43-45, 47, 59, 64, 67, 76, 87, 94, 97-98, 102, 105-107, 112-113, 115-116, 118, 155, 159-162, 164-165, 167-170, 173, 175, 178-182, 184-187, 191, 211, 213, 215-216, 220, 222, 225-226
noncompliance 38
nonexperts 86, 159
nonlinear 50
non-proficiency 170, 174, 176, 180, 185

INDEX

nonroutine 55
nontechnical 126, 139-140
novice 46-50, 52-54, 58-63, 83-84, 113
novice-to-expert 46-47, 50, 52, 58
numerical 179

O

objective 3, 12, 46, 49, 57, 69, 118, 120
objectively 64
objectivity 33
observable actions 45, 66, 71-73, 75-76
observation 32, 44, 47, 71, 80, 118, 123, 126, 130, 192-194
obsolescence 160, 170, 178
obsolete 3, 161, 168-169, 171
officers 26, 105, 114, 125, 127, 149, 172, 201
offshore 184, 197
OJT 110-111, 210, 220
onboarding 78, 104, 212, 220
on-the-job training 85, 104, 110, 204
operate 126, 169
operating 69-70, 93, 111, 173
operating readiness 111
operation 8, 13, 20, 27-28, 37, 46, 57, 97, 139, 151-152, 161-162, 165, 167, 171, 174, 176-177, 180-181, 191-193, 195, 207, 211, 213, 218-221, 227
operational metrics 8, 13, 161-162, 165, 211, 213, 218-219, 227
optimizations 229
orchestration 78, 227
order 55, 61-63, 71-72, 79, 85, 87, 93, 130, 134, 166-167, 169, 171, 185, 209
organisation 3-4, 6-8, 11, 13, 33, 38, 40, 46, 59, 63, 65, 87, 97, 118, 127, 137, 164-165, 170, 174, 185, 191-192, 225-226
organization 3-7, 11-14, 31, 37-40, 45-46, 51, 57, 64, 66-67, 69, 71-72, 78, 80, 86-89, 93-94, 96-99, 101, 103, 106-107, 110-111, 115-116, 118, 125-126, 137, 144-145, 153, 155, 159-161, 163-166, 169-170, 172-175, 177-182, 186, 211-213, 219, 225-227
organized 6
outcome 34, 38-42, 45, 53-55, 62-64, 66-75, 77-80, 82-83, 88-89, 109, 111, 113-118, 173, 227
outcome performance 38-39, 41
outsourcing 145

P

participant 11, 14-17, 29, 33, 113
path 5, 65, 93, 106
pathway 26, 149, 201
pattern 30-31, 43, 50, 55, 69, 123
peer 33, 39, 49, 73-74, 195, 199
perception 52, 54-55
perform 42, 44, 53, 57, 61, 64-65, 68, 72, 77-78, 80, 93, 97, 115, 160, 168, 172, 178, 180
performance 3-5, 7, 13, 37-52, 54-55, 59-61, 64-80, 82-89, 93-98, 103, 106-107, 109, 112-114, 117-118, 123-125, 154, 159, 161, 171, 175, 178, 183, 186, 193, 195, 198-200, 202, 205, 214-215, 220, 225, 227
performance development 46
performance improvement 106, 113-114
performance level 70, 75, 78, 82, 89, 97
performance measurement 94
performance measures 59, 64, 106
performance of the workforce 93

performance specifications 72, 75
performance thresholds 65, 82, 88
performed 30, 67, 74
performer 43-44, 48, 52, 54-55, 63, 65-67, 69, 71, 75-76, 81-82, 85, 88, 104-105, 114-115, 117-118, 120, 175, 195-196
performing 45, 49, 67, 74, 79, 84, 106, 115, 120, 144, 174, 193, 195
personnel 27, 165, 171
petrochemical 25-27, 148-149, 198-200, 220
petroleum 27, 143-144, 151, 205, 210
pharmaceutical 19-20, 25-26, 127, 134-136, 140, 143, 148, 198-199, 209, 220
phenomenal 212, 220
phenomenon 99, 102-103
plane 124
plant 25-27, 128, 143-144, 148-150, 152, 198-200, 204, 206, 210, 220-221
population 84, 181, 193-194, 205-206, 209, 211, 216-217
power 27, 58, 98, 144, 152, 206, 210
practice 6, 11-13, 31-32, 34, 49, 53, 55-56, 58, 81, 83-88, 102, 104, 115, 117-118, 123-124, 159, 179, 194-196, 226-227, 229
practitioners 13, 46, 57, 67-69, 73, 89, 93-94, 113-114, 191, 225
precision 21, 26-28, 132, 138-140, 179-180
predefined 45, 65-66, 115
predetermined 45, 65, 69, 94
prevalence 26, 33, 149, 177-178, 201, 217-218
problem 3-4, 20, 25-27, 29, 43, 46, 48-49, 52, 54, 56, 83, 97, 107, 125-126, 129-132, 138, 141, 144-145, 153, 160, 169, 185-186, 192, 225-226
production 20, 26-28, 104, 128-129, 138-140, 143-144, 149-152, 162, 167, 172, 180, 204, 210, 218, 221
productive 44, 65, 68, 72, 79, 94-95, 111, 113, 125, 169, 180, 202, 220
productively 88
productivity 7-8, 68, 72, 75-76, 93-96, 174-175, 180, 197-198, 201, 203, 205, 211, 213-216, 218-222, 227
profession 17, 48-49, 53, 56, 61, 108, 169, 185
professional 4, 15, 20, 26-27, 33, 43, 48, 56-59, 84, 87, 136, 140, 149-151, 200, 203, 205, 213, 220-221
proficiency 3-7, 11-14, 18, 31-32, 34-35, 37-53, 56-83, 86-90, 93-120, 123-124, 127-133, 135-138, 142-143, 153-155, 159-160, 163, 170-171, 173-174, 176-177, 179-185, 192-194, 197, 199, 206, 208-211, 213, 215, 217, 225-227
proficiency acquisition 52, 57-58, 100, 102
proficiency growth 100
proficiency measurement 44, 49, 71
proficiency scaling 47, 58-61, 63
proficiencyrelated 37
proficient 3, 7, 37, 43-45, 48, 55, 59, 63-65, 67-70, 72, 74-76, 79-81, 83, 87-88, 96-98, 104-105, 112, 115, 119, 131-132, 161, 166-168, 170, 172, 174-175, 182, 185, 194-196, 218
proficient performance 7, 37, 64, 69, 75, 83, 87, 112

INDEX

proficient performer 43-44, 55, 63, 81, 175, 196
proficiently 41, 168
profit 5, 37, 211-212, 220
program 5, 16, 26, 45, 98, 106, 110-111, 129-130, 137, 146, 149, 155, 173, 177, 185, 192-193, 195, 200, 213, 220
progress 46, 48-49, 51, 61, 200, 203-204, 206, 208, 210
progression 37, 44, 46-52, 55-56, 58-59, 62, 64, 69, 81-82, 153
progression of development 81
progressively 46, 49
project 4, 7, 13-15, 18-19, 21-26, 29-33, 45, 65-81, 87-88, 101, 103-113, 115-119, 125-138, 140-143, 145-147, 153, 160, 162-168, 170-173, 175-180, 182-185, 187, 191-197, 208-219, 222, 226-227
purposive sampling 14

Q
qualification 49
qualified 55, 61, 85, 99, 161, 170
qualified workforce 161, 170
qualify 147
qualifying 37, 48
qualitative 13, 29, 33, 46-47, 59-60, 86, 211
qualitatively 48-49, 63, 69, 84
quality 29, 44, 72-73, 76-77, 98, 172, 183, 197, 214
quantifiable 13
quantification 57
quantified 59, 211
quantify 63, 229
quantifying 222
quantitative 29, 47
quantitatively 63
questionnaire 14, 29

quickly 3, 75, 99, 108-109, 111, 115-116, 127, 162, 167, 169, 172, 181

R
rapid 161, 163-167, 179-182
rapidize 110
rapidly 76, 159, 170, 184
ratio 213, 221
readily 102, 110-111, 114, 127, 161-163, 165-168, 170, 173, 176, 182, 191-193, 195, 197, 199, 201, 203-204, 206, 211-212, 216, 220
redevelop 168
reduce 4-6, 8, 12, 14, 29, 32, 34, 75, 97-98, 100-102, 106, 110-111, 113, 118, 155, 160-161, 165-166, 170, 173-175, 177, 180, 185, 187, 191-195, 197-198, 204-206, 208-211, 213-222, 226-227
reduce time to proficiency 6
reduce TTP 29, 34, 113, 118, 160, 165, 177, 185, 191, 208, 219, 226-227
reducing the TTP 12, 106, 214, 216
reducing TTP 4, 100, 218
reduction in the TTP 191, 208
Reduction in TTP 8, 29, 34, 191, 209-210, 214-215, 217, 219, 222, 226
regulations 61, 181
reliability 34
reliable 61, 68, 93, 95, 99
reliably 70, 124, 159
repair 25-27, 128-129, 138, 142-144, 146-152, 168, 172, 197-198, 200, 202-206, 208-210, 214, 217-221
repeat 32, 69, 85, 109, 159
repetitions 73-74, 76

represent 39, 41, 61, 71, 110, 165, 216
representative 25, 27, 74-75, 86, 124-125, 127, 143, 148, 151, 194, 199, 202, 204, 209, 212, 220-221
representative tasks 86, 124, 194
reproducibility 86
require 3-4, 14, 18, 29, 38, 43-45, 49, 53, 55, 64, 66-68, 70-71, 73, 77-81, 85, 88, 94, 97-98, 104-107, 109, 112, 114, 116, 118, 123, 125, 127-128, 130-131, 143, 146, 154, 160-162, 164, 166-171, 175-182, 184-185, 211, 218, 227
research 6, 11-13, 15, 19-20, 25-26, 32, 34, 37, 44, 50, 56, 60, 62, 83, 103, 135-136, 140, 149-150, 159, 178, 191, 210
researcher 7, 12, 16, 42, 46-47, 49-50, 53, 56-58, 60, 62, 64, 77, 79, 83, 86, 88, 95, 117, 123, 128, 153, 159, 165, 191, 212
resource 3, 15, 19, 28, 65, 89, 97, 135, 138, 222, 226, 229
respondents 32, 96
result 3, 18, 29, 31, 39-41, 66-68, 71-75, 77-80, 85, 105, 108, 110, 113-114, 124, 169, 172, 192-194, 205, 212, 214, 220, 227
retention 86, 109, 117, 170, 175, 211, 213, 220-221
retention 86, 109, 117, 170, 175, 211, 213, 220-221
retire 181
retirement 128, 161, 170-171, 180-181
revenue 65, 90, 164, 166, 174, 176, 178, 182, 202, 211-212, 215-216
review 6, 32-33, 76

risk 70, 155, 175-176
role 4, 7, 11, 18, 31, 44-45, 47, 65-68, 70-72, 74-75, 77-78, 81-83, 87-89, 94, 96, 101, 103-107, 109, 111-112, 114-115, 119-120, 125-128, 130-131, 143-144, 146, 153-155, 162, 166, 182, 192-193, 195, 208, 210, 225, 227
running 167, 172, 176, 218

S

sale 20, 25-28, 38-39, 71, 75-76, 109, 111-112, 125-129, 132, 139-140, 143, 147-152, 163, 165-166, 178, 182, 197, 199, 201-206, 209, 211-212, 215-216, 220-221
sample 6, 32-33, 72
sampling 14, 18
scale 4, 7, 25, 47, 59, 83, 98, 125-126, 144, 146-147, 153, 160, 197, 219, 225-227, 229
scale of TTP 7, 144, 146-147, 225, 229
scaling 47, 58-61, 63-64, 145
scholarly 68
school 26, 39, 57-58, 77, 149, 173, 200
science 86, 178
scientific 20, 25-27, 62, 127-129, 140-141, 147-149, 152
semiconductor 3, 15, 19, 25-27, 134, 136, 141-142, 145-147, 149-152, 167-168, 197-198, 200, 203-206, 208-209, 217-219, 221
senior 64, 95, 99-100, 127-128, 160, 171
seniority 59, 100
short 99, 109, 113, 133-134, 162, 171, 175, 182, 210

INDEX

shorten 4, 6-7, 11, 13, 37, 97-98, 104-105, 110-111, 119, 176, 186, 192, 221-222, 226, 229
shorten time to proficiency 6
shortened 110, 191, 194, 202, 212, 221
shortening 5-7, 13-14, 18, 34, 81, 100, 107-108, 110-111, 116, 119, 160, 165, 172, 185, 191-193, 211-212, 217, 227
shortening training 110, 217
shortening TTP 5-6, 13, 18, 34, 81, 107, 116, 160, 165, 172, 185, 191-193, 211, 217, 227
shorter time 13, 102, 107-109, 117-118, 166, 168, 171-172, 179, 182-184, 199, 201-204, 206, 209, 211-212, 218, 220
shorter TTP 8, 13, 101, 109, 120, 155, 160, 170, 174-175, 179, 184-185, 191, 210-212, 216, 222, 225-226
significant 48, 56, 133-134, 153, 160, 164, 174, 181, 195, 204, 206, 209, 226
simulated 76, 198, 201, 205, 207
situation 43, 48, 50, 52-56, 73, 77, 113-114, 117, 174, 176, 180
situational 52, 54-55
skill 3, 7, 11, 18, 20, 24, 27, 30-31, 41, 44-53, 55-63, 67-70, 76-86, 88-89, 96-99, 102, 104, 109, 114, 118-119, 124-125, 129-132, 137-138, 159-161, 164-172, 176-184, 186-187, 198, 203, 211, 213, 218-219, 226
skill acquisition 52, 56-57, 83-84, 102, 118
skilled 47, 83-84, 162, 165, 170
skilled workforce 162, 165
skill focused 118
skillful 44, 49

software 15, 19-20, 25-27, 74, 96, 128, 134-136, 141, 147, 149-150, 163, 167-168, 184, 197, 200, 203, 214, 219-220
solution 29, 56, 96-98, 107, 112-114, 118, 164, 182
solve 53, 56, 169
solving 20, 25-27, 48-49, 56, 83, 97, 129-132, 138, 141, 225-226
special 61, 83-84
specialist 16, 62-64, 87, 94, 112, 124, 128
specialty 20, 136, 138, 148, 150
specifically 14, 115, 221
specification 66, 71-73, 75-76, 116
speed 3-7, 46, 67, 71, 93-94, 97-99, 101-102, 109, 111-112, 145, 153, 161-167, 169-171, 176-182, 184, 186, 202-205, 226
speed to proficiency 3, 5-7, 71, 93, 97-99, 101
speed up 67, 112
speed up proficiency 67
speeding 4, 6, 13, 108, 112
speed related 161, 165, 168
speed-related competitiveness 7, 161, 164, 166, 178-180, 182, 184, 226
sports 27, 70, 80, 84, 86, 124, 159
stage 37, 43-44, 46-58, 60-61, 63-64, 68-69, 80-82, 88, 93-95, 99-100, 112, 159
staged 46, 48, 51, 57-58, 64
stages of proficiency 48, 53, 58
stages of skill acquisition 56
stakeholder 89, 106, 116, 154-155
state 44-46, 50, 66, 68-70, 75, 80-82, 88, 90, 96, 103, 107, 110, 115
statistics 213

274

strategic 20-21, 26-28, 51, 127-129, 132, 138-140, 148-149, 151-152, 176, 204, 212, 221
strategists 3
strategize 175
strategizing 26, 149, 201, 220
strategy 6, 11-14, 28-29, 32-34, 39, 44, 55, 58, 73-74, 98, 105, 111, 113-114, 119, 130, 152, 159, 170, 176, 185, 193-196, 207-208, 221-222, 226-227, 229
studied 125, 153
study 4-7, 9, 11-15, 17-18, 32-34, 37-38, 40-42, 44-45, 47-48, 50-52, 56-59, 65-66, 68-71, 74, 78-87, 94-95, 103-105, 107-108, 110, 113-116, 118, 123-125, 131, 142, 159-160, 162, 165, 169-170, 173-175, 191, 194-195, 210-212, 216, 219, 226-227
study participants 15, 17
success 14, 18, 20, 24, 29, 31, 64, 75-76, 89-90, 98, 119, 131-132, 161, 164-165
successful 12, 18, 29, 85, 108, 113, 165, 199, 226
sufficient 94
superior 41, 84, 86, 118
superior performance 41, 84, 86
supervision 39, 44, 55
supervisor 94, 220
supervisory 21, 25-27, 129, 131-132, 138, 148, 150
supply 20, 26, 28, 139, 149, 152, 200, 220
surgeon 70, 114
surgery 86
surgical 28, 152, 206, 209
survey 95-96, 125, 165, 168
synthesis 103
system 8, 19, 22, 26, 98, 126, 133-135, 143, 150, 163, 167, 169, 180-181, 185, 193, 203, 209, 216, 220, 222-223, 225-227, 229
systematic 127

T

tacit 55-56
talent 96, 155
target 14, 45, 58, 89, 94, 97, 110, 112, 146-147, 153-155, 166, 168, 182, 200, 203-206, 208, 226-227
target proficiency 45, 58, 153
task 37-45, 48-49, 52-55, 57, 59, 61, 63-68, 74, 76, 78-82, 85-87, 89, 94-96, 98, 104, 115-116, 124, 168, 194, 204
task performance 38, 40-42, 49, 65, 79, 82, 94
task related 38
taxonomy 62-63
teach 61, 111
teacher 26, 85, 149, 200
teaching 21, 25-26, 132, 140
team 37-39, 65, 71, 75, 98, 105, 116, 120, 137, 155, 165, 170, 212
technical 20, 25-28, 46, 74, 82, 116, 126, 128-129, 132, 134, 138-141, 143, 147-152, 163, 166, 177-178, 180, 182, 209
technicians 26, 128, 143, 149, 172, 202, 210, 214, 220
techniques 30-31, 33, 109
technological 97, 162, 164
template analysis 33
thematic 30, 33
theme 30-33, 75, 77, 118-119
theoretical 50-51, 98
theorists 48
time 3-7, 11, 13-14, 18, 31, 45-46, 49-50, 52, 54, 62, 65, 69-71, 76, 78, 80, 82, 86-87, 89, 93-

INDEX

104, 107-115, 117-119, 123-125, 128-130, 132-133, 135-136, 138, 142-143, 145-146, 154, 159-166, 168, 171-172, 174-179, 181-187, 191-195, 197, 199, 201-206, 208-212, 214-215, 217-220, 226
time and speed 4, 6, 186
time to competence 7, 93, 96, 104, 113, 201
time to proficiency 3, 5-7, 14, 18, 93-94, 96-97, 101, 129-130, 132-133, 135-136, 138, 142-143, 182, 193, 197, 208-210, 215, 217
time to readiness 176, 191-193, 195, 197, 199, 201, 203-204, 206
Time to training 129-130, 132-133, 135-136, 138, 142-143, 197, 208-210, 215, 217
time to training 129-130, 132-133, 135-136, 138, 142-143, 197, 208-210, 215, 217
timeframe 171, 184
time related 162, 176
time-related pressures 7, 161-163, 166, 168, 172, 176, 178, 182-183, 185, 226
time-to-market 4, 164-165, 178-179, 186, 219
traditional training 112, 116-117
train 53, 99, 117, 181, 183, 198
trainer 16, 25, 76, 104, 113, 115
training 5-6, 12-16, 20-21, 25-26, 49, 53-54, 59, 76, 80-81, 84-86, 96, 98, 102, 104, 107-119, 123, 127, 129-130, 132-133, 135-138, 140, 142-143, 145-146, 149, 159, 161-164, 168, 172-175, 183-185, 187, 192-193, 195, 197-200, 204, 206, 208-211, 213-217, 219, 221

training and development 164
training duration 107, 110-111, 133, 143, 161-162, 173-174, 192, 195, 210-211, 214-217
training event 85, 112, 117
training intervention 80, 107, 110, 112-114, 116-118
training objectives 118
training programs 129-130, 137, 185, 195
training specific 81
trajectory 50, 102
transition 46-47, 50, 58, 61, 199
triangulation 33
trigger 5, 7-8, 34, 121, 160, 177, 225, 228
troubleshoot 20, 25-27, 74, 128, 131-132, 139-144, 146-151, 163, 168, 172, 197-198, 200, 202-205, 208-210, 214-215, 217-221
TTP figures 125
TTP improvement 103, 222
TTP measurement 103, 119
TTP metrics 5, 11-12, 94, 103, 107
TTP reduction 191, 193, 197, 208-210, 215, 217, 222
turnover 166, 183-184

U
uncertain 169
unprepared 175
unskilled 181
unstructured 56, 111
unsupervised 55, 61, 64, 93, 95, 99
untrained 86
up to speed 4, 153, 162-163, 170-171, 179, 181-182, 202-205
up-to-speed 5
urgency 161, 165, 167, 172, 180
utility 19-20, 27, 134-135, 141, 143, 152, 159, 171
utilization 32

V
validate 31-32, 62
validation 32, 34
validity 32, 57
variable 18-19, 29-31
variants 3
variation 31, 137, 194-195
verifiable 73-74, 76

W
weapon 98
within-case analysis 30-31
work 4, 11-12, 14, 18, 37-40, 45, 55-56, 58, 61, 64-65, 67, 71-74, 76-77, 81, 83, 85, 87, 93, 95, 98-99, 107, 111, 114, 123, 125, 127, 137, 153, 162, 175, 180-181, 183, 193, 200, 203-204, 206, 208, 210, 213, 218, 222, 226, 229
worker 61, 68, 93, 97, 114, 165, 181
workforce 6, 11-14, 37, 46, 93, 98, 102, 112, 118, 120, 125, 144, 160-162, 164-165, 170-171, 173, 179, 181, 184, 186, 215-216, 220, 225
workforce proficiency 46
workplace 5, 7, 14, 37, 45, 58, 64-66, 69, 77, 81, 87, 97, 102, 108, 114, 117-119, 160, 169
workplace performance 37

THE AUTHOR

Dr Raman K Attri is a global authority on speed in personal and professional space. He is a performance and learning leader with over 25 years of international experience. His specializes in equipping professional and organizations with proven competitive strategies to speed up human learning, expertise, and performance by 2X. An accomplished business researcher, he is one among few experts in the world who have cracked the code to reduce time to proficiency of employees by 50%. An organizational learning leader, he manages a Hall of the Fame training organization, named one among the top 5 globally, at a $40bn technology corporation. Passionate about learning, he holds two doctorates in human performance apart from earning over 100 international educational credentials and being nominated for some of the world's highest certifications. An inspiring personality, he speaks internationally to guide leaders and professionals on research-based best practices, models, and frameworks to solve tough workplace performance problems. A prolific author of 20 multi-genre books, he writes about the deeper aspects of human excellence and capabilities. A powerhouse of positivity, despite his disability since childhood, he made his mission to teach others how to accelerate the path to excellence and walk faster in all walks of life.

LinkedIn https://www.linkedin.com/in/rkattri
Facebook https://www.facebook.com/DrRamanKAttri
YouTube https://www.youtube.com/RamanKAttri
Website http://ramankattri.com
Contact raman@ramankattri.com

FROM THE SAME AUTHOR

DESIGNING TRAINING TO SHORTEN TIME TO PROFICIENCY: Online, Classroom and On-the-Job Learning Strategies from Research

ISBN: 978-981-14-0633-1 (e-book)
ISBN: 978-981-14-0632-4 (paperback)
ISBN: 978-981-14-0645-4 (hardcover)

Available with major retailers, distributors and market places

ACCELERATE YOUR LEADERSHIP DEVELOPMENT IN TRAINING DOMAIN: Proven Success Strategies for New Training & Learning Managers

ISBN: 978-981-11-8991-3 (e-book)
ISBN: 978-981-14-0066-7 (paperback)

Available with major retailers, distributors and market places

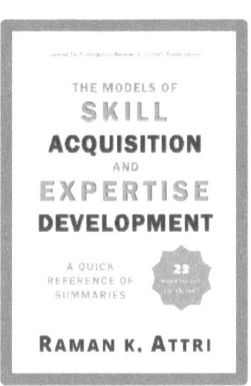

THE MODELS OF SKILL ACQUISITION AND EXPERTISE DEVELOPMENT: A Quick Reference of Summaries

SBN: 978-981-11-8988-3 (e-book)
ISBN: 978-981-14-1122-9 (paperback)
ISBN: 978-981-14-1130-4 (hardcover)

Available with major retailers, distributors and market places

TRAINING EFFECTIVENESS MEASUREMENT FOR LARGE SCALE PROGRAMS: DEMYSTIFIED! A 4-Tier Practical Model for Technical Training Managers

ISBN: 978-981-11-8990-6 (e-book)
ISBN: 978-981-11-417672 (paperback)

Available with major retailers, distributors and market places

ACCELERATING COMPLEX PROBLEM-SOLVING SKILLS: Problem-Centered Training Design Methods

ISBN: 978-981-11-8991-2 (e-book)
ISBN: 978-981-14-1766-5 (paperback)

Available with major retailers, distributors and market places

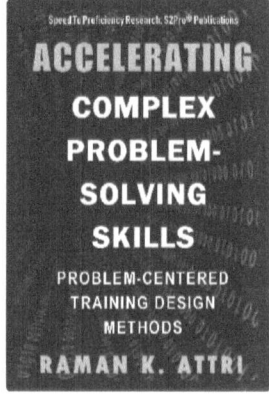

SPEED TO PROFICIENCY IN ORGANIZATIONS: Model, Practices and Strategies to Shorten Time To Proficiency

ISBN 978-981-14-0753-6 (e-book)

Available with major retailers, distributors and market places

ACCELERATED PROFICIENCY FOR ACCELERATED TIMES: A Review of Key Concepts and Methods to Speed Up Performance

ISBN: 978-981-14-6276-4 (e-book)
ISBN: 978-981-14-6275-7 (paperback)
ISBN: 978-981-14-6274-0 (hardcover)

Available with major retailers, distributors and market places

MODELLING ACCELERATED PROFICIENCY IN ORGANISATIONS: Practices and Strategies to Shorten Time-to-Proficiency of the Workforce

Published at Southern Cross University

MODELLING ACCELERATED PROFICIENCY IN ORGANISATIONS

Practices and Strategies to Shorten Time-to-Proficiency of the Workforce

Dr Raman K Attri